*The South African Churches
in a Revolutionary Situation*

To Our Parents

The South African Churches in a Revolutionary Situation

MARJORIE HOPE AND JAMES YOUNG

ORBIS BOOKS

Maryknoll, New York 10545

Portions of this book first appeared in the *National Catholic Reporter* under the following titles: "Durban Bishop Courageous" (Nov. 2, 1979); "S. Africa's First Black Archbishop 'Unflappable' " (Nov. 9, 1979); "South African Rulers Fear Christian Workers" (Nov. 16, 1979); "South Africa: Apartheid Stays, Fury Escalates" (Nov. 30, 1979). They are included here with permission of the National Catholic Reporter, P.O. Box 281, Kansas City, MO 64141. The section on Bishop Tutu first appeared as "Desmond Mpilo Tutu—South Africa's Doughty Black Bishop" in *The Christian Century* (Nov. 28, 1979) and is included here with the permission of The Christian Century Foundation.

The Catholic Foreign Mission Society of America (Maryknoll) recruits and trains people for overseas missionary service. Through Orbis Books Maryknoll aims to foster the international dialogue that is essential to mission. The books published, however, reflect the opinions of their authors and are not meant to represent the official position of the society.

Library of Congress Cataloging in Publication Data

Hope, Marjorie.
  The South African churches in a revolutionary
situation.

  Includes bibliographical references.
  1. Christianity—South Africa. 2. Christian
sects—South Africa. 3. Church and race relations—
South Africa. I. Young, James, 1916-
II. Title.
BR1450.H6   280'.0968   81-9584
ISBN 0-88344-466-6 (pbk).   AACR2

Contents

Preface

Why did we decide to write this book? A primary reason was to focus on an explosive issue that touches on the lives of Americans and others to a far greater extent than most people realize.

It has frequently been predicted that World War III will be a racial one. South Africa might well be the tinderbox. In a world of diminishing natural resources, the extraordinary mineral wealth of that country acquires increasing importance to the United States, and to other nations as well. From a military viewpoint, too, the Republic of South Africa possesses strategic importance, poised as it is at the convergence of the Atlantic and Indian Oceans.

In a sense, rounding the Cape of Good Hope from the Atlantic has always meant entry into a world that westerners by and large fail to understand. Along the east coast of Africa it is of course a world ruled by Black peoples—save at the southernmost tip, where a White minority still holds out against the inevitability of majority rule. The so-called colored peoples of the world view the regime with abhorrence—as countless resolutions passed by the United Nations General Assembly and by global conferences of nonaligned states attest. Even if a violent racial conflict in South Africa were to remain a "limited" rather than a global war, it would inevitably trigger conflict—and probably bloody rioting—in the United States.

The "South African problem" is not only an economic and political issue, it is also a moral one. Although followers of realpolitik are correct in their belief that politics is a matter of power, it is also true that when human beings are moved by moral passions—as our own founding fathers were—they can become bonded into a community with power.

Sometimes that community is a church. Certainly the church as institution has enormous potential to promote—or to hinder—social change. In South Africa the multiracial churches have not lived up to the challenge of practicing the essential message of the gospel. Yet, as we shall see, they represent the one large social institution where Blacks and Whites can meet on equal terms, and where Blacks can acquire positions of power.

Our subject is a complex one, for it is impossible to examine the Christian churches in South Africa without some consideration of the historical, political, psychological, economic, and sociological forces at work. Volumes have been written on single aspects of our subject. Space considerations, then, have placed limits on the scope of this book.

For example, we could not include Namibia (South-West Africa), Botswana, Lesotho, or Swaziland, although South Africa has administered

Namibia since 1953, and the other three territories are indirectly controlled, both politically and economically, by South Africa. Moreover, most of the churches in these lands are linked through some form of federation.

By the same token, we could not include Angola, Mozambique, Zambia, Zimbabwe, and Malawi, although South African leaders in Pretoria view them as part of the South African sphere of influence, and have intervened in their affairs.

Because it is crucially important to understand how South Africa got into what many call a "quagmire," we have devoted several chapters to historical background. Because our focus is on the churches, and on the relations between colonizers and colonized, we have had to exclude the fascinating history of Africans before the arrival of the Whites.

Due to space limitations, too, we have given considerably less attention to the Indian and Colored ethnic groups than to Black Africans. The last-named are by far the most populous of the so-called non-White groups, and have taken the lead in pressing for socio-political change. Moreover, Black Consciousness leaders among the Africans have managed to convince many younger Coloreds and Indians to identify themselves as "Black."

Unfortunately, most writers who examine and diagnose the "South African problem" are either South African Whites or visiting Whites. Inevitably, they have a White perspective. South African Blacks are frequently eloquent. Steve Biko, Nelson Mandela, Mangaliso Robert Sobukwe, and Albert Luthuli are only a few of the men whose polished and impassioned oratory has stirred their listeners and other concerned persons around the world. Although the writings of Percy Qoboza, Noel Manganyi, Es'kia Mphalele, Steve Biko, and many others are a testament to the literary gifts of Africans in the Republic of South Africa, it is nevertheless true that because of their oral tradition (and the constant threat of censorship) Africans tend to rely more on the tongue than on the pen. It is our hope that in the future more Africans—tired of being analyzed by White researchers from White universities—can turn to the written word as a further means of becoming subjects of their own destiny.

No White person can ever truly *know* what it is like to be a Black person in the land of apartheid. But we have tried to listen. We have listened not only to Blacks, but also to Coloreds, Asians, and Whites from all walks of life and positions on the political spectrum.

It has been a privilege for us to know some of these remarkable men and women. We have wished to share that experience by making this a book describing not only institutions and events, but the lives and hopes of individuals immersed in the struggle.

Among the many South Africans who generously gave of their time and shared their thoughts with us, we are particularly grateful to Dr. Allan Boesak, Dr. Alex Boraine, Dr. David Bosch, Archbishop Peter Butelezi, Chief Gatsha Buthelezi, Bishop Manas Buthelezi, Canon M. J. D. Carmichael, Dr. John de Gruchy, Fr. Gerard de Fleuriot, Sheena Duncan, Sr. Brigid

Flanagan, the Rev. Abel Hendricks, Archbishop Denis Hurley, Dudley Horner, Wolfram Kistner, Shimani Khumalo, Vusi Khanyile, Douglas Lolwane, Deborah Mabiletsa, Dr. Ntatho Motlans, Thomas Manthata, Leonard Mosala, Bernadette Mosala, James Moulder, Bishop Stephen Naidoo, Revelation Ntoula, the Rev. Jimmy Palos, Benjamin Pogrund, Percy Qoboza, John Rees, the Rev. Rob Robertson, Michael Rantho, Tony Saddington, Fr. A. D. Scholten, O. P., the Rev. Unez Smuts, Fr. Lebamang Sebidi, Bishop Desmond Tutu, and the many others who cannot be named here, because it could cause problems for them in South Africa.

We also wish to thank Jeanne Liggett, Lenna Mae Gara, Douglas Steere, Lewis Hoskins, Mary Kay Bray, Rena Van Nuys, Helen Weeks, David Mesenbring, and Mary Blackburn for help and criticisms of the manuscript. Our editors—Philip Scharper, John Eagleson, and William Jerman—have been particularly helpful.

Throughout this study we shall be following the usage of many political and religious leaders in referring to all non-White persons and related concepts (African, Colored, Asian) as Black. The umbrella term has political connotations, reflecting the emergence of Black Consciousness in the early 1970s, and is intended to suggest the solidarity of all oppressed peoples in South Africa.

The government, of course, does not use "Black" in this sense. In everyday life, too, most South Africans use either "Black" or "African" to designate the indigenous people of the country; they do not generally call Coloreds (in South Africa, persons of racially mixed ancestry) or Asians "Black." White South Africans seldom refer to themselves as "Africans," although, paradoxically, the word "Afrikaner" means African! Some confusion is unavoidable.

The term "Brown" also occurs now and then in South African literature and in this book. It refers to Coloreds or Indians. Neither Coloreds nor Indians who have been conscientized would ever refer to themselves as "Brown."

Contrary to the prevailing tendency in American publishing, we capitalize the terms "White," "Black," "Brown," and "Colored," to highlight—paradoxically—the fact that *color* has virtually nothing to do with the designation. By South African law and the everyday usage that derives from it, the terms "Black," "White," and "Colored" are used to refer to certain specified *human groupings*—hence our use of capital letters—having little to do with skin color. Individuals have even been reclassified officially from Colored to Black, or vice versa, by governmental decision.

Acronyms

ABM, American Board of Missions
AICA, African Independent Churches Association
AME, African Methodist Episcopal (Church)
ANC, African National Congress
ASB, Afrikaanse Studentebond ("Afrikaans Student Union")
AZAPO, Azanian People's Organization
AZASO, Azanian Students Organization
BCM, Black Consciousness Movement
BCP, Black Community Program
BOSS, Bureau of State Security
BPC, Black People's Convention; *also* Bantu Presbyterian Church
CCSA, Christian Council of South Africa
CI, Christian Institute
COSAS, Conference of South African Students
CPSA, Church of the Province in South Africa (Anglican)
DRC, Dutch Reformed Church (= NGK)
DWEP, Domestic Workers Employment Project
ELCSA, Evangelical Lutheran Church of South Africa
ELCSA(-SER), Evangelical Lutheran Church in Southern Africa (-South Eastern Region)
FEDSEM, Federal (Theological) Seminary
FELCSA, Federation of Evangelical Lutheran Churches in Southern Africa
FMC, Federal Mission Council
FOSATU, Federation of South African Trade Unions
GK, Gereformeerde Kerk (Dopper Kerk)
GKN, Gereformeerde Kerken van Nederland
GMC, General Missionary Conference
HK, Hervormde Kerk
ICU, Industrial and Commercial (Workers) Union
IDAMASA, Interdenominational African Ministers Association
IFOR, International Fellowship of Reconciliation
LMS, London Missionary Society
LWF, Lutheran World Federation
MCSA, Methodist Church of Southern Africa
MCT, Methodist Church of the Transkei
MWASA, Media Workers Association of South Africa
NGK, Nederduitse Gereformeerde Kerk (= DRC)

NGKA, Nederduitse Gereformeerde Kerk in Afrika (DRC, for Blacks)
NGSK, Nederduitse Gereformeerde Sending Kerk (Dutch Reformed Mission Church, for Coloreds)
(N)HK, (Nederduitse) Hervormde Kerk
NIC, National Indian Congress
NUSAS, National Union of South African Students
PAC, Pan-Africanist Congress
PCR, Program to Combat Racism
PCSA, Presbyterian Church of Southern Africa
PEBCO, Port Elizabeth Black Civic Organization
PFP, Progressive Federal Party
PRP, Progressive Reform Party
PSC, Program for Social Change
RCA, Reformed Church in Africa (= DRC, for Indians)
RSA, Republic of South Africa
SABA, South African Black Alliance
SABRA, South African Bureau of Racial Affairs
SACBC, Southern African Catholic Bishops Conference
SACC, South African Council of Churches
SACLA, South African Christian Leadership Assembly
SACOS, South African Council of Sports
SACP, South African Communist Party
SACTU, South African Congress of Trade Unions
SAIC, South African Indian Congress
SAIRR, South African Institute of Race Relations
SASO, South African Students Organization
Spro-cas, Study Project on Christianity in Apartheid Society
SWAPO, South West Africa (Namibia) People's Organization
TNIP, Transkeian National Independence Party
UCCSA, United Congregational Church of Southern Africa
UCM, University Christian Movement
UELCSA, United Evangelical Lutheran Church in Southern Africa
UELCSWA, United Evangelical Lutheran Church of South West Africa (Namibia)
UNISA, University of South Africa
UP, United Party
WCC, World Council of Churches
YCS, Young Catholic Students
YCW, Young Catholic Workers

SOUTHERN AFRICA 1981

PRETORIA
JOHANNESBURG
TRANSVAAL
SWAZILAND
KURUMAN
ORANGE FREE STATE
NATAL
ULUNDI
BLOEMFONTEIN
LESOTHO
PIETERMARITZBURG
DURBAN
UMTATA
HOMELANDS
GAZANKULU
VENDA
LEBOWA
BOPHUTHATSWANA
TRANSKEI
KWAZULU
CISKEI
KANGWANE
QWAQWA
SOUTH NDEBELE
EAST LONDON
Cape Town
PORT ELIZABETH

SOUTH AFRICA 1981

Desmond Tutu, Anglican Bishop,
General Secretary of the South African Council of Churches

Introduction

South Africa has been called "the last bastion of White racism." It has also been called a bastion of Western civilization, a defense against the dark forces of communism.

It is a beautiful, yet often desolate country, governed by a people that enjoys great material comfort yet suffers from some of the highest rates of suicide, homocide, coronary disease, divorce, and alcoholism in the world. It is a land where racial bitterness simmers close to the surface, yet where small acts of love and cooperation across the color lines persist.

It is a nation apparently bent on a collision course, shaped by irrational leaders who seem prepared to commit suicide rather than share power with the Black majority. As an editor of the *Rand Daily Mail* has observed, "The first thing you've got to understand about South Africa is that it's completely crazy."

Some facts are completely clear. It is the only republic that has constructed a vast edifice of legislation that deliberately denies human rights to the majority of its people. Hundreds have died in prison, cases of torture (documented by Amnesty International and other groups) are reported regularly, and over the years the republic has held the world's record for the per capita rate of executions.

Ironically, the South African regime views itself as a Christian theocracy. Indeed, in the Republic of South Africa Constitution Act (1961) God is credited with having given South Africa "this their own" land and with having protected the South African people from threats and perils.[1]

In few countries are sex films, gambling, obscene literature, or any other publication "blasphemous or offensive to the religious convictions of any group" censored so rigidly.[2]

Sunday is indeed a holy day in South Africa. The streets are virtually deserted as citizens demonstrate their solidarity by gathering for worship. In the well-appointed Dutch Reformed churches* women in dresses and hats, men in somber business suits, and children in frocks or suits and ties, carrying

---

*In the broadest sense of the term, "Dutch Reformed churches" comprise (1) the original Dutch Reformed Church founded by the colonists and now generally referred to as the DRC or NGK (Nederduitse Gereformeerde Kerk), terms we shall used interchangeably, reflecting the practice in White South Africa's bi-lingual society, (2) the DRC mission churches, which now consider themselves full-fledged churches: DRC in Africa, or NGKA, for Africans; the Sendingkerk (Mission Church), for Coloreds; and the Reformed Church in Africa (RCA), for Indians, (3) the Hervormde (reformed) Kerk, a small Afrikaans church which split from the NGK in the nineteenth century, (4) the Gereformeerde (reformed) Kerk, an even smaller Afrikaner splinter group commonly referred to as the Doppers. (See Chapter 15.)

1

gloves and hugging Bibles to their sides, sit rigidly in their pews, eyes fixed on the pulpit. A few miles away, in the African independent (Black) churches, the faithful rock their bodies, clasp each other's hands, and dance as they make joyful noises unto the Lord.

In this explosive society the churches have been a power both for and against political change. The faith that purportedly unites all believers in one Body of Christ serves both to exacerbate and to mollify conflict between the races. For better or for worse, the Christian church is a potent political force in South Africa.

On the one hand, the main weight of the White Dutch Reformed churches, which over the years have served as the cradle of apartheid, continues to resist political and social transformation of the nation. On the other hand, since the banning of Black organizations in 1977, Africans, Coloreds, and Indians have come to view the multiracial churches as the only institution left where they can make their voices heard and exercise some measure of power. In these multiracial churches—a category that includes the Roman Catholic Church and most mainline Protestant denominations such as the Anglicans, Methodists, Presbyterians, and Congregationalists—Blacks are gaining influential positions. They are taking a more political stand, voicing most of the goals of the Black power organizations that the government tried to quell in 1977. The avowedly Christian regime is caught in a bind: it can ban "communist" or "subversive" organizations, but it can hardly ban the church of Jesus Christ.

A Profusion of Ironic Contrasts

On one side of Cape Town's Table Mountain, the visitor can see tropical gardens, shop windows filled with luxury goods, a beautifully landscaped transportation center, and Whites-only suburbs of comfortable homes. On the other side of the mountain, stretching to the East, stand shanties that Black married couples, condemned by law to live in single-sex hostels, have constructed—illegally—in order to remain together.

In White homes Black domestics dress the children of "madam" and "baas" and prepare food for their masters. Yet in most White business organizations even a college-educated Black employee is not permitted to use "Whites-only" toilets that are on almost every floor, and may have to take the elevator down to the courtyard in order to use antiquated facilities.

Driving through the Transkei, the first "homeland" to achieve so-called independence, the visitor notices that the rocky, barren stretches are inhabited by Blacks. Enclaves of green fertile land remain in the hands of Whites and are still parts of the Republic.

The White government continues to advertise in Western Europe for skilled White workers. Yet every day long lines of African workers, eager to upgrade their skills—indeed, desperate for any kind of work whatsoever—

queue up for jobs that are steadily diminishing in number. . . . At a city filling station, a car is washed by machine, then polished by three or four Africans, each of whom may work eighty-four hours a week for a wage equivalent to twenty-two dollars.

Coloreds and Indians in need of housing and able to pay for it must by law seek it only in "their" areas. And at night, when the White *burgers* retire to homes fortified by spiked fences, high hedges, and police dogs, the city sky-lines begin to glow with familiar neon: General Motors, Mobil, Ford, ITT, Firestone, Holiday Inn, Pepsi Cola. For a moment, American visitors might think themselves back in Chicago.

Paradoxically, South Africa still enjoys a relatively free press. However, radio, television, books, periodicals, and films are heavily censored. . . . City streets in "White areas" are filled with Blacks. . . . In a few churches today, one can see White infants being baptized by Black clergy. Scattered across the nation there are still homes where young Blacks and Whites— courageous enough to break the laws by living together communally—gather round a table each evening, sharing food, song, and hopes.

The struggle in South Africa is not a simple conflict between good and evil, justice and oppression. Individually, a great many members of the dominant Afrikaner group are friendly, generous people, hospitable to visitors, and—contrary to the prevalent stereotype—anxious to be accepted by the rest of the world. A growing number of them are questioning the ideol-ogy of apartheid. Although English-speaking Whites are generally consid-ered more "liberal," many are more bigoted than their Afrikaner counter-parts.

Many Indians and Coloreds refuse to get involved in anything political. Among the few Africans who have acquired a little money, a fair number are engaged in power struggles or even corruption. Most Blacks, understandably, are striving for the ecologically wasteful lifestyles of Whites in South Africa and the United States.

As Ernie Regehr aptly observes, it is more useful to examine the conflict in terms of incompatibilities: "When one group desires something that can be obtained only at the expense of what another group also desires, their in-terests are clearly incompatible."[3] The conflict in South Africa is primarily over resources and power, and secondarily over ideology or abstract stand-ards of justice. Such a struggle of interests has many parallels in other so-cieties, including the American.

It may also be useful to see the dominant Afrikaner *volk* as prisoners of their own turbulent history. They have carried into the twentieth century atti-tudes that served their survival in the colonialist nineteenth century, but ulti-mately can only destroy the *volk* in the future. Preoccupied with preserving their identity and obsessed by fear of the *swartgevaar* ("Black danger"), they seem bent on fulfilling the conditions that will justify their worst fears. Thus the Afrikaners have become captives of a system that dehumanizes both the oppressed and the oppressors.

The System

In South Africa—a country one-eighth the size of the United States—some 4.3 million Afrikaans- and English-speaking Whites control the destiny of 22 million voteless Black Africans, 2.5 million mixed-race Coloreds, and 750,000 Asians (mostly of Indian descent).

Since 1948 the country has been ruled by the National Party, the vast majority of whose members are Afrikaners, descendants of the Dutch pioneers who came to Cape Town more than three hundred years ago. Although Afrikaners constitute only 60 percent of the electorate (the other 40 percent being English-speaking Whites), in 1977 the party drew 64.5 percent of the votes for members of Parliament—representing a steady increase based largely on the number of English-speaking Whites who have shifted to the right as their fears of Black domination have risen. Even White voters do not choose the prime minister, who is named by the party caucus (an elitist group of members of Parliament) and can hold the office for life. In recent years the party has increasingly usurped the functions of Parliament as the link between the electorate and the executive.[4]

The White minority controls the lives of over 25 million non-Whites by means of complex laws (to be described in greater detail in subsequent chapters). Fundamental to implementing apartheid is the Population Registration Act, which requires that every person carry an identity card specifying whether they are White, African, Colored, or Asian. Coloreds are further divided into subgroups and Africans are divided into tribal groups—Zulu, Xhosa, Tswana, and so on. Although many urban Africans do not identify with any tribe and reject such a label, it is stamped into every African "pass."

Laws require every African over sixteen to carry their "reference book" detailing their name, tribal origin, where they are permitted to live, and what sort of work they are permitted to do. An African cannot move without that pass, and failure to have an official stamp on it entitling them to be where they are can lead to imprisonment. (There are more than half a million prosecutions a year under the pass laws.)

Extremely important is the Group Areas Act, which zones land so rigorously that hundreds of thousands of Blacks have been ordered out of their houses and businesses and moved miles beyond the city limits to dreary housing in "townships." Moreover, if African workers lose their jobs, they may be "endorsed out" to a tribal homeland even if they have never seen it and even if the working spouse remains behind, thus splitting the family.

Laws forbid interracial marriage; sexual relations across the color line are a crime. A job reservation policy that literally differentiates between "civilized labor" and that done by "people who are barbarous" sets aside the best jobs for Whites.

Despite official rhetoric about "separate development," the entire economy depends on cheap Black labor. Hence the millions of Africans—domestics, laborers, clerks, and a few professionals—living in townships outside White cities. In addition, Blacks come to the cities to work in White-owned enterprises as migrant laborers. They must leave their families behind in the homelands and live in huge, concrete "hostels," seedbeds of prostitution, homosexuality, venereal disease, alcoholism, and malnutrition.

The Bantu Education Act restricts Africans to inferior primary and secondary schooling that, unlike White education, is neither free nor compulsory. By law Africans cannot attend school until they are seven years old.

All these laws, and many others, are buttressed by various acts empowering the police to arrest whom they wish, keep them incommunicado from their families and lawyers, and detain them without issuing any charge whatsoever. The draconian police network includes informers, some fifteen thousand of whom are said to be Blacks paid or blackmailed to report on their own people. In addition, the Republic maintains the most powerful military force on the continent. It can put two hundred thousand troops into the field and is reputed to possess nuclear weapons.

The rationale behind this policy rests on the theory of "separate development," a refinement of "apartheid," a term that arouses opprobrium around the world. In theory, separate development posits a power bloc of ethnically rooted independent states, linked together by common interests. In practice, it means that although Africans have not been consulted about the arrangement, each is attached to one of ten tribal "bantustans," or homelands, decaying rural slums that have become dumping grounds for women and children, the old, infirm, and unemployed.

The homelands make up 13 percent of the national territory, leaving the White minority in control of the remaining 87 percent, the "White" areas. Paradoxically, Blacks constitute the majority in "White" South Africa because they make up the bulk of the labor force—yet they are considered "visitors."

The result of this policy is that all South Africans—both Black and White—live in "ghettos." As one White Quaker put it, "I, too—I live in a White liberal ghetto. I seldom move into an Afrikaner, or even a Black liberal ghetto. The tragedy is that South Africans are not communicating with each other."

The South African Churches

Nationalist leaders have thundered against Black clergymen and their White "liberal" counterparts for mixing politics and religion. The reality is that politics and religion have always gone hand in hand in South Africa. Afrikaner church leaders themselves have proudly described apartheid as the child of the Dutch Reformed Church (DRC), which is often referred to as "the National Party at prayer." Nationalist politicians tend to equate nation, church, and party. "Without hesitation," writes one of the party's frankest historians, "it can be said that it is principally due to the Church that the Afrikaner nation has not gone under. . . . With the dilution of this philosophy, it [the Afrikaner nation] must inevitably disappear."[5] And in the words of David Bosch, a leading contemporary Afrikaner theologian, "Above all, the Afrikaner is a religious animal."

But so are the Black Africans. To them religion permeates every aspect of life; they cannot understand the Western dichotomy between the political and the spiritual. Moreover, Christianity is growing all over the continent. Far more than Western intellectuals and politicians, African leaders feel compelled to explain it to themselves and to others if they are not deeply committed Christians. Tanzanian Julius Nyerere and Zimbabwean Robert Mugabe are pious Catholics; Zambian Kenneth Kaunda, son of a Presbyterian minister, exhorts his people by religious appeals. These are only a few examples of the seriousness with which African nationalists take the faith brought by Whites.

In South Africa, even the many Blacks who blend certain elements of traditional animist religions with the teachings of Jesus of Nazareth tend to identify themselves as Christian. In 1970 only 18 percent of the African population declared that they did not belong to a church. Moreover, since its inception in the late nineteenth century, South African Black nationalism has had strong Christian undertones.

It is true that many young Blacks, particularly in the townships, are becoming increasingly alienated from the church as *institution*. They criticize it for "indoctrinating our people into servility," for "destroying our customs," or for "the hypocritical way it teaches Christian principles but fails to practice them." Yet the Black Consciousness Movement itself emerged out of a religious context. Black consciousness leaders turn to the clergy for support and counsel, some young militants are studying theology because they see it as a source of guidance and as a way of reaching people, and some of the outstanding Black leaders today are activists who are articulating Black theology.

It is also true that with the growth of affluence and secularization in society in general, the power of the Dutch Reformed churches vis-à-vis government policy has declined somewhat. Nevertheless, it remains one of the most unifying elements of Afrikaans culture, and furnishes a rationale for apartheid. Its *potential* as an agent of change can hardly be overestimated, for the DRC extends into every town and *dorp* ("village"), and socializes citizens from the cradle to the grave. It could serve as a potent force in preparing Whites for the political change that now seems inevitable. However, as we shall see in subsequent chapters, it is extremely unlikely that the DRC will utilize this potential.

It is in the so-called English-speaking multiracial churches that Blacks and Whites can meet in the land of apartheid. To be sure, the majority of English-speaking Whites are scarcely more open to transformation of South African structures than their Afrikaner counterparts. It is also true that because of residential segregation, Blacks and Whites rarely meet in parish churches.

Nevertheless, from their ministers, from their synods, and from the South African Council of Churches, Whites can hear official church statements that challenge their personal resistance to change.

Certainly, changes are occurring. Most parks and public libraries and a growing number of first-class hotels, restaurants, theaters, and sports events are no longer segregated. Most Africans are acquiring collective bargaining rights. More reforms are promised. A spirit of greater pragmatism and greater willingness to engage in dialogue characterizes Prime Minister Pieter Botha's administration.

But the right to enter a five-star hotel is meaningless to a hungry person, Black leaders emphasize. There have been virtually no fundamental changes in "Bantu" education, security laws, residential segregation, the right to vote, the pass system, or the homelands policy. To most Blacks, the changes that have occurred have been too few, too late, and too superficial.

To most Whites, on the other hand, these changes and the speed at which they are taking place are frightening. Yet the fact that their pragmatic leaders have espoused reform and that the bulk of the White citizenry has followed indicates some alteration in the White South Africans' view of the world and their own place in it.

In this process the church is not the primary agent of change. Economic and political pressures are far more fundamental. Especially since the formation of a Black regime in Zimbabwe, it has been clear that such pressures will be emerging from outside the country with increasing frequency. They will also emerge from the inside, for today the tide of events in southern Africa and closer communication with the rest of the world have raised the expectations of the Black majority and endowed their leaders with greater confidence.

Slowly but surely, Blacks are taking the initiative. Despite their military might, Whites are being thrust into the defensive position of reacting to Black demands.

Most White South Africans seem to recognize this phenomenon, albeit dimly. A study conducted in 1978 by Theo Hanf of the Arnold Bergstraesser Institute[6] of Freiburg, Germany, reveals that most Whites expect Black majority rule in South Africa by the year 2000. Yet very few White respondents had any conception of how that would happen, and most of them appeared unwilling to think about it.

This is not to say that Blacks are unified in their ideas of how to get from here to there. The leading Black nationalist groups—the African National Congress, the Pan-Africanist Congress, the Black Consciousness Movement, and Inkatha—are plagued by rivalry with each other and by internal quarrels. Some Blacks envision enjoying a piece of the pie, gaining access to the fruits of the capitalist system. Others, including many religious leaders, want to change the system itself and are seeking to develop a level of awareness that can create Black institutions that will eliminate White political privilege and build new economic structures.

To many Whites this vision of a society based on a more equitable distribution of resources is far more threatening than sharing their neighborhoods with Blacks. It is easy for them to convince themselves that these visions of an alternative society are the work of "communists."

Although the church is not the primary agent of change, it plays an extremely important role. The multiracial churches, some segments of the African independent churches, the Black (formerly "mission") churches of the DRC, and even some leaders of the White Afrikaans churches are already assuming a more prophetic stance, and could play a mediating role in the inevitable conflict.

However severely outsiders may criticize the church for not opposing apartheid more vigorously, the truth is that the church has gathered within itself an impressive number of women and men, Blacks and Whites, who take heroic risks to fight for an end to oppression. No police system can suppress them. They return from imprisonment or banning and quietly go back to their work. Even in their absence, others come forth to take their place.

They know that theirs is a thankless task; seldom do they find genuine recognition either at home or abroad. They know that even when a new regime emerges they will be called on to fight other injustices. They often feel that the endeavor to change hearts and minds is hopeless. Yet they continue to hope against hope.

Notes

1. Monica Wilson and Leonard Thompson, eds., *The Oxford History of South Africa* (London: Oxford University Press, 1971), Vol. 2, *South Africa 1870–1966,* p. 371.

2. Loraine Gordon et al., eds., *A Survey of Race Relations in South Africa, 1977* (Johannesburg: SAIRR, 1978), p. 174.

3. Ernie Regehr, *Perceptions of Apartheid* (Scottdale, Pa.: Herald, 1979), p. 7.

4. Heribert Adam and Hermann Giliomee, *Ethnic Power Mobilized: Can South Africa Change?* (New Haven: Yale University Press, 1979), p. 206.

5. G. D. Scholtz, *Het die Afrikaanse Volk 'n Toekums?* (Johannesburg: Voortrekkerpers, 1953), pp. 80–81.

6. Theo Hanf et al., *Südafrika, Friedlicher Wandel?* (Munich: Kaiser, 1978). This work is commonly referred to as the "Freiburg Study."

Part One
South Africa from Its
Origins to 1960

CHAPTER ONE

History to 1900

Although it was a Portuguese, Bartholomeu Diaz, who discovered the Cape of Good Hope in 1486, the Dutch were the first Europeans to settle in South Africa. In 1652 the Netherlands East India Company set up a halfway station at the Cape for its sailors on their seven-month journey to the Orient. The company, a powerful mercantile empire unto itself, had little interest in settlement, but in 1657 did permit a few sailors and soldiers to leave its service and farm their own land.

Afrikaners are fond of saying that they were in South Africa long before Blacks arrived from the north, but there is ample evidence that in 1652, yellow-skinned Hottentots and Bushmen were already living on the Cape. The Bushmen were great hunters, and have left behind fascinating rock paintings in caves. With their poison-tipped arrows they resisted the settlers but were gradually forced northward into the Kalahari Desert.

More "civilized" than the Bushmen were the Hottentots, who called themselves Khoikhoi, "men of men." At first they met the Whites on amicable terms, exchanging their cattle and sheep for European beads and copper. But as the newcomers sought more and more territory, the indigenous Khoikhoi found themselves dispossessed of grazing land. Some retaliated with cattle theft—providing the Whites with reasons for punitive measures and seizure of more land.

The Dutch Reformed Church (DRC) became the established church. Indeed, until 1804 Catholics were not allowed to practice their faith even though the Reformation had never succeeded in making Holland exclusively Protestant. The first DRC minister arrived in 1665. Missionary work began very slowly, however, partly because the religious needs of the Dutch themselves were poorly provided for, and partly because in 1618 the Synod of Dort, the great confessional assembly of the DRC, had declared that the children of heathen were not to be baptized, even if they had been taken into Christian households. But the Cape consistory sometimes acted independently, allowing the baptism of children of slaves if a White person guaranteed that they would be brought up Christians.

Gradually the number of Europeans increased as Dutch and French Huguenots fled religious persecution in their homelands. Although the Huguenots shared the Calvinist base of the Dutch Reformed Church, the governor of the colony at first refused the French permission to have their own pastor. It was already clear that even minor differences in religion had political significance. Moreover, although German Lutherans arrived in the colony during the first century of White settlement, it was only in 1778 that the East India Company permitted them to worship in public.

Because labor was needed, the company brought in slaves from East and West Africa, and from Malaya. Eventually many Malays mingled with White settlers and indigenous peoples, forming a subgroup of people who today are known as Coloreds. Some descendants are Muslim; a great many others belong to the N.G. Sendingkerk (Dutch Reformed Mission Church).

The tyrannical rule of the company was deeply resented, and many settlers moved eastward. The Khoikhoi put up fierce resistance, which lasted until after the British takeover in the early nineteenth century. Eventually, however, they became laborers in homes and on farms.

Living on large tracts of half-arid plains, separated from neighbors and cut off from their European roots, the hardy Dutch Boers ("farmers") turned in upon themselves, looking only to their own resources and to the Old Testament for guidance. They were particularly attracted to the stories of the patriarchs, whose lives seemed most akin to their own in their treks through the wilderness among wild beasts and wild aborigines, with no protection but their rifles and their God.

Mission Beginnings

The first missionary on the Cape was a Moravian, Georg Schmidt, from the religious community of Herrnhut. After his arrival in Cape Town in 1737, Schmidt moved to Genadendal, and patiently tried to convert the Khoikhoi. His difficulties with them were many, but his greatest obstacle was the opposition of DRC ministers to baptizing the heathen. He was forbidden to perform the sacraments; frustrated and disappointed, he returned to Europe in 1744.[1]

Missionary work disappeared in the Cape for nearly fifty years. But in 1786, a young DRC minister began to arouse his flock to the necessity for missionary work among slaves and Khoikhoi.

In 1792 the Moravians were allowed to reopen the Genadendal station. Although a half-century had passed, many Khoikhoi remembered Schmidt, and had continued to say their prayers. The mission expanded rapidly, and by the middle of the nineteenth century it comprised seven stations and over seven thousand members. These stations were disciplined communities on the Herrnhut pattern: enclosed settlements where the "heathen" could learn skills, elementary education, the dignity of labor, and the standards of civilized living. This pattern of converting Africans from one way of life to another and establishing new communities where they were to remain for the rest of their lives was to become a permanent feature in South African missionary work.

In 1795 the British occupied the Cape. They were ousted in 1803, but returned in 1806. Officials of the Dutch Batavian Republic determined to institute reforms in the spirit of the Enlightenment, and in 1804 declared the DRC no longer the state church. Because, however, it possessed the largest membership and was a helpmeet of the government, it was given certain privileges. To this day formal freedom of worship has continued in South Africa.

The tiny Jewish community did not take advantage of the opportunity for public worship,[2] but the Catholics did. In 1804 three Roman Catholic priests arrived in Cape Town. They were expelled two years later, however, when the Cape was recaptured by the British, for the new major general was a Scots Presbyterian who shared the feelings of the Calvinist Dutch toward Catholics.

After 1814 the Anglican clergy were allowed more freedoms, such as the right to perform the marriage service. In 1820 thousands of immigrants—working-class townspeople rather than farmers—arrived from England, and by 1830 the colony had acquired a settled British population. But a curious situation prevailed: the English church was the official church of the government, whereas the Dutch church was the official church of the colony.

When the number of Dutch Reformed ministers declined, because it was difficult to import them from what had been formerly the homeland but was now a foreign power, the colonial government tried to find suitable candidates from Scotland. Like the Cape Reformed Church, the Scots Church was Presbyterian and Calvinist. At the DRC synod of 1824, it was even suggested that there should be some sort of union with the Church of Scotland. The proposal was defeated, but Scottish ministers continued to be employed in White congregations and exerted considerable influence on the Dutch church in South Africa.

Mission Growth

By the 1820s, missionary work was well under way. As early as 1821, two Presbyterian ministers, William Thomason and John Bennie, were sent out by the Glasgow Missionary Society and paid by the government to work among the Africans along the eastern Cape frontier. Bennie became a pioneer in putting the Xhosa language into written form and publishing the literature of that tongue, and later helped found the famous Lovedale institution.

The Lutheran Church was strengthened by German, Scandinavian, and American Lutheran mission societies. Greatly influenced by the methods of the Moravians, they formed self-supporting, close-knit communities. In 1829 the Rhenish Mission Society, representing the Lutheran, Reformed, and United churches of Germany, began work in the Cape Colony. Five years later the Berlin Mission arrived.

The nondenominational Paris Missionary Society also sent three men to the Cape in 1829. One settled with Huguenot descendants near Wellington to devote himself to the slaves, and the other two moved north to the land of the Bechuana.

One of the most famous of the mission societies that sprang up as the result of the eighteenth-century evangelical movement in Europe was the London Missionary Society (LMS). Originally it united Anglicans, Methodists, Presbyterians, and independents; each minister decided the form of religious organization best suited to his situation. Eventually, however, Anglicans, Methodists, and Presbyterians set up their own mission societies and the support of the LMS fell largely upon Congregationalists. The American Board of Commissioners for Foreign Missions (ABM) was also interdenominational in origin, but finally came under the aegis of the Congregationalists.

The first LMS missionary, Johannes Vanderkemp, arrived in the colony in 1799. When he established a place of refuge for the Khoikhoi at Bethelsdorp, the local Boers were incensed. Khoikhoi were being lured away from their proper position as farm laborers; Bethelsdorp was a nest of idleness and vice! To make matters worse, Vanderkemp dressed and ate like a native, and even married a young slave from Madagascar. Some mixed marriages had occurred in the earliest days of the colony, but as Whites came to perceive that cultural assimilation would be accompanied by social integration, mixed marriage and the baptism of slaves began to meet resistance within the framework of a deliberate antiassimilation policy.[3]

One of his successors, Dr. John Philip, was a better administrator, but likewise a champion of the Khoikhoi. In 1828 he influenced the government to issue Ordinance 50, declaring that vagrancy was no longer punishable, that Khoikhoi could give or withhold labor, and that all free persons of color were to enjoy the same legal rights as White colonists. In the same year he published a book delineating charges of White cruelty. As time went on, he came to believe ever more strongly that the Khoikhoi ought to live in "places of refuge" until they had been civilized and trained in new roles so that they could take their place as full citizens.

To farmers who saw such a high proportion of Khoikhoi (at one time up to a third) living on missions, such ideas were revolting. Missionaries were the villains responsible for the shortage of labor! A pattern of thought and a pattern of power were growing: missionaries were seen as agitators.

Shortly after the second British occupation, Methodist missionary Barnabas Shaw arrived from England and began to work among the people of Namaqualand, beyond the Orange River. By 1826 he had established a thriving station with a permanent Christian community, from which other centers began to spread.

The real period of growth for Methodism began after the arrival of the 1820 settlers. One particularly zealous young minister, William Shaw, attempted to place a missionary with each important chief in the eastern part of the colony, and to establish a chain of connecting stations. By 1860 there were thirty-two Methodist missionaries and some five thousand converts in an area stretching from the coast around Grahamstown across the Kei River into independent "Kaffirland" (now the Transkei). This rapid expansion generated some conflict with the Anglicans, who were finally beginning to turn their eyes toward the eastern part of the province.

By 1830, the fundamental conflict between missionaries and settlers was evident. As John de Gruchy observes, "The basic reason that both Dutch and English settlers resented some missionaries was that the missionaries not only evangelized the indigenous peoples, but took their side in the struggle for justice, rights, and land."[4] A cleavage between settler and missionary churches emerged. Although the English-speaking churches eventually adopted a way of relating settler church and mission church that was different from the DRC's approach, in the nineteenth century the pattern was similar. The English-speaking churches were also divided along ethnic lines, even though this did not usually mean separate synods.[5]

The Great Trek

Meanwhile, a profound schism between Afrikaners and the British was growing, culminating in the Great Trek of the 1830s. Behind the schism lay a struggle for the land—a struggle that was to dominate the history of South Africa's nineteenth-century frontiers. It explains not only the conflict between the Boers and the British, but also the confrontation between Blacks and Whites.

To the Boers, the shortage of labor was due to the missionaries' influence on the government. Equally alarming were the attempts of the British colonial government to stop farmers from going into Kaffirland to retrieve stolen cattle, and its restriction of the size of farms so that the frontier could be populated more densely. It was clear to the Boers that missionaries, the Khoikhoi, and the government formed a coalition against decent Whites.

Then, in 1836, came the thunderbolt. England abolished slavery entirely, and offered compensation—obtainable only in London—of £1.25 million for slaves valued at £3 million. The outrage of the Boers is clear in the words of a Voortrekker woman, Anna Steenkamp:

> It is not so much their freeing which drove us to such lengths, as their being placed on an equal footing with Christians, contrary to the laws of God, and the natural distinctions of race and color, so that it was intolerable for any decent Christian to bow down beneath such a yoke; wherefore we rather withdrew in order to preserve our doctrines in purity.[6]

Hemmed in by the British colonial government on one side and Black tribes pushing south, the Afrikaners determined to go it alone, sustained only by faith in their God. In 1836 the Great Trek began as five thousand hardy souls set out northward in canvas-topped ox-wagons, leaving the eastern

coasts, climbing the mountains onto the great interior plain. Despite skir-
mishes with African tribes, especially the Xhosa, many settled in the area
between the Orange River and the Vaal River, and others pushed up across the
Vaal into present-day Transvaal.

One group, under Piet Retief, descended the Drakensberg escarpment into
Natal. On a peace-making mission to the Zulu King Dingaan, Retief and sixty
followers were murdered. Then the king sent ten thousand warriors to the
Voortrekker camp, where a few men had stayed behind to guard the women
and children, and slaughtered them all.

But a new Voortrekker leader had already appeared: Andries Pretorius
(after whom Pretoria, South Africa's administrative capital, was named). On
December 9, 1838, the commandos gathered for their regular evening prayer-
meeting, and entered into a sacred covenant with God: should he grant them
victory in the coming struggle, a church would be built and the day kept holy
forever. On December 16, the Zulus attacked. Positioning their ox-wagons in
a circle, a *laager* ("camp"), the men kept firing, while their women loaded the
guns. The Zulus were driven off, and the Ncome became a river of Zulu
blood—henceforth to be known as Blood River. Some three thousand Zulus
had been massacred, and—miraculously!—only three of the commandos
had been wounded. To the Voortrekkers, it was proof that the Almighty had
responded to their vow—and that they were God's chosen people.

The Great Trek divided South Africa politically into British colonies, Boer
Republics, and African tribal lands, although frontier wars raged until the
end of the nineteenth century. After their victory at Blood River in 1838, the
Voortrekkers established the Republic of Natalia. It was short-lived, however, for in 1841 the British annexed the land. Most of the Voortrekkers then
trekked back over the Drakensberg escarpment, and Natal, as a result of
British immigration, became the largely English-speaking province it is today
(if one considers only the White population). In 1848 the British took control
of the territory between the Orange and the Vaal Rivers and it became known
as the Orange River Sovereignty. Again the Trekkers, in their search for
freedom, had encountered the greater strength of Britain.

In 1854, however, the English gave up the Orange River Sovereignty, which
became the Trekker Republic of the Orange Free State. Two years later the
Transvaal became the South African Republic.

When Sir George Grey arrived in the Cape in 1854, his intention was to
federate the three British possessions (Natal, the Cape, and British Kaffraria)
and the Boer Republics (the Orange Free State and republics north of the
Vaal) as a protection against barbarism.

He hoped to entice chiefs to retire by offering them handsome pensions
and to put White magistrates in their place, then inject wedges of White settlers into African areas. Christian mission stations were to be used to bolster
his policy of pacifying and civilizing the eastern frontier. This "integra-
tionist" plan was opposed by Theophilus Shepstone, administrator of native
affairs in Natal, who believed that Africans should be gathered in vast "loca-

tions" where they could live according to their own laws and customs, yet learn something of the civilized life.

Hinchliff points out that there were pronounced differences in both political and missionary theory. There were those who believed that separation of Black from White was the only way to secure justice for the former or safety for the latter. Others believed that the races must live together, either because Africans should provide labor for White landowners or because peaceful coexistence was right and good.

In the matter of missionary strategy, some believed that the right thing to do was to convert Blacks from their "heathen" culture and settle them where they could absorb civilization and Christianity together. Others believed that converts should be left in their own community, that they should be encouraged to go out as missionaries among their own people, and that African tribes and the African way of life should be Christianized as a whole.

Often political "separationism" went with missionary beliefs of the second type, for if one maintains that African culture ought to be retained but Christianized, then it will seem that the only way to retain the culture is to isolate the Western influence. In practice, however, such insulation was never really achieved.

Moreover, the attempts of successive White governments to stop interaction between White colonists and the Bantu were doomed to failure. Many Europeans considered it an obligation to teach the gospel to every human being, intermarriage between non-Whites and White farmers or missionaries was not uncommon, the urge to trade was compelling on both sides, and—most important—White farmers depended on "native labor."

In 1857, before Grey's plans to spread the missions and pacify the frontiers could be put into effect, the Xhosa people was decimated by an undertaking that embodied their desperate hope of getting rid of Whites and recovering their land. Their prophets had promised that if the Xhosa would kill their cattle and destroy their crops, their ancestral spirits would return on a certain day, give them new cattle and endless supplies of food, and drive the Whites into the sea. The day came, but no such miracle occurred.

Despite the efforts of the government and missionaries to supply food, thousands of Blacks died. The Xhosa were a broken people. Survivors came into the colony looking for work, and White colonists were settled in the newly depopulated areas. Yet some missionaries rejoiced that good had come out of evil, for the chiefs' power had been one of the obstacles in the way of their work.

The relationship between missionaries and the government was becoming closer and more complex. Although missionaries were usually instructed not to meddle in "politics," many could not fail to be moved by compassion for homeless tribal Blacks and by goodwill to the colonial administration. They tried to act as intermediaries and even came to be used, officially and unofficially, as government agents with tribes beyond the Kei River. Was this politics?[7]

When Britain annexed Kaffraria, missionaries of all denominations welcomed the move. Even where there was no open antagonism with tribal chiefs, missionaries who required their converts to forego African institutions such as polygamy and witchcraft felt compelled to provide a society in which they could live in relative peace. Many missionaries also felt it their Christian duty to protect refugees escaping from African justice who claimed that they were being persecuted for supposed witchcraft. Hence it is hardly surprising that most missionaries worked for the day when British order and justice would prevail over all southern Africa.

David Livingston paved the way toward fulfillment of this vision. Beginning his work in South Africa as a member of the London Missionary Society, he became determined to set non-White peoples free and to help Africans meet Whites on more equal terms. In his explorations, he came to feel that his special calling was to open up the whole of Africa to the missionaries. Indeed, by the time of his death in 1873, he had penetrated the wilds of both southern and central Africa, making it possible for missionaries to reach hitherto unknown parts of the "darkest continent."

Divisions within the DRC

During the mid-nineteenth century upheavals shook the DRC. The Great Trek had sowed the seeds of division in that church. In 1837 the synod of the Cape DRC denounced the exodus. The Voortrekkers were convinced that the Cape church had adopted the viewpoint of the colonial government. Moreover, the Cape church still made no official distinction between White and non-White members. Trekkers came to see this as another example of undue "missionary" and "government" influence on the church. The Cape church had also refused to send an accredited minister of their church to accompany them. (Eventually three ministers from other denominations ministered to them, including an American Presbyterian, Daniel Lindley, who quit his work with the Matabele people and joined forces with the Boers in Natal.)

As early as 1839, White members of a DRC church at Stockenstrom in the eastern Cape asked their presbytery for permission to have separate communion. The presbytery responded with a firm *no* and referred the issue to the church council. It agreed with the presbytery and referred the matter to the General Synod, which upheld the decision of the two lower bodies: such a proposal would run counter to Scripture and the unity of the church.

However, the question surfaced at every synod thereafter, for during this period the Boers were shaken by the emancipation of the slaves, the Great Trek, and splits in the DRC itself. In 1857, after a long debate, the synod finally decided to allow individual churches to have separate communion and separate services. Yet the decision was seen as a concession to the "weakness" of White brothers who did not have the moral strength to accept the presence of Coloreds and Africans. This was only a temporary measure, declared the synod; as Blacks became more acceptable in society, church services should again become integrated. Gradually, however, the prescription was turned around: when *society* became ready, then Blacks would become more acceptable. Thus the way was paved for the emergence, several decades later, of separate DRC "daughter" churches for Coloreds, Indians, and Africans.[8]

Religion remained supremely important to the Trekboers. Indeed, they felt they had to rely on God because there was no one else to whom to turn. The Trekkers had come to liken themselves to the Israelites of the Old Testament led by the Almighty into the wilderness, beset by dangerous enemies, but destined to be guided into the Promised Land.

As Hinchliff notes, their faith was patriarchal rather than sacerdotal. The father of the family, the leader of each group, must provide the necessary devotional exercises. Hence, as in the case of Sarel Cilliers, who administered the covenant on the eve of Blood River, the patriarchal figure of the leader of each Trekker group became the prototype of the religious leader. All this created a schism in experience and viewpoint between the Trekkers and the Cape church.

After the South African Republic (the Transvaal) became independent, in 1856, it was not the DRC, but a conservative offshoot, the Nederduitse Hervormde Kerk (NHK), that became the *volkskerk* ("people's church") in the newly freed land. (It remained the state church there until 1910.) At its inception in 1853 and for many years thereafter, there was no intention to separate from communion with the Cape church; the NHK simply rejected organic union.

Differences between the two churches were more political than doctrinal: the Trekkers sought independence and many felt that the British colonial government was trying to use the Cape church to get its hands on the Boers again. Only later did real schism emerge, with the result that today the NGK (DRC) and the NHK exist side by side in the Transvaal. The constitution of 1856 not only recognized the NHK formally, but also asserted that there was to be no equality of Black and White in either church or state.

Religious conflict among the Voortrekkers themselves was growing, however. Some Transvalers, stimulated by theological controversy in Holland, broke away from the NHK and in 1859 established the Gereformeerde Kerk—the "Dopper Kerk"—in Potchefstroom. Strictly puritanical, they vowed adherence to the standards of faith and morals laid down by the Synod of Dort, and even raised strident objections to hymns, declaring that only the recitation of psalms was acceptable in the eyes of God.

Eventually the Dopper faith became associated with the neo-Calvinism of Abraham Kuyper, the Dutch theologian who fought for the separation of church and state, insisted that each sphere of life has a sovereignty over its own affairs under God, and laid the theological foundation for later Afrikaner nationalism. It was this "Dopper Kerk," not the Dutch Reformed Church, that was truly Calvinist, says de Gruchy. Today the Doppers' theological school at Potchefstroom University for Christian Higher Education is the fountainhead of ultra-Calvinist thought.

In the 1860s and '70s the DRC in the Cape was subjected to a bitter, complex struggle between liberals and conservatives. The central figure in the drama was Andrew Murray, Jr., a Scotland-educated conservative who led a widespread revival movement. For a number of reasons—including the development of an indigenous seminary at Stellenbosch that produced "orthodox" ministers of strongly Calvinist fundamentalist persuasion—the number of liberals dwindled. In Hinchliff's words, "The Cape church had become in ethos and outlook more like the churches of the Boers in the North. . . . The triumph of conservative theology had meant that a simple, fervent, old-fashioned piety, quite different from the usual trends that developed in most Christian churches in the nineteenth century, had become the norm in the Cape church."[9]

Missionary Societies

By 1860, missionary societies were engaged in subtle competition for souls of the "heathen."

In the Cape Colony the Moravians, the Presbyterians, the Rhenish missionaries, the Methodists, the Anglicans, the Congregational Union, and the London Missionary Society were particularly active. In Natal the Norwegian Mission, the Hermannsburg Mission, the Methodists, the Church of Sweden, the LMS, the American Board of Missions, and the Anglicans dominated the scene.

Rhenish missionaries were taking over the Methodist and LMS stations in Namaqualand (the desert area that straddles the border of present-day Namibia and the northern Cape Province). Penetrating even farther north the Finnish Mission Society began operating among the Ovambos, the most populous ethnic group in Namibia today. In nearby Bechuanaland (now Botswana) the LMS was actively serving the Griqua people (Coloreds of mixed Boer and Khoikhoi ancestry), as well as African tribes.

Having failed in its work with a tribe in Bechuanaland, the Paris Evangelical Missionary Society had begun work in Basutoland (now Lesotho). For some twenty years, until the arrival of the Roman Catholics from Natal in the 1860s, they were the dominating force in that area. At Thaba Nchu (not far from Lesotho) the Methodists set up a thriving center for Barolong tribes uprooted by the expansion of the Zulu empire, and the Berlin Missionary Society worked among Hottentots in what was to become the Orange Free State.

In almost all these areas other missionary groups were also at work, but rivalry was not intense. In the Transvaal, however, conflict was more evident—conflict among the Cape DRC (which was moving somewhat belatedly into the task of converting Africans), the Methodists, the Anglicans, and the Berlin Society.

More important were the conflicts of attitude. Should indigenous Christians live in their own village settlements or in integrated communities?

Should the native churches develop along independent lines or be brought into organic connections with the European churches of the same denominations? Not only the DRC, but the Lutherans and the Baptists believed it necessary to keep native and European churches apart, because Christianity ought to become thoroughly African and presented in such a form that Africans could understand it and accept it as something of their own. The Lutherans and Baptists later adopted multiracial unions but kept separate congregations and work projects.

On the other side, the issue of separate churches for different groups did not arise among the Catholics or Anglicans: their doctrinal stances precluded it. The Anglican attitude was reinforced by the fact that it had moved closer to early Catholic doctrine and ritual when it supported the Tractarian Movement, which opposed tendencies toward evangelical Protestantism in the Church of England. In 1870 the Anglicans claimed the status of a Province, and founded the Church of the Province in South Africa (CPSA). (The CPSA and the original but greatly reduced Church of England in South Africa coexist today, and they are often confused.)

Although neither the CPSA nor the Catholic Church established separate racial or language congregations, it is nonetheless true that discrimination in subtle forms did exist in both churches, and that their overall policy had the effect of creating "missions" where the congregation was Black and "parishes" where the congregation was White.

The situation of the Presbyterians was more complex. Like the ABM's Bantu Congregational Church and the LMS's mission church in Botswana, the churches that evolved from the Presbyterian missions among the Bantus and the Tsonga were dependent on foreign missionary leadership, but independent of the settler churches. Moreover, in 1893 the first Black minister of the Free Church of Scotland formed his own all-Black Presbyterian Church of Africa, known today as the Mzimba Church. Yet separation of the races was by no means complete, for in 1897 the settler churches and some Black congregations agreed together to declare autonomy from Scotland, and formed the multiracial Presbyterian Church of South Africa (now, of Southern Africa).

Is it true, as some Africans allege, that the missionaries were agents of conquest—indeed of cultural imperialism?[10]

Certainly educational institutions like Lovedale, Marianhill, Healdtown, and Saint Matthews gave Black South Africans better education than was available elsewhere on the continent until the 1950s, and were agents of change. Founded by the Presbyterians in 1824 in the eastern Cape, Lovedale was open to all races and all donominations. During the nineteenth century this was not uncommon in the Cape, for mission schools there were not segregated, though government schools were for Whites only. At Lovedale, Black and White pupils ate at separate tables and slept in separate dormitories, but attended classes together.

Like most mission schools in South Africa, Lovedale accepted girls as well as boys. Hence the great disparity between education of Black men and women, so marked elsewhere on the continent, never emerged in South Africa. Since educational facilities were scarce in the colony, White parents were happy to send their children to mission schools. Lovedale graduates included teachers, nurses, academics, administrators, clergymen, physicians, a minister of agriculture, a general manager of De Beers (a large mining company), a judge, two chief justices of South Africa, and even Black consciousness leaders such as Steve Biko.

In the early nineteenth century both the DRC and the Anglican authorities had discouraged Catholics from taking up missionary work. By the middle of the century, however, they were beginning to grow with amazing rapidity.

Marianhill, the most famous Catholic mission center, was founded in 1880. Originally a Trappist settlement modeled on the monastic missions of medieval Europe, Marianhill put the religious community at its core. Manual work was regarded as an essential part of real civilization for monks and Bantu alike. Boys were taught to farm and to make implements and homes for themselves; girls were prepared to become not servants but good wives and mothers. A Bantu community could thus become self-supporting.

Eventually a high school and a teachers' training college were formed, as well as a seminary to train African priests (thus giving birth to an African Catholicism). Moreover, the Trappist balance of contemplation and manual work earned the admiration of the Zulus; several chiefs asked the monks to establish schools—communities—for their people, and by the year 1909 the abbey had twenty-eight dependent settlements.

Lovedale emphasized academic learning and interracial education; Marianhill stressed manual training and formation of a total community. With their differing approaches, they shared the common goal of bringing Africans into "civilized society"—a goal with potential for new kinds of conflict.

By learning to read the Bible and other texts, converts moved into a literate society. Africans also learned more efficient cultivation of the land, and new skills ranging from carpentry to teaching and the ministry. To people whose simple needs might be met with only a few hours of labor every day, an ethic exalting work as a virtue in itself was new and strange. And with the concept of work came a new concept of time—as something that should be used, and was somehow linked to "progress."

European missionaries collided head-on with certain tribal customs and thought patterns, particularly sorcery, ancestor cults, and the time-honored tradition of polygamy. In the long run, family relations and even the political structure were radically changed by the condemnation of polygamy. Social relations too were changed. In some tribes, for example, men accustomed to grazing cattle began to join their womenfolk in cultivating the land. New tastes were formed—new "needs" for trinkets, cloth, sweets, and guns. (Hence the argument that missionaries were the advance agents of imperialism.)

All these changes produced conflicts of values. With the gospel of work and the acquisition of new kinds of goods came a certain competitiveness; communal values (such as communal land tenure) gave way to individualism.

More pronounced were the conflicts of loyalties. Many converts were caught between loyalty to their own chiefs and communities, and to the White missionary who taught them. In the end, some refused to fight on the side of their tribe, and then took refuge with missionaries.

Chiefs might be caught between their attraction to the gospel and their need to maintain status and power by keeping a number of wives. Their authority could also be undermined by their renunciation of tribal initiation ceremonies denounced by missionaries, by the refusal of some converts to fight with their tribes, and by the flight to mission stations of transgressors of tribal laws—not all of whom were innocent victims of witch-hunts.

Most of the missionaries expected their converts to wear a western style of clothing, to build square rather than round houses, to settle a village around the church and school rather than in scattered homesteads, to change the division of labor between men and women, and to abandon ancient festivals.

Many missionaries thus seemed to equate Christianity with western civilization. Many also practiced social apartheid. Even the few African clergymen trained by the church complained that they were treated as second-class citizens by their White brothers in Christ.

On the other hand, there can be no doubt that Africans were enormously enriched by the message of universal fellowship in God's family, the challenge of social justice, and the establishment of schools on the premise of a moral universe. Many of the outstanding older "moderate" Black political and religious leaders of today are products of mission schools. Black consciousness leader Steve Biko and Black newspaper editor Percy Qoboza, for example, attended Marianhill. Most Black graduates also seem to retain warm, vivid recollections of their White teachers. Between these Blacks and the embittered youth who have experienced only a narrow Bantu education lies a painful generation gap.

On balance, it would seem that few missionaries consciously attempted to impose a foreign culture. As Monica Wilson observes, the force compelling the Christian tradition was religious conviction, not cultural chauvinism. Moreover, the Africans sought the trappings of that culture, while at the same time struggling to maintain their own traditions.[11]

Clearly, the missionaries did soften the resistance of Africans to conquest. And yet, says Fergus Macpherson, a missionary writing about southern Africa as a whole:

Though the simultaneous arrival of the evangelist and the alien ruler made it seem that the former called people to close their eyes in prayer while the latter grabbed the land, it is clear that the situation would have been far worse if the missionaries had not come. The Christian agencies released forces which produced a creative tension in the minds of African people, which in turn sharpened their awareness both of injustice from White to Black and of their territorial and consequently continental oneness.[12]

In the long run, by educating African men and women and helping them realize their potential, Christian missionaries were partly responsible for creating frustration and tensions—for fomenting a revolution of rising expectations.

The Shaping of Things to Come

Other seeds of that revolution were sown with the discovery in 1867 of a diamond near the Orange River. The Orange Free State claimed the area, but a Griqua chief named Nicholas Waterboer also claimed it, won the case in arbitration court in 1871, and then "asked" the British to take over the territory.

In 1877, Selukini, the Bopedi chief who had made desperate attempts to prevent the Berlin Missionary Society from proselytizing his people, attacked the Transvaal. Arguing that it was necessary to prevent a general outbreak of native wars, the British seized control of the area. The action succeeded in antagonizing the Boers throughout South Africa and stimulating the movement to use the unifying name "Afrikaner." The annexation lasted only until 1881, for after the first Boer War for Independence, self-government was restored (although the Transvaal was subject to the suzerainty of Queen Victoria). Swaziland was made independent of the Republic and placed under British protection.

The discovery of diamonds and gold had a dramatic impact on life in South Africa and became the major determinant of its future economic and political patterns. By 1910 the country was producing 98 percent of the world's diamonds. Cecil Rhodes, the "empire builder," became not only the millionaire owner of vast diamond and gold fields, but Prime Minister of the Cape Colony and head of the British South Africa Company, which was the proprietor of the Rhodesias.[13] South Africa was catapulted into a new age of technology, cities, industries, railroads—and the machinations of imperialist industrial capital.

Skills were in the hands of the White workers; pick-and-shovel labor was to be done by Blacks at below-subsistence wages. Because many Africans had little liking for mining work and often left after two or three months, the government levied head and hut taxes on them. Hence the natives accustomed to living outside a money economy had no choice but to work for wages in order to pay the tax. Pass laws (first used, somewhat unsystematically, in the early nineteenth century on the Cape) were reintroduced and strengthened as a means of gaining control over African workers and binding them to contracts that, if broken, allowed Whites to apply criminal sanctions. Land tenure laws were tightened, for as long as Africans had access to relatively plentiful land, it was difficult for either the mining industry or White farmers to satisfy their labor needs. Moreover, thousands of Chinese, as well as Blacks from other southern African countries, were recruited to work in the mines.

To be sure, the dependency on cheap labor to make higher profits was only part of the process that had been going on since the seventeenth century. In 1717 the Council of Policy of the Netherlands East India Company decided that the settlement should be based not on free White, but "servile colored labor." The majority condemned White workers as lazy and incompetent and more expensive than slaves. After the abolition of slavery, Africans were seduced into working for wages. From 1860 to 1911, Natal sugar planters also imported indentured workers from India. Today most of the Indians and other Asians still live in Natal. Some continue as laborers on sugar plantations and in factories; others have moved upward to become small business entrepreneurs, but are still classified as second-class citizens.

Barracks-type lodgings were provided for Black miners. On a visit to South Africa, James Bryce, author of *The American Commonwealth,* described the compounds as "huge enclosures, unroofed, but covered with a wire netting to prevent anything from being thrown out of them, and with a subterranean entrance to the adjoining mine. . . . Every entrance is strictly guarded, and no visitor White or native is permitted, all supplies being obtained from the store within, kept by the company."

The discovery of the glittering dust also precipitated a gold rush into the Transvaal on the part of English and other European *uitlanders* (literally, "outlanders", i.e., "foreigners"), who soon outnumbered the Boers. The latter wanted to have the tax money of the new arrivals, but did not want to share power.

In 1899, the conflicts that had been building up since the early 1800s culminated in the Anglo-Boer War. Bent on victory, the British did not hestitate to burn farms and put women and children into concentration camps, where thousands of them died. Three years later the Boers were defeated, and their leader, the redoubtable Dopper Paul Kruger, took refuge in Holland. The defeat climaxed what the Boers, in their bitterness, came to call the "century of wrong."

Notes

1. Peter Hinchliff, *The Church in South Africa* (London: SPCK, 1968), p. 10.
2. The Jews had no synagogues until 1841, and totaled only some sixty families in 1860.
3. Hinchliff, *The Church in South Africa,* p. 6.

4. John W. de Gruchy, *The Church Struggle in South Africa* (Grand Rapids: Eerdmans, 1979), p. 13.

5. Ibid., p. 46.

6. Ibid., p. 19.

7. Ibid., p. 84.

8. Ibid., p. 8.

9. Hinchiff, *The Church in South Africa,* p. 84.

10. Colin Bundy, in *The Rise and Fall of the South African Peasantry* (Berkeley: University of California Press, 1979) observes from a Marxist perspective that "the 'Cape liberal' merchant/ missionary axis favored the creation of a class of Black rural producer-consumers." But, Bundy continues, the African peasant producer was destroyed by capitalist mining and farming interests that needed cheap labor for their rapidly expanding territories. Hence the underdevelopment of African farming, says Bundy, was "the other side of the coin of capitalist development in South Africa."

11. Monica Wilson and Leonard Thompson, eds., *The Oxford History of South Africa* (London: Oxford University Press, 1967), Vol. 1, *South Africa to 1870,* p. 267.

12. Fergus Macpherson, *Kaunda* (Lusaka: Oxford University Press, 1974), pp. 60–61.

13. The Rhodesias included present-day Zimbabwe (Southern Rhodesia) and Zambia (Northern Rhodesia). The Rhodes-dominated British-South Africa Company (BSA) also came to assert controlling interest in Malawi (Nyasaland).

CHAPTER TWO

The Genesis of Afrikaner Civil Religion

In 1910 the four colonies—the Cape, the Orange Free State, the Transvaal, and Natal—merged into the new self-governing Union of South Africa, within the British Empire. With the end of imperialism, the country seemed ready to enter a new era of goodwill.

The English and Dutch languages were declared equal. The Cape was to keep its nonracial franchise, which included several thousand Colored and African voters (who met stringent educational and economic qualifications), but this was not to be extended to the other three provinces. All four agreed that whatever the voting rights of non-White people, no non-White could be elected to either house of Parliament.

Although talk of goodwill filled the air, and the first three prime ministers (Louis Botha, James Hertzog, and Jan Smuts) were former generals who had led the Boers against British troops but now believed in peace between the two White groups, many Afrikaners continued to resist reconciliation.

Why? Certainly the Union, created with the connivance of Britain, made no pretense of sharing power with non-Whites. Indeed, the blame for racial injustice in the twentieth century cannot be placed on the Afrikaners alone, for if Britain had bequeathed a steadily widening nonracial franchise to the young Union, the history of South Africa might have been very different. The new Parliament had only White members. In 1911 it passed the Color Bar Act, extending the government's power to determine who could do skilled work in mining and engineering. In 1913 came the Native Land Act barring Blacks from acquiring terrain outside the "reserves," which constituted just 13 percent of South Africa and was generally poor land as well.

The real intent of the legislation was not only to insure that the minority acquire a guarantee in perpetuity to the better land, but that the Native Reserves become a vast labor pool. The 1926 Labor Act defined two kinds of labor: civilized (that done by Europeans) and uncivilized (that done by "people who are barbarous"). Master-and-servant legislation forbidding Blacks, under pain of prosecution, from leaving their jobs without permission was taken over from the former colonies, and existing pass laws were made more stringent.[1]

27

Despite this common front against the threat of non-White power, most Afrikaners were still consumed by memories of the "century of wrong," which they also saw as an heroic age of revolt in reaction to attacks from both African tribes and the powerful British. They became obsessed with guarding Afrikaner traditions, history, religion, philosophy, language, and culture. While welcoming the recognition of Dutch, they pushed for the recognition of Afrikaans (a mixture of High Dutch, Malay, a few tribal words, and new idioms emerging from the rugged life of the Boers), and that impulse was concretized in resistance to anglicization. The die-hards opposed South Africa's entry into World War I on the side of the British, even though it was an Afrikaner, General Botha, who led the country into the war.

From Inferiority to Political Control

In the process of defeat and postwar reconstruction the traditional agrarian Boer society had been shaken to its foundations. Afrikaners began making up for their economic and cultural disadvantages. One symptom was the founding of movements to reunite Afrikanerdom. Another was emigration to the cities. At the turn of the century, only about 10 percent of the Afrikaners were living in urban areas; by 1970 only about 12 percent were still on farms.

In 1910 about two-thirds of the White population was English-speaking. (Afterwards, this proportion gradually decreased.) Moreover, trade, commerce, and industry were in the hands of Anglo-Saxons. As de Klerk describes it, "The new immigrant Afrikaners were in fact strangers in their own country: hesitant, fearful of using their own language in shops and businesses, and confined very largely to the humbler areas and jobs."[2] Inferiority bred resentment, which in turn bred a new kind of nationalism.

When the Union was formed in 1910, Louis Botha became its first prime minister. Although a member of Botha's cabinet, James Hertzog scorned the Botha-Smuts policy of conciliaton with the English-speaking sector. He became the unofficial spokesman of Afrikaner separatism, and by 1914 had formed the National Party. In 1920 the National Party became the strongest single party, although it still did not command a majority.

Three years later Hertzog entered an election pact with the small, predominantly English-speaking Labor Party. As W. H. Vatcher observes, essentially the pact "was a White man's front against the Africans created for the purpose of raising White wages and insuring jobs for the 'poor Whites,' the overwhelming majority of whom were Afrikaners."[3]

The pact was formed in reaction to a series of bloody strikes in the Transvaal in 1922 by White workers opposing mine owners who wished to abolish the color bar, put Blacks into jobs reserved for Whites, and thus lower costs of production.[4] When the "pact government" came to power in 1924, it passed a series of laws to protect White labor. Then Hertzog's new regime, pursuing a planned economy, imposed protective measures for White farmers such as export quotas, import duties, and minimum-price controls.

When Afrikaans became an official language (replacing Dutch), in 1925, the earlier regulation making English and Dutch (now Afrikaans) necessary for employment in the civil service began to be enforced. Afrikaners had a great advantage, for many more of them were bilingual.

Afrikaner "poor Whites" who had been deprived of their land with the industrialization of agriculture were migrating to the cities, settling in slums with Africans and Coloreds. The situation was so frightening to the Afrikaner *volk* that eventually the Hertzog government offered privileged employment for White workers.

In 1929 the National Party won an outright parliamentary majority on its own, and Hertzog began to feel that the time had come for a broader White unity, a South African rather than an exclusively Afrikaner nationalism. In 1934 he and Smuts fused their parties into the United Party. Three of the four provincial National Parties voted in favor of fusion, but the Cape party, under the leadership of D. F. Malan, opposed it. A long struggle between Fusionists and the opposition ensued, a struggle from which Malan was to emerge victorious fourteen years later.

Who was this new leader? Significantly, Malan was a former NGK minister who had left the pulpit to become a newspaper editor and politician because he felt the calling to lead his people through the wilderness. In 1915 he founded *Die Burger*, the first daily newspaper in Dutch. In 1924 he became minister of the interior, health and education in the pact government.

Hertzog failed to understand the new movement that was gathering momentum during and after World War I. Eager young intellectuals were gathering in the Koffiehaus in Cape Town, students and professors were engaging in fervent debate at the Afrikaans universities, and even Dutch Reformed ministers and theologians were speculating on the divine mission of the Afrikaners. Indeed, it was a professor of divinity at Stellenbosch University, J. M. Potgieter, who expressed that calling succinctly: "God saved the Afrikaner people at Blood River and allowed them to carry on to where they are today."[5]

As René de Villiers points out, "Calvin divided the human race broadly into the elect and the rest. Afrikaner leaders, however, interpreted his doctrine to refer not to individuals alone but to nations, and they applied this formula to their own people."[6] De Klerk emphasizes that the Afrikaners' "Calvinist" philosophy is aligned not with the Calvinism found in the *Institutes*, but with later, Puritan mutations. True Calvinism stresses the value of the individual, and condemns the slavery of women and the poor—indeed, all hierarchy among human beings.

Yet the new ideology had an enormous appeal to members of the NGK (to which 90 percent of the Afrikaners belong). The rallying cry of an NGK theologian is typical: "We believe that God . . . has made merciful provision for our people. But in any case our choice remains that of rather perishing on the way of obedience than to melt into the non-Whites, to forfeit our identity and our sacred calling."[7]

To Malan, "the history of the Afrikaner reveals a will and a determination which make one feel that Afrikanerdom is not the work of men but the creation of God."[8]

A treatise by Dr. Nicolaas Diederichs, a professor of political science and philosophy, epitomized nationalism as a worldview. "The individual in itself is nothing, but only becomes itself in the nation as the highest (human) community." The new nationalism, he declared, was a "spiritual attitude, which worked in us like a form-giving, compelling power. It was our love for our nation which formed our love for and our responsibility for our fellow human beings of the same descent we were."[9] "Nationalism finds its final justification and anchoring in the religious belief that the very ground of the being of a nation is in the will and love of God."[10]

NGK theologians have written millions of words in support of this *Weltanschauung*, asserting that the fact that God had given to nations their separate existences clearly implied that they should remain separate. And they cited passages from Deuteronomy, Acts, and especially Genesis. (Did Jehovah not upset the builders of the Tower of Babel by a confusing of tongues, ordaining the distribution of nations all over the earth?)

Thus grew a civil religion based on a doctrine of history, culture, and mission designed to uphold the Afrikaner people in its struggle for identity, survival, and power against all odds.[11]

De Gruchy reminds us, however, that although the English in South Africa had few leaders with a sense of national calling, some regarded that country as crucial to the designs of British imperialism, and for this they claimed religious sanction. Cecil Rhodes, for example, wrote that only one race approached God's ideal type, his own Anglo-Saxon race. God's purpose, then, was to make the Anglo-Saxon race predominant.[12]

The Broederbond

Lurking in the stage wings during the rise of Afrikaner nationalism was a stealthy actor, a secret organization known as the Afrikaner Broederbond ("brotherhood"). The full extent of its power came to be known only since the publication of two books, *The Super-Afrikaners*, by Ivor Wilkins and Hans Strydom, and *Brotherhood of Power*, by J. H. P. Serfontein.[13] They trace the influence of the Broederbond throughout the whole of Afrikaner society from the smallest *dorp* ("village") to sophisticated Johannesburg. The five prime ministers since 1948 have been members. Originally designed as a service organization to help Afrikaners through the alienation they experienced as newcomers to Anglo-Saxon cities, it soon came to dominate the political sphere.

A number of other Afrikaners were violently opposed to the Bond. Smuts is said to have labeled it a "kind of Gestapo"; Hertzog called it a "grave menace," and added, "I know of few towns and villages in the Free State where the Broederbond has not established for itself a nest of five, six, or more Broeders to serve as a focal point for Bond propaganda."[14] Their efforts to suppress the Broederbond were to no avail.

In more recent years, however, the Broederbond has "come out of the closet." The key leaders, Dr. Gerrit Viljoen, the rector of Rand Afrikaans University, who became administrator general of South-West Africa/Namibia; Dr. Carel Boshoff, former head of the South African Bureau of Racial Affairs (SABRA); and Dr. Willem de Klerk, editor of *Die Transvaler,* neither deny that they are members nor remain reticent about their opinions on current policy.

From the beginning, the Bond included many ministers and teachers of religion. There is evidence, too, that the Broederbond sometimes attempted to tell NGK members what to do at church meetings. Indeed, it was the quasi-religious mystique that bound theologians, intellectuals, and politicians together in this peculiar brotherhood.

Perpetuating the Color Bar

The impetus behind Afrikaner nationalism was not only resistance to domination by British political symbols, culture, and economic interests, but awareness of *color*: the growing Black and Brown proletariat in the cities. Many Nationalists took violent exception to legislation sponsored by Hertzog in 1936 enlarging the "native" reserves—even though this was done largely as compensation for the transfer of all African voters to a separate roll. The legislation allowed Africans to have White representation in the Senate, and kept Coloreds as part of the White electorate. To the Nationalists, permitting Whites and Coloreds to mix was a serious threat to the survival of the Afrikaners.

After the outbreak of World War II, in 1939, Smuts convinced Parliament to join the Allies, a move bitterly opposed by Prime Minister Hertzog and other Afrikaners who saw it as "England's War." Many of them admired from afar the principles of German national socialism. (Some of the diehards interned for their anti-British, pro-Nazi sympathies later became government officials—among them, future prime minister Balthazar Johannes Vorster.) Smuts took over after Hertzog resigned, and the latter formed an uneasy alliance with Malan. After encountering opposition from Nationalist intellectuals, however, Hertzog retired from politics.

In 1948 Malan and the Nationalists confounded the pundits by defeating Smuts and the United Party. This was the first all-Afrikaner government in South Africa; at last the humiliation of the Anglo-Boer wars had been wiped out. It should be noted, however, that as a result of gerrymandering—

through an earlier agreement that a rural constituency might be underloaded up to 15 percent and an urban area overloaded up to 15 percent—actually the Nationalists won a minority of votes.

The Nationalists triumphed because they promised to solve the racial problems of South Africa by the methods of apartheid—indeed, *wit baasskap* ("white boss-ship") was the electoral slogan. On the strength of this policy, Malan served six years. He was succeeded in 1954 by J. G. Strijdom, who in turn was followed in 1958 by H. F. Verwoerd.

As de Gruchy puts it, the Nationalist victory did not introduce segregation to South Africa, but it transformed an *ad hoc* traditional way of life into a closed ideological system that claimed theological justification.[15]

The Legislation of Separate Development

During the first twelve years of Nationalist rule, a tremendous amount of legislation was passed to buttress apartheid. Only the most significant portion of this legislation can be described here.

The word "apartheid" itself, which had begun to evoke odium throughout the world, was eventually replaced by "separate development," with its connotation of leading each race to its own destiny. According to that grand design, Blacks under the tutelage of Whites, but also by their own efforts, would develop their own system of values, culture, morality, and worldview. This would require complete separation of the races. Only thus could the White race make certain of the purity of its blood and assure a home for its posterity. Hence segregation must penetrate every aspect of life in South Africa.

The cornerstone of separate development was the Group Areas Act (1950), which clearly demarcated residential areas for the various racial groups. Whole populations were shifted, many from areas where they had lived for generations. In addition, the Resettlement of Natives Act (1954) empowered the government to uproot some hundred thousand Africans from slums in Johannesburg and resettle them in a new area called Meadowlands twelve miles from the city, later to be known by the acronym Soweto (Southwest Township).

After a bitter parliamentary and legal struggle, Coloreds were removed from the common roll between 1951 and 1957. (Afterwards they were allowed representation in Parliament by Whites, but in 1969 this was abolished.) The parliamentary representation by Whites finally offered the Indians in 1946 was removed by the Malan government in 1948, although the Indian community had decided to ignore the earlier concession in any case.

Although there had never been much crossing of the color line, it was made even more difficult by the Prohibition of Mixed Marriages Act (1949) and the Immorality Act (1950), which proscribed sexual intercourse between Whites and *all* non-Whites. Because it was often virtually impossible to distinguish between darker-skinned Whites and lighter-skinned Coloreds, the Population Registration Act (1950) set up a racially classified national register. The Reservation of Separate Amenities Act (1953) compelled the various racial groups to use separate restroom facilities on buses and trains, and in other public places.

To control the movements of individual Africans, in 1952 came the Abolition of Passes and Co-ordination of Documents Act (a grossly misleading name), which rationalized existing pass laws and required that a "reference book" be carried by all African men.

Of great importance was the Bantu Education Act (1953) empowering the government to take control of all African schools receiving state aid. The new policy was aimed at ensuring that African education have its roots in the reserves. All education, with the exception of foreign languages, should be through the medium of the tribal mother tongue for the first eight school years, and mother tongue instruction should gradually be extended to secondary schools and training institutions. Just enough English and Afrikaans should be taught to enable the Bantu child to follow oral or written instructions and carry on simple conversations with Europeans about work and other subjects of common interest.

Bantu education involved a different syllabus, neglecting subjects such as mathematics, and emphasized tribalism and stereotypes of Africans living in rural conditions with their sleek cattle and fertile maize fields. Now that knowledge of Afrikaans was also required, the chances for adequate training in English were limited; English was particularly desired by Africans because they felt that "the whole world speaks English."

The emphasis on vernacular instruction was explicitly designed as the main instrument to promote separateness. Indeed, Verwoerd criticized the former system as having created a class of Africans that "feels that its spiritual, economic, and political home is among the civilized community of South Africa."[16] Moreover, urban-based high schools and trade schools (which potentially could train Blacks to compete with White labor) were extremely limited.

Most Blacks bitterly opposed these moves to further reduce the quality of non-White education and were joined by many liberals and church leaders. To missionary schools that had offered good educational opportunities to non-Whites the act spelled disaster, for they depended heavily on state subsidies. During the late 1950s most of them were forced to close. Only the Catholics resolved to carry on without government aid.

The Extension of University Education Act (1959) barred "White" universities (except by way of special permit) to all Africans, Coloreds, and Indians, who would now have to attend their own institutions of higher learning, most of which were situated in isolated rural areas.

Because special powers seemed needed to combat political activity against such laws, the Suppression of Communism Act (1950), the Criminal Law Amendment Act (1960), and the Unlawful Organizations Act (1960) provided severe penalties for any activity deemed communist.

To implement the political separation of races, the Bantu Authorities Act (1951) set up structures for African self-government in the various Bantu-stans (now called homelands). The Promotion of Bantu Self-Government Act (1959) terminated African elected representation (by Whites) in Parliament and, more importantly, refined plans for the eight Bantustans.[17] Now the grand design could be implemented, inasmuch as the future homelands were defined as offering "independence" to Africans.

It would be a mistake to assume that the Afrikaners were a monolithic group. A number of courageous Afrikaner men and women did what they could to work against the racial separatism they felt would lead to disaster. Afrikaners played a considerable role in the Torch Commando, a short-lived but numerically large movement organized in the early 1950s to oppose what they saw as the government's lack of concern for constitutional law.

A few Afrikaner women joined their English-speaking sisters in the Women's Defense of the Constitution League, generally known as the Black Sash because of their practice of wearing black sashes during silent public demonstrations. This small compact group also undertook practical assistance to Blacks needing help with problems arising from the pass laws and economic troubles. Still another organization where Afrikaans- and English-speaking persons worked together was the South African Institute of Race Relations (SAIRR), a multiracial association founded in 1929 to work for goodwill and practical cooperation between South Africa's races.

Neither these movements nor the political opposition became strong enough to withstand the growth of the *laager* mentality as the waves of African nationalism elsewhere on the continent began to lap the borders of the republic. By 1960, an elaborate scaffolding for the majestic new edifice of separate development had been erected. The architects of this grand design seem to have been sincere men possessed of a quasi-religious vision. The ideology of apartheid was buttressed by an enormous amount of theological, philosophical, sociological, anthropological, and political writings, all arguing for the validity of the Afrikaner's secular faith.

The most articulate spokesman for this doctrine was Dr. H. F. Verwoerd, the brilliant sociology professor and editor who succeeded Strijdom in 1958. His eloquent speeches emphasized the Whites' Christian duty to accept responsibility for the well-being and development of non-Whites, and reverberated with such statements as "We shall keep on fighting for the survival of the White man at the southern tip of Africa and the religion which has been given to him to spread here."

Notes

1. Benjamin Pogrund, "The Anatomy of White Power," in *Atlantic* (October 1977): 56.

2. W. A. de Klerk, *The Puritans in Africa: A Story of Afrikanerdom* (London: Rex Collings, 1975), p. 110.

3. Monica Wilson and Leonard Thompson, eds., *The Oxford History of South Africa* (London: Oxford University Press, 1971), Vol. 2, *South Africa 1870–1966,* p. 379.

4. The Smuts government called out the troops. After 247 Whites were killed and 591 wounded, the revolt was suppressed. Afrikaner strikers sang not only the Republican *Volkslied* but the "Red Flag," and their slogan was "Workers of the world unite—and fight for a White South Africa."

5. Wilson and Thompson, *Oxford History,* Vol. 2, p. 371.

6. Ibid.

7. de Klerk, *Puritans in Africa,* p. 233.

8. Ibid., p. 204.

9. Ibid., p. 205.

10. Ibid., p. 203.

11. John W. de Gruchy, *The Church Struggle in South Africa* (Grand Rapids: Eerdmans, 1979), p. 32.

12. Ibid., p. 34.

13. Wilson and Thompson, *Oxford History,* Vol. 2, p. 396.

14. Hennie Serfontein observes, "The whole philosophy of the Broederbond has a powerful religious basis; the philosophy of Christian nationalism forms its very foundations. The Broederbond and Afrikaner religion and the church have over the years been inseparable" (J. H. P. Serfontein, *Brotherhood of Power* [Bloomington: Indiana, 1978], p. 47).

15. John W. de Gruchy, "The Relationship Between the State and Some of the Churches in South Africa," in *Journal of Church and State* 19 (Autumn 1977): 445.

16. Wilson and Thompson, *Oxford History,* Vol. 2, p. 78.

17. In 1980 they numbered ten: Transkei, Bophuthatswana, Venda, Ciskei, KwaZulu, Qwa Qwa, Lebowa, Gazankulu, Swazi, South Ndebele. The Transkei, Bophuthatswans, and Venda have all become "independent" in the last five years, but no nation other than South Africa recognizes their independence. In November 1980, residents of the Ciskei, heavily influenced by their chiefs, voted for independence. The Quail Commission, a White advisory group appointed by Chief Lenox Sebe, has reported that the Ciskei economy is almost wholly dependent on South Africa, however.

CHAPTER THREE

The Rise of Black Nationalism: 1900 to 1960

The seeds of African nationalism were sown in the nineteenth century, with the growth of urbanization, industrialization, education, and conversion to Christianity. Two social strata were important in the development of the movement: the urban proletariat and educated Christians. The latter, attracted to Western culture, became the main carriers of African nationalism, initiating the movement and shaping its ideology.[1]

Peter Walshe distinguishes several influences in the late nineteenth century: Christian missions, awareness of the Negro struggle in the United States, the nonracial qualified franchise in the Cape, increasing economic integration, and a belief that tribal organizations had been a preparation for parliamentary government processes in which Africans had a right to participate.[2]

To mission-educated Africans, Christian values were a source of political ideas. Brotherhood meant a shared, if racially diverse, society. The old tribal society was weakened as converts learned that a new cohesive force transcended the tribe: the spiritual brotherhood of all Christian believers. For many Africans, the new faith also functioned as a guide for cultural, political, and social judgments. Christianity furnished a language of protest.[3]

In the late nineteenth and early twentieth centuries, at least forty mission-educated Christians went on to higher education in the United States. Prior to the founding of University College of Fort Hare by the Presbyterians, in 1915, there was no such institution of higher learning in South Africa for Blacks. Many African leaders came to feel that they could learn much from the Black experience in the U.S.A.

The emergence of the "Ethiopian" churches in the late nineteenth century was one of the earliest expressions of African nationalism, although the ideology, combining Pan-Africanism and Black solidarity, remained vague.[4] Resentment of the color bar in the White settler churches was an abiding factor in the movement.

The first secession, which did not last long, occurred in 1872, when 150 members of the Paris Evangelical Missionary Society congregation at Mt. Hermon declared themselves no longer bound by rules other than those made by themselves.[5] Twelve years later the Methodist minister Nehemiah Tile, a Tembu, quarreled with the superintendent of his circuit and set up the Tembu National Church.

Only in 1892 was the word "Ethiopian" first used, when a Methodist minister named Mangena Mokoni set up his Ethiopian Church in the Transvaal in reaction to racial segregation in the Methodist conference. He interpreted the passage in Psalm 68:31—"Ethiopia will stretch out her hands to God"—to mean the evangelization of Africa under African leaders. At that time, Ethiopia and Liberia were the only independent African countries.

Eventually an American connection was formed; in 1896 Mokoni's group formed a union with the all-Black African Methodist Episcopal (AME) Church. But a rival, James Dwane, got to America first and was made general superintendent. Mokoni was eclipsed in his own movement. The AME continued to exert an important influence, for it saw South Africa as important missionary territory and sent Black clergymen and visiting bishops to instruct and ordain Africans.

Ethiopianism frightened a great many Whites, who saw in the rejection of White control a sinister new movement. Colonial officials were deeply concerned, and the Natal government placed restrictions on African clergy who were "not under European control." However, the tendency of the Ethiopian churches to fragmentation was so great and their acceptance of the missionaries' religious ideas so deeply entrenched that little direct involvement in African political movements occurred.[6] The real impetus to African nationalism lay elsewhere.

It was the Indians in Natal, under the leadership of Mohandas Gandhi, who pioneered nonviolent action against the government. Indeed, Gandhi's concept of "passive resistance" originated in South Africa with the founding of the Natal Indian Congress in 1894. Before his departure from the country, in 1914, the Mahatma launched three major civil disobedience campaigns against a variety of discriminatory legislation. Prime Minister Smuts felt compelled to reach an accommodation with Gandhi on most of these issues. At this stage there was no political cooperation between Indians and Africans, however.

Birth of the African National Congress

The earliest Black organizations emerged in the late nineteenth century, launched by the few members of the middle-class intelligentsia that then existed.[7] In 1912, in angry reaction to the failure of the British to include extension of the Cape franchise in the new Union constitution, the first strong Black nationwide movement was created—the South African Native National Congress, later renamed the African National Congress (ANC).

Through most of its life the political composition of the ANC was varied, ranging from Marxists, through liberals, to African nationalists. The over-riding emphasis was moderate and gradualist, in the pursuit of nonracial justice. The main movement of African nationalism, then, never embraced Black racism.

From its beginning, the movement had a nonviolent base, for its leaders combined a religious faith that truth shall overcome with a pragmatic recognition of the difference between White and Black power. They also saw that although some social forces were separating the races into mutually hostile groups, economic forces were drawing them together. Africans were repelled too by the exclusive quality of Afrikaner nationalism. ANC's ideology included interracial cooperation, while emphasizing solidarity among Blacks.

Over the years the ANC campaigned for abolition of the pass system, urban freehold, economic and civil rights in the urban areas, and inclusion of all citizens in social security and welfare services. Its activities included petitions and deputations to the South African government and nations overseas, participation in the developing labor movement, various forms of noncooperation, and organizing for non-European unity.

The first action occurred in 1913, when African women in Bloemfontein demonstrated against the extension of pass laws to women in the Orange Free State. The protest spread to other towns and went on for many years, with some minor successes.[8] In 1914 Africans sent out petitions against the Natives Land Act excluding them from 87 percent of the South African land, an act striking at the very basis of African life. The petitions had very little effect, however.

During the following three decades, Africans staged several large demonstrations—most of them nonviolent—that were brutally repressed by government forces. Albert Luthuli, president of the ANC from 1951 to 1961, has written that in 1920 twenty-one strikers were killed at Port Elizabeth alone; in the following year, 163 were struck down at Bulhoek; in 1924 "a hundred Hottentots were butchered for refusing to pay an incomprehensible tax on dogs."[9]

After the end of World War I, four new ideological influences emerged on the scene: the Industrial and Commercial Workers Union (ICU); the Joint Councils; the ideas of the Jamaican, Marcus Garvey; and the South African Communist Party.

The multiracial ICU was concerned with wage levels, the color bar in industry, and equality in every walk of life. Despite a spectacular growth, by the late 1920s the union was collapsing.[10]

The Joint Councils were committees of Blacks and Whites who opposed the native policy, but relied not on mass action but on educating society at large. Their faith in ultimate justice, already eroding, was shattered in 1936 when Prime Minister Hertzog successfully did away with the Cape common roll, replacing it with representation of Africans by White members of parliament.[11]

Garvey's slogan "Africa for the Africans" affected only a small group of radicals, but led to heightened race consciousness. Moreover, "Africa for the Africans" began to circulate in tandem with the Communist Party's slogan "Independent Native Republic." Formed in 1921, the South African Communist Party (SACP) fostered a new concept—predominant political power for Africans. In the long run, it declared, Africans might have to carry responsibility for the reform and governance of society.

By 1928 communists had risen to high positions in the ANC. James Gumede, who had been to Russia in 1926, had become its president; J. A. La Guma, a high union official, was also with the ANC. The ANC's relationship with the SACP has continued to the present, with much of the dissension revolving around White membership in the ANC and foreign White domination of the SACP.[12]

By the 1930s the ANC had fallen into organizational chaos. The All African Convention, a new umbrella body including the ANC, was created in 1935 to oppose the hated Hertzog bills. After 1937 it began to move toward a united front with the Coloreds and Indians.

In the early 1940s the faltering ANC set out to develop mass support and regain its primary position in African politics by establishing a well-organized network voicing more assertive claims for justice. Under the vigorous leadership of A. B. Xuma, president general from 1940 to 1949, the congress called for recognition of African trade unions, abolition of the color bar in industry, abolition of pass laws, freehold tenure, equal welfare services, and a per capita allocation of funds from general revenue for education. Although World War II was bringing further integration of the economy, and people of different racial groups were mingling in the cities, Prime Minister Smuts turned a deaf ear to these claims.

Africans were not quiescent. According to Horrell, there were sixty illegal strikes between the introduction in 1942 of War Measure 145, which prohibited strikes by Africans pending awards by arbitrators, and the end of 1944.[13] In 1946, a strike of some fifty thousand African miners was cruelly suppressed.

During and shortly after the war, many Indians and Coloreds were seeking political cooperation with Africans. On the other hand, in 1943, when conditions were favorable for such cooperation, there arose within the African National Congress itself a more militant and exclusively Africanist wing—the ANC Youth League, under the leadership of Anton Lembede. Arguing that because South African Whites looked at the country's problems through the perspective of race, Blacks should do the same, the League declared that Africans were oppressed as a nation, and under conditions different from those pertaining to Indians and Coloreds. Although willing to cooperate with other non-European groups on common issues, League members believed that Africans could do so only when they themselves had achieved unity and created a national liberation movement.[14] Eventually, the Youth League took up Pan-Africanism, an issue that had been of minor importance in earlier decades, despite some interest in the Pan African Conferences convoked by the much revered American activist-intellectual W. E. B. Du Bois.

The 1948 electoral victory of the Nationalists checked the trend toward racial unity and ushered in a period of continuous erosion of law, assumption of extraordinary powers by the state, and attempts to reverse the processes drawing the racial groups toward a common society. The government was deliberately trying to divide them through residential and educational segregation, and to splinter African unity by segregating "tribal groups" into language groups in urban residential areas and schools, and into separate Bantu authority structures in the reserves. Yet protests continued.

In 1950 ANC activists staged three major demonstrations, all with interracial support and active participation of schoolchildren. In the following year, Coloreds in the Cape area carried off an effective strike against legislation aimed at them.[15] The climax came in 1952, when the ANC, the South African Indian Congress, and the Franchise Action Council (Colored) launched a nationwide Defiance Campaign to commit breaches of certain discriminatory laws. Rural action, industrial strikes, and a final drive were to culminate in mass action. Following the classic tenets of nonviolence, letters were sent to the authorities announcing plans for the campaign, lists of volunteers were often politely handed in, and discipline was excellent—so much so that, according to Luthuli, nonviolent volunteers sometimes took charge of traffic control when authorities were unable to maintain order.[16]

Many of the demonstrations took the form of prayer meetings, and at political gatherings speakers stressed the affinity between nonviolent resistance and the Christian ethic.[17] One African speaker declared, "These people are Christians but they eat people. . . . If they represent God, then they represent a false God. And if God is like that, then God is no good for Africa." Yet this speaker used a biblical text as the setting for his remarks. Like many other Africans, he held fast to a Christian faith in terms of which he judged the White man's piety and hypocrisy.[18]

The orderly demonstrations for the Defiance Campaign gathered momentum; more White sympathizers, especially university students, joined in with defiance songs and other forms of protest. The government began to feel seriously threatened. When riots finally broke out—almost surely unrelated to the campaign, and quite probably instigated by the government—authorities used them as a pretext to smash the movement. The campaign was officially ended in 1953 by Luthuli, the newly elected ANC president.

A new period of reaction and repression set in. Students were refused readmission to school, workers were fired from their jobs, clergymen were denied certain privileges, and the minister of justice was empowered to bar all public meetings within a specified area for a stated period of time. Despite these intimidations a few local economic boycotts and other acts of resistance continued on a minor scale.

In 1955 delegates from the ANC, SAIC, the South African Colored People's Organization, the Congress of Democrats (leftist Whites), and the interracial South African Congress of Trade Unions (SACTU) met at Kliptown (now part of Soweto) for a nationwide Congress of the People. Here they adopted the Freedom Charter, which proclaimed that "South Africa belongs to all who live in it, Black and White"—thus implicitly denying the idea of "Africa for the Africans." This alliance also proposed the transfer of mineral wealth, banks, and monopoly industry to the ownership of the people as a whole. The government responded with raids, political bans, and the mass arrest of 156 leaders on charges of treason.

Despite the Treason Trials, which dragged on for five years, and the government's success in crippling resistance organizations, protests continued, especially in the reserves. As early as 1954 the Africanist movement inside the ANC had enjoyed a clear victory with a bus boycott in Evaton. (When the Montgomery, Alabama, bus boycott began, in late 1955, many Africans thought that Martin Luther King, Jr., must have been inspired by the success of the Evaton action.)

This was followed in 1957 by a massive bus boycott in Alexandra township, near Johannesburg. It was so successful that soon afterward the ANC launched a wide economic boycott of Nationalist-controlled firms and their products. The campaign did little to cause the government to change its policies, however.

Between 1956 and 1958 the Black Sash, the interracial Federation of South African Women, and *ad hoc* groups of African women continued to demonstrate against the nationwide extension of pass laws to women. Although most of the protests were countered by brutal force, on at least one occasion women devised a successful nonviolent tactic: when ordered to disperse, they fell to their knees and began to pray. The police did not know what to do.[19]

In 1958 the Youth League (the "Africanists") seceded from the ANC, and in the following year formed the Pan-Africanist Congress (PAC), under the dynamic leadership of Mangaliso Robert Sobukwe, a teacher and Methodist lay minister. At a time when the ANC was already preparing for new demonstrations against the pass laws, the young PAC seized the initiative and on March 21, 1960, began a nationwide campaign.

It is interesting that the PAC militants chose a nonviolent strategy. In the words of Peter Molotsi, a PAC organizer who fled into exile after the campaign:

The idea was to *fill* the jails all over the country till they simply overflowed with prisoners demanding arrest for violating the pass laws. To get at least a million arrested. If there was no place to put us, we reasoned, the system would break down. We'd show our people they'd have nothing to fear. And when you remove that fear, you remove the whole basis of the system. The Whites' only alternative would be to kill us. And they couldn't kill a million people, we thought. The other African states wouldn't take that.[20]

At one of the townships, Sharpeville, police tried to break up the crowd with tear gas canisters and armored Saracen cars, but the orderly, well-disciplined crowd failed to disperse. After a few hours of this, a few Africans broke discipline and began throwing stones at the police. Without a word of warning and without firing a warning shot, the police sent a rain of 476 bullets into the crowd. Sixty-nine African men, women, and children were killed on the spot, three others died later, and a hundred eighty were wounded.[21]

The events surrounding Sharpeville have been well documented elsewhere. Suffice it to say here that violent disorder as well as nonviolent demonstrations and strikes continued, and the ANC called for a day of mourning on March 28 for solidarity with the victims. The government responded by unleashing a reign of terror. Some nineteen hundred persons of all races (mostly members of the ANC, PAC, the Liberal Party, and the Congress Alliance) were detained for three or four months; an additional twenty thousand Africans were detained on charges of vagrancy. Luthuli was jailed, then banned; Both the PAC and the ANC were banned; many of their leaders, including PAC's Robert Sobukwe and ANC's Nelson Mandela, were sent to prison.

Sharpeville shocked people of compassion and concern around the world. Black African countries denounced the killings, and the Afro-Asian nations at the United Nations brought the issue before the Security Council, which passed a resolution condemning South Africa. The U.S. State Department, too, deplored the political measures taken against Blacks. Yet there were few organized protests among the American people.

Communism and Christianity in the ANC

During the 1940s, says Peter Walshe, the South African Communist Party enjoyed very little direct influence on the ANC. Only by the 1950s were a few key persons able to gain some limited influence. But they were held in great suspicion by the vast majority of ANC members, who felt that their communist colleagues upheld a foreign revolutionary creed, worked for a predominantly White central executive committee, and were trying to take over leadership of the nationalist movement.

After the party was outlawed in 1950, a few members remained in the freedom movement, and eventually developed some common ground with members of the Congress Youth League. The result was the increased use of Marxist vocabulary, especially in explaining economic exploitation. Thus to the eclectic sources of ANC political attitudes was added a new ideological factor. The class emphasis helped to check any degeneration into Black chauvinism. However, the use of some Marxist analysis among the wider influences on African political thought did not mean that the nationalist movement had "gone communist."[22]

In contrast, Christianity played a vital part in the resistance to apartheid. The African Ministers Federation worked in close cooperation with the African National Congress. Foremost in the long list of Christian leaders was Albert Luthuli—a tribal chief, teacher, lecturer in the United States for the North American Missionary Council, leader in Christian councils, and Nobel

Peace Prize winner—who testified eloquently to the relevance of his Congregational faith to his work in the freedom movement. Anton Lembede, founder of the Youth League, was a devout Roman Catholic. Dr. Walter Rubusana, one of the founders of the ANC and the first African to be elected to the Cape Provincial Council, was moderator of the Congregational Union of South Africa. American-educated John Dube was a Congregational minister who became the first president of the ANC, and founded Ohlange Institute as the Natal counterpart of Booker T. Washington's Tuskegee Institute. Zaccheus Mahabane, a Methodist minister, was twice president of the ANC.

Yet these leaders had to counter growing mistrust of the church, particularly among the young, as well as some ambivalences within themselves. As Kuper observes, the manner in which the Dutch Reformed Church sanctioned apartheid had the effect of clothing naked oppression in Christian vestments. The feeling about White Christians might be summed up: "Their deeds speak so loudly that their voices cannot be heard."[23] The novelist Ezekiel Mphalele put it thus:

> For years I have been told by White and Black preachers to love my neighbor; love him when there's a bunch of Whites who reckon they are Israelites come out of Egypt in obedience to God's order to come and civilize heathens. . . . For years now, I've been thinking it was all right for me to feel spiritually strong after a church service and now I find it is not the kind of strength that answers the demand of suffering humanity around me. It doesn't even seem to answer the longings of my own heart.[24]

Nevertheless, for most African nationalists the disillusion seems to have been more with the churches than with Christianity itself.

Notes

1. Monica Wilson and Leonard Thompson, eds., *The Oxford History of South Africa* (London: Oxford University Press, 1971), Vol. 2, p. 433.

2. Peter Walshe, *The Rise of African Nationalism in South Africa* (Berkeley: University of California Press, 1971), p. 1.

3. Ibid., pp. 9–10.

4. Zionists, a later movement, comprise the other basic type of independent churches; see Chapter 16.

5. Peter Hinchliff, *The Church in South Africa* (London: SPCK, 1968), p. 90.

6. The Pan-Africanist Congress (PAC) made efforts to recruit members of the independent churches in the late 1950s. Gail Gerhart notes: "There was a clear affinity between the PAC's 'go it alone' spirit and the anti-White mood of the independent churches. . . . Had the PAC not brought about its own demise . . . so prematurely, it might eventually have succeeded in redirecting some of the energies of religious separatism into political channels" (*Black Power in South Africa* [Berkeley: University of California Press, 1978], p. 202).

7. Benjamin Pogrund, "The Anatomy of White Power," in *Atlantic* (October 1977): 56.

8. Wilson and Thompson, *Oxford History,* Vol. 2, p. 445.

9. Albert Luthuli, *Let My People Go* (New York: McGraw-Hill, 1962), p. 93.

10. Peter Walshe, *Black Nationalism in South Africa* (Johannesburg: Ravan, 1973), p. 20.

11. The Joint Councils were started by a group of Christian liberals, including Howard Pim, a Quaker, and J. D. Rheinallt Jones. After the formation of the South African Institute of Race Relations (1928), the Joint Councils worked under it.

12. Walshe, *Black Nationalism,* pp. 21–22.

13. Muriel Horrell, *South African Trade Unionism* (Johannesburg: SAIRR, 1961), p. 69.

14. Wilson and Thompson, *Oxford History,* Vol. 2, p. 458.

15. Luthuli, *Let My People Go,* p. 251.

16. Ibid., p. 117.

17. Leo Kuper, *Passive Resistance in South Africa* (New Haven: Yale University Press, 1957), p. 117.

18. Ibid.

19. Luthuli, *Let My People Go,* p. 219.

20. Marjorie Hope, *Youth Against the World* (Boston: Little, Brown, 1970), p. 125.

21. These are the official South African government figures; others are higher.

22. Walshe, *Black Nationalism,* pp. 34–35.

23. Leo Kuper, *An African Bourgeoisie: Race, Class, and Politics in South Africa* (New Haven: Yale University Press, 1965), p. 195.

24. Ezekiel Mphalele, *Down Second Avenue: Growing up in a South African Ghetto* (New York:Doubleday, 1961; reprint Magnolia, Mass.: Peter Smith), p. 178.

CHAPTER FOUR

The Churches: 1900 to 1960

How did the Christian churches respond to racial issues during these six decades of upheaval?

It is not easy to speak of the response of the churches; as David Bosch points out, the South African scene has been characterized by a multiplicity of denominations. This was due to several factors. One was the fact that new migrants, in successive waves, brought their churches with them. Moreover, almost every British and continental European missionary society, as well as several from the United States, undertook work in the subcontinent. Finally, many new denominational bodies took root in South African soil.

Following the typology suggested by Professor Bosch, we divide the churches into (1) the Afrikaans Reformed Churches; (2) the member churches of the South African Council of Churches (until 1968 known as the Christian Council)—that is, the Methodist, Anglican, Lutheran, Congregational, and Presbyterian Churches; because all of them, except the Lutheran, originated in Britain, they are known as the "English-speaking" churches, although a fair number of members are Afrikaners, and most members are Black people whose mother tongue is not English; (3) the Roman Catholic Church; (4) the conservative evangelical churches; (5) the African independent churches.

The Afrikaans Reformed Churches

After 1857 no more Colored congregations were affiliated with the NGK synods for Whites, and in 1881 the first "daughter church"—the Sendingkerk (mission church) for Colored people—was established at Wellington. In 1951 a separate church (the DRC in Africa, or NGKA) was created, and in 1968 one for Indians, the Reformed Church in Africa (RCA).

Racial attitudes were hardening. In 1891 even the synod of the comparatively liberal Cape Province declared that the conversion of heathen must be followed by setting up a church for converts. The mother church must not try to frustrate aspirations toward full independence, or destroy their indigenous

45

culture. Therefore an independent, separate church was the answer.

Today the mother church and her three mission "daughters" are joined in the Federal Council of Dutch Reformed Churches.

Throughout this period the White DRC supported the government's racial policies. The daughter churches were too timid and powerless to voice much opposition. It was only in the 1970s that they became bold enough to rebel against their "mother."

The Doppers (Gereformeerde Kerk) were also convinced that almighty God had decreed the separation of races. Indeed, it was only in 1910 that the first Dopper missionary was ordained. By 1958 the church had five White and nine indigenous missionaries.

The Hervormde Kerk, which clearly states that it is a church for Whites only, did not set up its first missionary commission until 1916. Its policy still follows the same guidelines: White workers are not sent among Blacks; only White members are allowed into the Hervormde Kerk, and entirely separate churches are maintained for the "indigenous peoples."

Despite the official view favoring separation of the races, some White DRC clergy and laypersons were distressed over what they considered to be evil ways in which a generally good policy was implemented. During the 1920s and '30s the DRC initiated several Bantu-European conferences at which speakers voiced concern over the effects of the migrant labor policy on African family life.

After the advent of official apartheid in 1948, concern mounted.

On the whole, dissent generally took the form of "secret" delegations to the Prime Minister to protest against specific legislation. In 1957, for example, a DRC delegation objected to the Native Laws Amendment, which would have decreed that certain churches in "White" areas that admitted even a single African worshiper could continue only with the permission of the cabinet minister, given concurrence of the local authority.[1]

The three White Afrikaans Reformed churches have shown flexibility and willingness to change on certain fronts. They moved toward greater cooperation among themselves by forming an Inter-Church Commission in 1958. The DRC also joined two Reformed World bodies, the World Alliance of Reformed Churches and the Reformed Ecumenical Synod. The Cape and Transvaal DRC synods became members of the World Council of Churches, and, despite objections to some World Council statements on apartheid, remained until 1961.

The DRC had (and still has) the most extended mission program of all the Christian churches in South Africa, contributing much more financial support per member than any other church in the country. While the emphasis has been on evangelization, medical and educational needs receive considerable attention. The DRC has also obtained considerable financial aid from the government for mission hospitals and other endeavors, a policy that has led to resentment in other churches. There are those who see in these missionary efforts a profound religious fervor. There are others, like one African interviewed by Leo Kuper, who feel that the mission of the DRC is to "indoctrinate a people into servility."[2]

To coordinate the mission policy, the Federal Council of the Dutch Reformed Synods in 1942 established the Federal Mission Council (FMC). Its declared aims were to study DRC mission policy, plan joint mission strategy, and organize mission conferences.

Although the FMC expressed interest in working with other Protestant denominations, repeated efforts of the Christian Council at cooperation during the 1940s came to nought. Indeed, only the DRC of the Transvaal joined the Christian Council, and it withdrew in 1941.

In 1950, two years after the Nationalist victory, the FMC held a large conference at Bloemfontein. It included the four DRC provincial synods, three mission synods, the Gereformeerde Church (Doppers), and the Hervormde Kerk, as well as representatives of the government and of the Christian Council. No Black participants, however, were invited to this conference on the future of South African Blacks; White missionaries represented the mission synods.

The conference came to the conclusion that the only just and permanent solution to the racial situation lay in separation: Africans would have no rights in the White areas and Whites would have none in Black areas. In short, the DRC was confirming its traditional rejection of racial injustice and discrimination while accepting the policy of separate development.*

As de Gruchy points out, outsiders tend to consider apartheid and separate development as synonymous. Traditional DRC theologians maintain that the Scriptures teach the essential unity of humankind and the fundamental equality of all peoples—and also teach that ethnic diversity is in accordance with the will of God. The ultimate restoration of the unity of humankind, which has been shaken because of human sin, will occur only at the final coming of the Kingdom of God. Meanwhile, however, in the words of one synodal document, "The church must exert itself to give concrete substance to the blessings of the gospel in the life and social structure of a people."[3] The role of the DRC thus becomes that of insisting that separate development be implemented in a just manner.

Assuming that the official DRC policy is the work of sincere persons, and that the political partition of South Africa sounds fine in theory, one still has to face the question of its feasibility. It is interesting that in a sharp retort to the FMC conference, Prime Minister Malan asserted he had "clearly stated that total territorial separation was impracticable under present circum-

---

*De Gruchy emphasizes that Calvin's stress on the prophetic role of the church has been tempered by the neo-Calvinist Kuyper's teaching on the "sovereignty of separate spheres." This doctrine that the state is under God, and the church is likewise sovereign in its own sphere, is quite similar to the Lutheran concept of the "two kingdoms." The Nationalist government seems to operate on Kuyper's premise, insisting that the church restrict itself to its "spiritual tasks" (John W. de Gruchy, *The Church Struggle in South Africa* [Grand Rapids: Eerdmans, 1979], p. 90). However, it is obvious that in practice the NGK is a powerful political force.

stances in South Africa, where our whole economic structure is to a large extent based on Native labor."[4]

Christians in South Africa waited for the DRC to reply. They waited in vain. Although the DRC sometimes challenged, in private, the Nationalist government on particular laws during the following years, never again did the government take the challenge of the church seriously.[5]

Eight years later, one of the chief architects of the conference, Prof. G. B. A. Gerdener, still clung to the idea of separation as the only honest solution. White South Africans, he declared, would have to be willing to pay the price: they would have to learn to work, to be willing to surrender their fortune.[6]

Another conference was held at Bloemfontein in 1951 and, for the first time in DRC history, African leaders were delegates. A cooperative spirit reigned throughout. Three other such conferences were organized in the following three years. Church leaders from other denominations were invited to the 1953 conference.

The dialogue, both cordial and frank, witnessed to the dividing lines that separate Christians in South Africa even today: some considered racial separation as scriptural, some as blatantly unscriptural, and others as pragmatically necessary, but not the ideal. These differences cut across confessional lines; some DRC delegates attacked apartheid as un-Christian. After the conference, too, DRC delegates such as Ben Marais and B. B. Keet continued to cut through the racial myths that dominate not only South Africa but the West.

The 1959 conference drew representatives from more races and denominations than ever before, and seemed to many observers to be a turning point in church relations in the Union. A continuation committee was set up to work toward a council of churches that would include those in the Christian Council and those in the FMC.

All these high hopes were crushed, however. In 1960 the Sharpeville massacre shocked millions of people around the globe, precipitating a call by the World Council of Churches for a consultation at Cottesloe with its eight South African member churches about the situation. The eight conferring churches (including the DRC synods of the Transvaal and the Cape) also reached a certain consensus in urging racist reforms. To many observers the Cottesloe Report was a series of weak statements. To the DRC synods, however, it was revolutionary; they rejected the statements, and the DRC delegates who stuck to their guns were ostracized.*

Churches Belonging to the SACC

In 1949 the Christian Council (predecessor of the South African Council of Churches) convened a conference at Rosettenville near Johannesburg. The

---

*See Chapter Six for an account of the Cottesloe Consultation and the Christian Insitute.

first ecumenical conference since the National Party came to power, it drew up resolutions that characterized the position of the English-speaking churches at the time, and highlighted their differences with the Afrikaans Reformed churches. Among other things, they stressed that "beyond all differences remains the essential unity" and "the real need of South Africa is not apartheid but *eendrag* (unity through teamwork)."

Although the somewhat paternalistic affirmations reached at Rosettenville did represent an attack on the unfolding policy of apartheid, it did not mean that the English-speaking churches had been unflinching champions of equality for Blacks before 1948, nor that they would adopt an unwavering posture in the apartheid era. Each church has had its own history, its own vision, and its own way of compromising with ideals.

Church of the Province in South Africa (Anglican)

As we have seen, although the CPSA was organized as one church for all its members, the system of missions was such that there were "missions" where congregations were Black and "parishes" where congregations were White. As the century advanced, however, society became increasingly urbanized, with the result that in cities and towns with a mixed population, congregations also became increasingly mixed. (Residential segregation, of course, limited this trend.)

During the first half of the century Anglican mission work—including the building of churches, hospitals, schools, and colleges—developed rapidly. The number of clergy increased greatly. Indeed, by 1960 nearly two-thirds of the clergy had been born or trained in South Africa. (Yet it was still looked upon by many as an "English," not South African, church.)

The CPSA has the longest and most consistent record of protest against discriminatory legislation. During the post-Union, pre-apartheid period, virtually all the resolutions of the synod were related to the race problem, especially issues of land distribution, African education, better housing and living conditions, and the need for consultation with Africans on matters affecting them.[7] After 1924, it leveled criticism at Hertzog's laws, reiterating the Christian commitment to "the full development of all men, irrespective of race."[8] In 1930 the synod of bishops declared, "We believe that the rights of full citizenship in any country are not dependent on race or color, but on men's fitness to discharge the responsibilities which such citizenship involves."[9] In 1938 it stated its opposition to interference with the rights of Colored persons.

In 1949 the synod supported extension of some effective voice in government to persons of all races "who have attained an adequate standard of education." A year later a statement affirmed that "every churchman should be assured of a welcome in any church in our communion." And in 1948, after the Nationalist victory, the synod condemned racial discrimination, affirmed universal human rights, and condemned the newly proposed apartheid legislation.

Although these statements, and many others, were courageous, they were not often backed up by demonstrations, petitions, deputations to the government, or other forms of nonviolent direct action. Nor was the CPSA critical of *all* racially discriminatory legislation. Finally, it did not practice what it preached. For example, Anglican private schools in Cape Town refused to admit Colored children, and there were no Black Anglican bishops until Alphaeus Zulu was made suffragan bishop of St. John's Diocese in the Transkei in 1960. Six years later, he became the first Black bishop when he was appointed to the Diocese of Zululand and Swaziland.

Yet the number of Black delegates to the synods did increase, and overall the Church of the Province seems to have been more consistent in practicing its ideals than most other South African churches. One reason is that many of its bishops, priests, and missionaries were influenced by Anglican Christian socialism in England.

A number of distinguished White Anglican bishops and priests became famous for their courageous witness to social justice. In the 1940s, Bishop Lavis of Cape Town spoke out repeatedly against the color bar, which he described as a "blasphemous parody of trusteeship."

The missionary priest Trevor Huddleston, who gained international repute with the publication of *Naught for Your Comfort*, was a beloved figure among his African flock before he was recalled to England by his religious order. The fiery cleric ran adult education classes on church and society, exposed the suffering of Africans evicted from their homes in the township of Sophiatown, and became the advocate of Africans imprisoned for pass violations or other status offenses. "He would come down to the jails and announce to the police, 'I'm taking with me *that* man and *that* one and *that* one.' And the officials would not dare to protest," recalls a Black exile.

Ambrose Reeves, Anglican bishop of Johannesburg, roundly criticized the government's reaction to Sharpeville, and engaged two attorneys to prepare evidence for the commission of inquiry investigating the massacre. The two lawyers were detained. Because he believed that he too would be imprisoned and he had information he thought should be made available to the world, Bishop Reeves escaped to Swaziland. When he returned to his diocese he was deported.

Even more famous was the Rev. Michael Scott. His long history of action against apartheid includes founding the Campaign for Right and Justice; being jailed for helping organize passive resistance to restrictions on South Africa's Indian population; living with Africans in a shantytown outside Johannesburg (an offense for which he was convicted); and investigating the ill treatment of Black farmworkers in the Bethal district of the Transvaal. In 1947 he began a sustained campaign to present to the United Nations the case of native tribes of South-West Africa who wished to return to their tribal lands, as well as a petition that the territory be placed under international trusteeship.

One of the most dramatic confrontations between church and state occurred in 1957, when Prime Minister Verwoerd decided to make churches as *institutions* observe apartheid, by proposing the aforementioned Native Laws Amendment Bill. Heated protest to this clause arose from the Anglicans, Methodists, Presbyterians, Baptists, and Catholics, as well as the Seventh Day Adventist Church.

The Anglican bishops, under the archbishop of Cape Town, Geoffrey Clayton, played a leading role by telling the Prime Minister that they could not obey the law, nor counsel their clergy or people to do so. According to Alan Paton, Clayton had taken a dim view of the nonviolent actions of Scott, Reeves, and Huddleston.[10] Now Clayton himself took the step of confronting the state. Not long afterwards, he collapsed and died in his study.

The confrontation made clear that not even the powerful Nationalist government could tackle organized civil disobedience by the churches. At that point the DRC, which had no intention of threatening disobedience, sent a deputation to the Minister of Native Affairs. This gave him the opportunity to amend the dangerous clause; among other changes, he made the worshiper, not the church, guilty of the offense. The clause has rarely been invoked, although an increase in confrontations of the state with individual church leaders was to follow. Moreover, other legislation made it virtually impossible to convene church conferences on a multiracial basis.

The Methodists

Although the Methodist Church differs from the Church of the Province by emphasizing individual conversion and involvement of the laity, both have made efforts to meet educational and health needs of non-Whites and to speak out against racial discrimination.

With a membership in 1970 of about two million, Methodists represent the largest of the "traditional" churches in the country. The early part of the twentieth century witnessed a tremendous growth in Black membership. By 1951 over a million Africans identified themselves as Methodists; Whites numbered two hundred twenty thousand, and the combined total of Indians and Coloreds was one hundred thousand.[11]

The overwhelming proportion of Blacks has naturally had an effect on church policy. Particularly since 1948, Methodists have adhered to a policy of one church, and thus one conference, for all members. On the parish level, however, congregations have usually remained uniracial. The multiracial character of the church is generally expressed only at the highest level.[12]

At that level, many bold attacks on apartheid were waged in the first six decades of the century. Like the Anglicans, the Methodists attacked the Hertzog bills, declaring that they were geared to the interests of the "guardians" and did not recognize the prerequisite for racial harmony—namely, a common citizenship for the inhabitants of a shared South Africa.

In 1948 the Methodist Conference asserted that no one should be deprived of rights on grounds of race, and in 1952 asserted that the policy of racial separation was impracticable and "inconsistent with the highest Christian principles."[13] At the 1956 conference delegates declared certain laws—especially the Group Areas Act—"unjust, un-Christian and inhuman." In 1957 the conference rejected the policy of separate development and laws that resulted in family disruption when members were reclassified into different racial groups. By 1960 the conference felt impelled to come out with a stronger statement, one that reflected on its own role in the problem:

> To assert a "spiritual unity" among Christians, while denying its expression in corporate liturgical and sacramental worship, savors of hypocrisy. We confess with shame that our church has been and is guilty of this hypocrisy, and we call upon our members to repent and to put into practice what we believe and assert.

During the late 1950s the Methodist Church started an educational campaign against racial discrimination and began to reform its own discriminatory practices. (At that time a White clergyman was receiving roughly twice the basic stipend of his Black counterpart.)

Such decisions of the more democratically organized Methodist churches, though taken with great difficulty, may be more significant for race relations than the clear and inspiring calls of bishops in the hierarchical Anglican Church.

The Presbyterians

We have seen that in 1893 the Rev. Pambani Mzimba formed the all-Black Presbyterian Church of Africa (the Mzimba Church), and that in 1897 the settler churches and several Black congregations agreed to take autonomy from the Scottish church and form the Presbyterian Church of South Africa, the PCSA (now of Southern Africa).

In 1923 the United Free Church of Scotland decided to give autonomy to its missions rather than encourage them to join the White-dominated PCSA. When the latter gave its Black congregations and presbyteries freedom to enter the new body, about half of them did so. Named the Bantu Presbyterian Church (BPC), it had (and still has) an all-African membership, except for a few White missionaries and some Coloreds in the Cape. To many Presbyterians the split was a source of sorrow. One minister called the BPC "a fine example of apartheid created by Scotland when Dr. Verwoerd had not even been heard of!"

In the 1870s Swiss missionaries had begun work in the Northeastern Transvaal. From this grew the Tsonga Presbyterian Church, which became autonomous in 1962 and is even more ethnically determined than the Bantu Presbyterian Church.

By 1934 efforts were being launched to join the PCSA and the Bantu Presbyterian Church. There were several obstacles. Whereas the Black and Colored congregations of the PCSA united with the majority Whites at the General Assembly level, they remained (and still remain) divided at the congregational level, to the embarrassment of some but the satisfaction of others.[14] Conflict also arose because the PCSA was carrying on missionary efforts in African urban areas that the BPC claimed as its territory. Nevertheless, the 1960 General Assembly affirmed the desire for union.

Considering all these divisions, it is hardly surprising that Presbyterians were not united on racial policy. In addition, the fact that the Presbyterians are also of the Reformed tradition and belong to the World Reformed Alliance of Churches has made some White Presbyterians reluctant to take issue with their DRC "brothers." Certainly the Presbyterians' statements on racial policy were far less frequent and forceful than those of the Catholics, Anglicans, Congregationalists, or Methodists.

Over the years, however, the Presbyterians became more convinced of the importance of taking a stand. In 1960 the General Assembly passed a lengthy statement affirming that "every man is of unique value to God," and that "therefore differences of color, race, class, or cultural background are irrelevant to Christianity in any fundamental sense." Racial tension had reached a point where "the non-White is often regarded not as a person, but as a means to an end." Specific laws were criticized on the ground that "they result in deprivations which hurt the dignity and restrict the opportunities of some for the protection and advancement of others."

The Congregationalists

Since the Congregational Church grew out of the London Missionary Society and the American Board, the greater part of its membership has always been African and Colored. By 1915 there were twelve African ministers and, as time went by, more responsibility was given to Black clergy.

This was in line with the policy of establishing an indigenous church that would be self-supporting. Such independence was fostered by Congregational forms of worship and by the changing role of the White missionaries, who were removed first from direct pastoral work and later from the position of superintendents, until finally they came to serve as advisors.

This identification with indigenous peoples has not saved the Congregational Church from separatism, the most notable secession being that of the African Congregational Church.

Especially after 1948, the Congregational Union consistently condemned all legislation that discriminated on grounds of color. In 1955, for example, the Public Questions Department reported that "any policy that seeks deliberately to limit the full and free development of human personality, or dis-

criminates against individuals because of the group to which they belong . . .
is morally indefensible and wrong."[15]

In 1961, reacting to Sharpeville, the assembly resolved that "we strongly
support every effort for the holding of multiracial consultation to plan for
better relationships and happier conditions and rights and privileges for all
people of this land."

In carrying out their beliefs in Christian fellowship, Congregationalists
built hospitals, established educational institutions for Blacks such as Adams
College and Inanda Seminary (a girls' boarding school), shared with Methodists and Presbyterians in training evangelists at Lovedale Bible School, participated in founding the Federal Theological Seminary for Black students,
and involved themselves in organizations such as the YMCA and YWCA.
Yet, like members of other denominations, White Congregationalists rarely
practiced the ideals of assembly resolutions in their parish churches or in their
day-to-day living.

The Lutherans

The image of the Lutheran Church in South Africa is more diffuse than
that of the four Anglo-Saxon orientated churches. One reason is that its extension work was usually carried out through mission agencies rather than an
established church.

Like their DRC counterparts, Lutheran missionaries believed in autonomous, indigenous churches, but they added the idea of *Volkskirchen*, or
ethnic churches. Especially in the period of German Romanticism, the concept *Volk* ("people" or "nation" as an ethnic entity) was seen as an order of
creation.

Moreover, a large proportion of the White congregations in both South
Africa and South-West Africa (a German protectorate from 1884 to 1915)
was composed of German immigrants, and German missionaries were part
of that community. Before the 1899–1902 Anglo-Boer War, the sympathy of
these missionaries was largely with the colonial and British governments.
That attitude changed after the war, partly because German theology at the
time encouraged acceptance of *Volkstum* ("nationhood," "nationality"),
and partly because of the Kaiser's sympathy with the Boer leader Paul Kruger.

During World Wars I and II, ill-treatment of the German community by
British elements of the population stimulated German Lutherans to side with
Afrikaner attitudes. The children of many missionaries associated themselves with the Afrikaans culture rather than with the English, and some
became ordained ministers of the DRC. Partly because of this leaning toward
the Afrikaans element, segregation of Lutheran congregations was strengthened.[16]

On the one hand, Lutheran training centers for indigenous ministers grew
during the first half of the twentieth century, as did interest in working with
migrant laborers, prisoners, and broken families in the industrial areas. On

the other hand, until the 1960s there was a remarkable absence of statements denouncing apartheid. According to Elfriede Strassberger, the daughter of German missionaries of the Rhenish Mission (but herself a lay minister of the Church of the Province), "the fact that there was much sympathy toward the Germans during World War II from Afrikaans-speaking South Africans is not without significance. The German missions were supported by the DRC in a magnificent way during the war."[17]

Thus the great majority of White Lutherans accepted the government's racial policy. Black Lutherans were increasing, however. Today they number over 760,000; White Lutherans, about 40,000. The shift was to spell confrontation in the 1960s and '70s.

The Roman Catholics

In the twentieth century the growth of Roman Catholicism in South Africa has been spectacular, especially among Blacks. In 1911 Catholics numbered approximately 50,000 thousand, about half of whom were Black. By 1969, the total Catholic population had reached one million; over 750,000 of them were Blacks.

This rapid expansion has been due to well-organized activity by missionaries all over southern Africa, who have taken linguistic and anthropological studies, as well as the training of indigenous leaders, more seriously than the clergy of any other denomination.[18] Lesotho (formerly the British protectorate of Basutoland) has had a particularly dense Catholic population, and its Pius VI Catholic University College located at Roma has attracted lay Catholics from all over the subcontinent.

After the publication of *Rerum Ecclesiae* (1926), the number of local-born bishops and clergy grew rapidly; by 1951, seven South African-born priests had become bishops, and nearly seven hundred South African women, including many Blacks, had become nuns. Seminaries were opened for Whites, Coloreds, and Africans. In 1951 Pope Pius XII created five ecclesiastical provinces, with archbishops at Cape Town, Durban, Pretoria, Bloemfontein, and Maseru (the capital of Lesotho).[19]

Since the Union of South Africa came into being (1909), Catholics have not played a very visible role in public life. In the words of William Eric Brown, "Political life in particular became more and more the preserve of Afrikaner culture, and Catholics did not force an entry."[20]

Over the issue of apartheid, however, Catholic church and lay leaders have collided with the government.

Catholics as a whole did not share the racial beliefs of the Dutch Calvinists. Hence the restriction of citizen rights to those of "European descent" (1909) dismayed Catholic leaders. When the DRC synods agreed in 1910 to virtually exclude Colored persons from equal rights in the church, the move exacerbated the long hostility between the Boers and the Catholics.

Jealousy compounded the tension. There was considerable mutual suspicion of educational methods, for example; both the Boers and the Catholics considered the other to be "indoctrinating" the young. Yet many Protestant and Jewish parents sent their children to Catholic schools.

Educational institutions were opened for Colored and African children in the townships. Great emphasis was laid by the Catholics on education, as well as social services such as hospitals and orphanages. Hence Catholics reacted very strongly to the Bantu Education Act of 1953, which resulted in the progressive withdrawal of government subsidies upon which mission schools were virtually forced to depend. Only Catholics declared their obstinate intention to take over the huge financial burden of their schools rather than close them to non-Whites who found them the avenue to a better life. Donations from overseas groups helped save many, but by June 1959 sixty institutions had closed, teacher training colleges and secondary schools suffering most heavily.

The Group Areas Act of 1950 was even more responsible for closures. Mixed schools were shut down as one area was declared "White," another "Bantu," and another "Colored" or "Indian." The common life of priests and religious was disrupted, as well as their cooperative efforts in educational projects.[21]

After 1948 Catholic bishops were among the first to denounce apartheid. This was true despite a traditional anti-Catholic bias in government attitudes, which led to a certain caution among Catholics and made the hierarchy perhaps more diplomatic than it might have been in a less zealously Protestant milieu.[22]

In 1952 the bishops issued a measured, not very radical, statement concluding that discrimination based exclusively on color is an offense against the right of non-Europeans to their natural dignity as human persons, and that justice demanded that non-Europeans be permitted to evolve gradually toward full participation in the political, economic, and cultural life of the country.

In 1957 they issued a far more severe condemnation of apartheid, declaring that "it is a sin to humiliate one's fellowman," that frustrated Blacks were being driven toward "atheistic communism," and that while change must be gradual, nevertheless "a change must come, for otherwise our country faces a disastrous future."[23]

In 1960, a month before Sharpeville, a pastoral letter emphasized that politics must be subject to God's law, cited Pope Pius XII's *The Rights of Man*, pointed out that the differing sections of the country were economically interdependent, and decried the Prohibition of Mixed Marriages Act, the Group Areas Act, and other legislation limiting free association.[24]

All these statements came from the hierarchy, however. On the parish level racial relations had a different dimension. As Strassberger notes, "Wherever Roman Catholic Christians exercise their free choice of association there does not seem to be any greater fellowship between Black and White Christians than in other denominations."[25] On the other hand, there can be no doubt that the Group Areas Act made it increasingly difficult for the races to mingle freely in their own parishes. In addition, the growing gap in education, language, and occupation engendered by Bantu Education, job reservation, and other aspects of apartheid made many Christians on both sides of the color bar feel that they had little in common.

By 1960 the Roman Catholic Church was ahead of the other churches in practicing racial equality within its own household. Forms of worship, finances, church discipline, training of priests, and stipends were uniform, regardless of race. Blacks were beginning to be heard at all levels of the church structure.

The Conservative Evangelical Churches

Inasmuch as these denominations are small, they will be mentioned here only very briefly. The English-speaking churches include Baptists, Free Methodists, Free Lutherans, the African Evangelical Church, the Church of the Nazarene, the Church of England in South Africa, and the so-called classical Pentecostal churches while the Afrikaans churches include the Apostolic Faith Mission and the Afrikaanse Baptiste Kerk, as well as many congregations of the Full Gospel church.

The African Independent Churches

A unique phenomenon, these churches will be described in a separate chapter. Suffice it to say here that although the "Ethiopian" churches are a manifestation of early African nationalism, by the mid-twentieth century it was clear that in both the "Ethiopian" and the "Zionist" churches, the chief concern was the welfare of their own members. Hence they tended to avoid involvement in the South African social and political situation.[26]

Conclusion

Particularly after 1948, the relationship between the Nationalist government and the churches that rejected apartheid took on the quality of a simmering feud. Yet as David Bosch points out, the fact that the members of the English-speaking churches were almost all supporters of the United Party meant that after 1948 Afrikaners perceived criticism by the churches as signs of unwillingness to accept the fact that the United Party had been defeated at the polls.

It is important to note too that most church opposition took the form of eloquent statements. Generally speaking, White Christians did not put multiracial policies into practice in their own congregations. It was church leaders at the synodical levels who spoke out. The great majority of the White laity were oblivious to such statements, or accepted the status quo, or were afraid to be isolated because of their "liberal" views. Hence the great majority of congregations remained segregated, stipends of White ministers were much higher than those of their Black counterparts, and the highest offices in synods and councils were usually reserved for Whites. Moreover, few parishioners engaged in protest actions, or even supported African trade unions.

Under these circumstances, some of the younger and more progressive White clergy left the ministry, disillusioned with the apparent unwillingness of the majority of church members to change. Even more Blacks, of course, reacted to racial separation in the church with bitter resentment. Some Blacks, especially among the intelligentsia, rejected Christianity entirely.

Yet despite this growing ambivalence, African membership in Christian churches rose to unprecedented heights. Even in the Dutch Reformed Church, African membership increased nearly eightfold, rising from 71,422 in 1911 to 556,898 in 1960.[27] Indeed, by 1960, nearly 24 percent of DRC members, 54 percent of the Anglicans, 63 percent of the Presbyterians, 70 percent of the Catholics, 77 percent of the Methodists, and 83 percent of the Lutherans were African.[28] Although figures for 1911 for the African independent churches are not available, their membership jumped from 1,089,479 in 1936 to 2,183,303 in 1960. By 1960 fully one-fifth of Black South African Christians were adherents of the independent churches.

It was partly in response to this phenomenal growth of the independent churches and partly in response to the growing number of Africans in their own denominations that the White-dominated churches began to learn from past mistakes and to make room for African feelings and initiatives. African nationalism found room and even a platform within the English-speaking churches. By 1960 a shift in the distribution of power was beginning to emerge—one that would have far-reaching consequences in the late 1960s and '70s.

Notes

1. Alan Paton, "Church and State in South Africa," in *Christianity and Crisis* 34 (September 30, 1974): 207.

2. Leo Kuper, *An African Bourgeoisie: Race, Class, and Politics in South Africa* (New Haven: Yale University Press, 1965), p. 201.

3. Elfriede Strassberger, *Ecumenism in South Africa: 1936 –1960* (Johannesburg: SACC, 1974), p. 181.

4. Ibid., p. 203.

5. Ibid.

6. Ibid.

7. Kuper, *An African Bourgeoisie*, p. 210.

8. Peter Walshe, *The Rise of African Nationalism in South Africa* (Berkeley: University of California, 1971), p. 161.

9. Strassberger, *Ecumenism in South Africa*, p. 30.

10. Alan Paton, *Apartheid and the Archbishop: The Life and Times of Geoffrey Clayton* (Cape Town: David Philip, 1971), p. 371.

11. Kuper, *An African Bourgeoisie,* p. 212.

12. Strassberger, *Ecumenism in South Africa,* p. 38.

13. Ibid., p. 39.

14. Ibid., p. 44.

15. Ibid., p. 55.

16. Ibid., p. 70.

17. Ibid., p. 76.

18. Ibid., p. 79.

19. Ibid.

20. William Eric Brown, *The Catholic Church in South Africa* (New York: Kennedy, 1960), p. 323.

21. Ibid., p. 341.

22. John W. de Gruchy, "The Relationship Between the State and Some Churches in South Africa," *Journal of State and Church* 19 (1977): 437–455.

23. Press Commission, *Pastoral Letters* (Pretoria: SACBC, n.d.), pp. 13–17.

24. Ibid., pp. 18–30.

25. Strassberger, *Ecumenism in South Africa,* p. 80.

26. David Bosch, "Racism and Revolution: Response of the Churches in South Africa," in *Occasional Bulletin of Overseas Ministries,* January 1979, p. 14.

27. Monica Wilson and Leonard Thompson, eds., *Oxford History of South Africa* (London: Oxford University Press, 1971), Vol. 2, p. 475.

28. Ibid., p. 476.

Part Two
The State and the Churches:
1960 to the Present

Manas Buthelezi,
Bishop of the Evangelical Lutheran
Church of South Africa

Unez Smuts,
Minister in the South African
Congregational Church

Rev. Smangaliso Mkhatshwa,
Secretary of the South African
Catholic Bishops' Conference

David Bosch,
Dutch Reformed Theologian

Membership in South African Churches*

Church Population: Approximately 70 per cent of South Africans (the figure is roughly the same for Whites and Blacks) identify themselves as adherents to a Christian church. The last complete census was taken in 1970 when, out of a total population of 21.4 million, 15.8 million identified themselves as Christian. The following shows the distribution of the Christian population according to race and denomination (1970 figures):

CHURCH	Whites	Coloured	Asian	Africans	TOTAL
NGK	1,487,080				1,487,080
NGKA				924,820	924,820
NG Sending		573,400			573,400
Indian DRC			830		830
Gereformeerde	113,620	3,940			117,560
Hervormde	224,400	1,620			226,020
Anglican	399,950	333,200	5,930	937,720	1,676,800
Presbyterian	117,250	7,570	320	329,320	454,460
Congregational	19,640	144,760	70	185,320	349,790
Methodist	357,410	115,810	2,540	1,676,080	2,151,840
Apostolic Faith Mission	110,960	52,380	590	138,360	302,290
Lutheran	40,620	83,510	250	759,740	884,120
Roman Catholic	304,840	195,630	13,820	1,329,980	1,844,270
African Independent				2,761,120	2,761,120
Other Christian	321,030	327,420	26,250	1,367,640	2,042,340
	3,496,800	1,839,240	50,600	10,410,100	15,796,740

*Figures are based on the 1970 census. Statistics from the 1980 census will not be published until 1983.

CHAPTER FIVE

The Political Scene: 1960 to 1980

The decade that had opened so ominously with the Sharpeville massacre was marked by increasing repression on the one hand and consolidation of White privilege on the other. Educational, cultural, and residential segregation laws became more detailed and stringent; for both Blacks and Whites, civil liberties were curtailed. At the same time White South Africans rose to unprecedented heights of prosperity and power.

In February 1960, a month before Sharpeville, British Prime Minister Harold Macmillan delivered his famous "winds of change" speech before the South African Parliament, emphasizing that the decolonization of the African continent was already underway, and South African Whites must come to terms with the Black majority. Most of his White listeners took umbrage. In October of that year, the all-White electorate, by a small majority (4 percent), voted that South Africa become a republic. The following year it withdrew from the British Commonwealth. The Afrikaner dream of complete liberation from the British was fulfilled at last.

At the same time, a group of African liberals and ex-members of the banned ANC and PAC convoked a new national convention to plan continuing nonviolent pressure against apartheid. Because Luthuli was banned, the conference chose Nelson Mandela, a Witwatersrand University law graduate and ex-ANC Youth Leaguer, as leader of the new National Action Council. The Council demanded that a convention of all races be held and threatened that if the government did not respond favorably it would call a general strike. When the government spurned the challenge, the strike took place—and failed. Mandela went underground to create a new militant wing of the ANC, *Umkonto we Sizwe* ("Spear of the Nation"), which devised plans to sabotage installations without taking human lives. Some twenty operations eventually were admitted to by its leaders. The PAC also sponsored an underground movement, *Poqo* ("We go it alone"), which did not shrink from taking human life.[1]

Faced with these threats, the government in 1963 established a Publications Control Board to forbid importation of works and films considered harmful to public morals and state security. The power of the police was extended to an extraordinary degree. They were allowed to detain suspects under conditions of solitary confinement, without formal charges, for single or successive periods of twelve days. (Later this was extended to an unlimited period of time if authorized by a judge—and even without authorization.)

In 1963 the government strengthened sabotage laws by passing a number of acts giving the Minister of Justice the authority to detain anyone suspected of "communist activity" for a period of up to 170 days, without any formal charge and without letting anyone know their whereabouts. In addition to its existing powers of banning, banishing, and listing individuals and organizations, the government already had authorization to hold suspects incommunicado and to make "unauthorized" reporting of prison conditions illegal; thus it was virtually impossible to corroborate widespread allegations of third-degree treatment of prisoners.

The newly refined legal system succeeded. In 1963, the police raided the underground ANC headquarters. Mandela (jailed after the 1961 banning of the ANC and PAC) was taken from his cell to join his companions on trial for conspiracy to overthrow the government. He was sentenced to life imprisonment on Robben Island. His testimony before the court is not only a brilliant attack on apartheid, but an eloquent affirmation of a democratic nonracist ideal.[2]

The Nationalist Party's rise to power had spurred the rise of Afrikaner capitalists, and by the mid-1960s they had "arrived." The "New Men," says de Klerk, were different from the semifeudal *plattelanders* ("flatlanders") living in serene self-sufficiency on their ancestral lands, from the intellectual and political elite who had contributed to the nationalist ideal, and from the small professional class. They were enormously energetic entrepreneurs who combined dedication to serving the Afrikaner community with a compelling drive for personal power. Anton Ruppert, founder of the worldwide empire of the Rembrandt Tobacco Group, is perhaps the prototype of the new Afrikaner tycoon.

Soon the ranks of the "New Men" were swelling in business, schools, clubs, restaurants, golf courses, and the other provinces of status-seekers. As economic growth became the watchword, there was a new accent on material success, and a deepening of "thing-mindedness." Not long ago, the cry had been against anglicization. Now the "American way" had intruded itself in almost all spheres of life.[3]

Partly because of the Afrikaners' new self-confidence, they no longer looked on their English-speaking compatriots as the prime enemy. Instead, the threat was seen to come from the Blacks inside the country and from British-American "liberals" abroad. For their part, English-speaking voters seemed to be retreating before the tide of African nationalism elsewhere on the continent, and seeking refuge in an increasingly armed *laager*. The Nationalists' new appeal to White unity against the twin forces of "liberalism" and "terrorism" bore fruit, for in the general election of 1966 they increased their parliamentary majority, winning 126 seats to thirty-nine won by the United Party and one by the Progressives.

Later that year the country suffered a shock: Dr. Verwoerd, as he sat at his desk in the House of Assembly, was stabbed to death by a parliamentary messenger. The assassin, a Mozambican of mixed Greek and mulatto descent, was declared insane. But the death of the charismatic Prime Minister did not leave a vacuum. As Davenport points out, the smooth transition to the leadership of B. J. Vorster, Minister of Justice, made it clear that Nationalist policies did not depend on the strengths of individuals, but on the collective determination of party men who had advanced to positions of authority only after careful ideological screening.[4]

Meanwhile, apologists for "separate development" could claim that by giving a form of self-government to the Transkei they were restoring to Africans a form of government rooted in their own soil. The constitution, however, was not drawn up in the Transkeian capital, Umtata, but in Pretoria. Moreover, the Assembly had a clear majority of chiefs over elected members, thus ensuring that the Republic's favorite for the premiership, Chief Kaiser Matanzima, was provided with a safe majority (although nearly all the elective seats in the first general election, in 1963, went to supporters of Matanzima's opponents).

Matanzima later founded his Transkeian National Independence Party (TNIP). Thus a new force entered the picture—a Black political ally committed to the policies of Pretoria. So few new jobs for Africans were created in the borders and the homelands that it became increasingly clear that the reserves would have little capacity to absorb African workers.

At the same time, the government tried to reduce the residential rights of Africans in White areas and increase labor migrancy. By making residential permits dependent on the availability of housing, and keeping houses in short supply, the government made it increasingly difficult for qualified Africans—shopkeepers, technicians, lawyers, and doctors—to get permission to work in "White areas," even if they wanted to serve their own people.

Pretoria also expanded the policy of "endorsing out" the so-called surplus dependents of workers—a policy resulting in the breakup of thousands of families and, for the "discarded people," a barren existence on inhospitable tracts of the reserves. Over 450,000 Africans from White areas were resettled by the end of 1968. Although the number of Africans increased in White areas, they came to consist more and more of contract workers without residence rights, living in crowded subhuman hostels.

To accommodate the "endorsed out" Africans, the government stepped up the development of resettlement villages in the homelands. Municipalities were authorized to make contributions from local revenue to Bantu homeland development, and 80 percent of the profits from municipal liquor sales to Africans were earmarked for this purpose. (Until 1961 only "kaffir beer" was legally available to Africans, and selling "European" liquor to "natives" was prohibited. In the 1960s the government discovered that encouraging liquor traffic would promote its own interests.)

Black and White critics of the resettlement schemes pointed out that the forcible removals were often carried out in a most brutal manner, that in the villages there was a general lack of amenities and jobs, and that the average old age pension (about $6.75 per month in 1970) was miserably inadequate.

In 1971 the Vorster government vested all urban Bantu administration in sixteen boards throughout the country, all reporting directly to Pretoria, thus acquiring greater power for controlling the growth of urban African townships and for directing the movement of contract workers. By way of "compensation," African control over the government of the homelands was increased, as attempts were made to attach citizenship in some homeland to every African, even if they had never lived there. African opposition to the whole concept of homelands, however, mounted steadily during the 1970s.

Nevertheless, in 1972 Lebowa and the Ciskei, as well as Bophuthatswana (which was a conglomerate of eight separate enclaves) spread across the north, and KwaZulu (formerly Zululand), a "nation" consisting of ten fragments, became "self-governing" (a step toward ultimate "independence").

Resistance and Its Suppression

The growth of repression met with some resistance on the part of both Whites and non-Whites.

The Progressives, formed as a result of a breakaway from the United Party in 1958 and committed to the middle-of-the-road principle that full citizenship should be given only to those who possess certain educational and economic qualifications, but without regard to color, criticized most of the racist legislation.

In 1966 Vorster introduced a bill to make it illegal for anyone to belong to any kind of mixed racial organization that intended to discuss political views. So great was the outcry that the bill was revised, and enacted to limit membership of political parties and attendance at political meetings, which henceforth were to be uniracial.

The small, multiracial Liberal Party, led by courageous men like Alan Paton and dedicated to the universal franchise, had already seen forty of its leaders banned over the years for "furthering the aims of communism." Now it was outlawed.

In 1968 the government erected a completely segregated political system for the Coloreds by setting up a Colored Persons Representative Council with forty elective members and twenty government nominees. Although most of the elective seats were won by the opposition Labor Party in the first general election, in 1969, the pro-apartheid Federal Party won just enough seats, with the support of government nominees, to take office. Government nominees included thirteen members who had been defeated in the election. All this destroyed the faith of many Colored persons in the future of the

Council. Several Labor Party confrontations with the government followed.

In the 1975 election the opposition won an outright majority, and the government invited Sonny Leon, the Labor leader, to take office. However, Labor Party members in the Colored Persons Representative Council decided not to appropriate funds allotted to the Council, on the grounds that the budget was racially discriminatory. Leon was removed from office and replaced by a government nominee who approved the budget.

During the early 1970s dissatisfaction grew as it became clear that Colored families were bearing the brunt of compulsory removals under the Group Areas Act. Some 45,000 Colored families had been moved by the end of 1972, many of them from land where their ancestors had lived since the days of the Dutch East India Company. Thousands of fisherfolk were ousted from their homes near the sea to flimsy new houses far from their source of livelihood. Large shantytowns (the scene of riots in 1976 and 1980) developed on the Cape Flats.

The Western Cape had been proclaimed a Colored labor preference area—which meant that Coloreds were to be hired in preference to "Bantu" whenever possible—but this only served to heighten antagonism between the two non-White groups. The policy was applicable even in places where the Colored population was but a small fraction of the African—and the latter was growing fast.

In view of the mounting tension, Vorster in 1973 appointed a commission under Professor Erika Theron of Stellenbosch University to inquire into "matters relating to the Colored population group."

In addition to opposition from liberal political groups, the government had to fight a fairly new source of dissidence, one within the Afrikaner world itself. In 1969, several very conservative *verkrampte* ("narrow") groups pulled out of the National Party to form the Herstigte ("restored") Nasionale Party, devoted to the old racial rigidities. In this conflict the Broederbond sided strongly with the National Party. Curiously, the pragmatic Vorster was coming to be seen as *verlig* ("enlightened") because of his willingness, in the face of mounting pressure from the outside world, to maneuver on relatively minor issues such as racially mixed sporting events and the admission of Black foreign diplomats. In order to be successful in its campaign against *verkrampte,* the government had to maintain a posture of constant assertiveness against the liberals, for it could not afford to be seen as lacking in conviction. The "liberals" under fire were not only the Liberal and Progressive Parties, but the English-language press, certain university groups, a number of creative writers, and many leaders of the English-speaking churches.

Although newspapers published by members of the Newspaper Press Union had avoided the threat of censorship by establishing their own Press Board of Reference, in 1967 the government tried the editor of the *Rand Daily Mail*, Lawrence Gander, and senior reporter Benjamin Pogrund for publishing statements on prison conditions that were held to be false (although attested on oath before publication). The sentences were nominal, but legal fees incurred by the newspaper in this "show trial" amounted to over $350,000.

Censorship of literary works provoked fierce criticism among South African writers. Prominent among those who described the human tragedy and pathos wrought by apartheid were Alan Paton, Nadine Gordimer, the Colored novelist Peter Abrahams, and the Black poet-playwright-novelist Ezekiel Mphalele. Even a few writers in Afrikaans—notably the *Sestigers* ("school of the sixties")—voiced defiance of the status quo. In 1974 came the first banning of a literary work in Afrikaans, André Brink's *Kennis van die And*.

Although the White English-language universities (Rhodes, Witwatersrand, Cape Town, Port Elizabeth, and Natal) had lost the fight over admission of non-Whites in the 1950s, student opposition to government policies toward the universities and public affairs continued. Most articulate was the National Union of South African Students (NUSAS). In 1966 it managed to invite Senator Robert Kennedy to South Africa, but on the eve of his visit the NUSAS president was served with a banning order. Afterward NUSAS and the English-language universities were subjected to increasing criticism from government authorities.

South African students were not unaffected by the worldwide upsurge of student radicalism at the time, and their criticism of apartheid, together with rejection of some aspects of conventional morality, made it possible for the government to appeal to the more conservative Anglo-Afrikaner electorate with the cry of "the nation in danger!"

In 1972 the Prime Minister appointed the Schlebusch (later, Schlebusch-LeGrange) Commission to investigate the affairs of NUSAS, the University Christian Movement (UCM), the South African Institute of Race Relations (SAIRR), and the Christian Institute. The Commission held its hearings in secret and was empowered to subpoena witnesses, find them guilty, and recommend punishment without recourse to any court of law.

The year 1972 was one of ferment on the Black campuses. The Black People's Convention (BPC) was formally launched in July, and O. R. Tiro, a student at the (Black) University of the North, was expelled for a public attack on White control of Black universities. The all-Black South African Students Organization (SASO) led the outcry against the expulsion.* Support for him swelled in the other English-language universities, Black and White, and NUSAS held protests in June.

In 1973 the Schlebusch-LeGrange Commission recommended no action against NUSAS as a body, but named eight leaders as dangerous to internal security. They were banned shortly afterward, together with eight SASO leaders. Tiro was murdered by a car bomb in Botswana.

The Schlebusch-LeGrange Commission also forced the multiracial Univer-

*For a description of SASO and BPC see Chapter Six.

sity Christian Movement to dissolve. Although several members of the Institute of Race Relations refused to testify, the organization survived, perhaps because it had always emphasized research and education more than action, and because it was supported by powerful industrialists such as Harry Oppenheimer, as well as American groups such as the Carnegie and Rockefeller Foundations.

The fourth target of the inquiry, the Christian Institute, perhaps posed the greatest threat to apartheid despite its small size, for it called for nothing less than a complete reconstruction of the White-ruled society.**

Escalation of Unrest and Indignation

The United Party (UP), which had been induced out of consideration for "public security" to take part in the quasi-secret Schlebusch-LeGrange Commission, found itself badly split. In 1975 the splinter Reform Party joined the Progressives. In 1977 the UP right wing broke away to form a new South African Party, the center renamed itself the New Republic Party, and the liberal wing joined the Progressives to form the Progressive Federal Party.

These shifts in political groupings were partly a reflection of the climate of growing unease. Until 1974 White South Africans were curiously complacent, for prosperity reigned. But in that year the Portuguese colonies of Angola and Mozambique came into majority rule. In the case of Angola, South Africa covertly sent in "advisors" and troops to support the anti-Marxist UNITA faction, and to defend the Cunene Dam that South Africa was building to supply Namibia and the Johannesburg area. The expedition was a fiasco.

At the same time, pressure was being exerted by the United Nations and the Western powers for South Africa to cede control of illegally-held Namibia. Ironically, Prime Minister Vorster was pressing Rhodesia's Prime Minister Ian Smith, albeit unsuccessfully, to move toward what Vorster would not accept for South Africa—majority rule.

The stepped-up guerilla activity in Rhodesia and Namibia, and on the borders of South Africa itself, prompted a general of the South African defense force—hardly a breeding ground for liberal thought—to declare that "the antirevolutionary struggle is 80 percent socio-economic and 20 percent military—the objective is no longer territory but the hearts and minds of men."[5]

Labor unrest has been growing, especially since 1972 when dockworkers struck in Durban and Cape Town. In 1973 there was a spate of unexpected Black strikes, particularly in the Durban area. By 1974 strikes had spread to the rest of the country and were continuing in the mines.

Despite these signs and the warnings from Black leaders such as newspaper editor Percy Qoboza, White authorities were unprepared for the Soweto up-

---

**For a description of the rise and fall of the Christian Insitutute, see Chapter Six.

risings that erupted in June 1976. These events have been well chronicled elsewhere. Suffice it to say here that this "children's revolt" was overtly a rebellion against the use of Afrikaans—the language of the hated oppressor—as the medium of instruction in schools, but clearly a furious rejection of the whole system. Many of the demonstrations began nonviolently but escalated to violence. Buildings went up in flames, at least 176 persons (almost all of them Black) died, and over twelve hundred were wounded in repeated clashes with the police.

The riots also spread to Colored areas on the Cape. (Some observers speculated that the Coloreds were reacting to the government's rejection of major proposals of the Theron Commission, which had been appointed to study the problems of Coloreds and had advocated reintegrating them into the White political system.) As a result of the riots, foreign investors and tourists were frightened, immigration dropped, emigration soared, and the military budget increased.

In 1977 the Black education system was still in a state of chaos, especially in postprimary schools of the townships and in African universities. Unemployment, especially among Africans, rose sharply. The arrest and detention of leaders of the Black Consciousness Movement continued. At least ten prisoners died in detention, from "suicide" or other mysterious causes such as "jumping" or "falling" from the tenth floor.

The most famous of these prisoners was Steve Biko, leader of the Black Consciousness Movement. His violent death had national and international repercussions, especially after a judge found no one responsible. A month after Biko's death, the government declared the Christian Institute and seventeen African organizations unlawful, placed seven persons under banning orders, and detained at least forty-two others.

That same year there was widespread indignation when the Bantu Affairs Administration Boards in the Western Cape and Port Natal decided to bulldoze the "illegal" shanty dwellings of thousands of African squatters during a particularly cold winter. Although they were offered free tickets to their homelands, the wives and children did not want to leave their menfolk. The government also moved to replace Bantu councils in urban African townships with community councils, but it became clear that their powers would be virtually the same and that urban Africans were increasingly skeptical of such bodies.

Forays in Constitutionalism

Yet the 1977 general elections returned the largest-ever majority for National Party members (the "Nats," in South African colloquial usage). The party proposed a "new political dispensation": a constitutional plan by which the White, Colored, and Indian ethnic groups would each have its own parliament, which would legislate on matters pertaining exclusively to the group concerned. Matters of mutual concern would be dealt with by a Council of Cabinets on which all three racial groups would be represented, but the African majority would be excluded from constitutional bodies.

During 1978, the Nats' plan was widely discussed, and a great many constitutional models were examined.

These constitutional proposals were drawn along the lines of "consociation"—that is, they were founded on the assumption of a plural society, based on ethnic groupings. Political decision-making would occur on the basis of communal representation rather than individual participation in the political process. At the top would stand a grand coalition of political leaders of all population groups, with mutual veto power over many types of decisions.

The National Party's version of "consociation" gave it dominance over other groups, for Black Africans were excluded and the Nats alone were to represent the Whites, thus preventing liberal and progressive elements among Whites from forming a successful alliance with Colored and Indian representatives. Moreover, the necessity of consensual decision-making favors the status quo: one group can veto another and the ensuing paralysis works to perpetuate legalized control of "the system."

The government's plan was opposed by the *verkrampte* ("closed-minded"), particularly by Andries Treurnicht, leader of the National Party's extreme right wing. On the other side, even leaders of the nonindependent homelands rejected both the idea of independent homelands and the new constitutional plan.[6]

In September Prime Minister Vorster announced his retirement for health reasons. He was succeeded by P. W. Botha. One of the latter's credentials was that he had been exonerated from the "Information Scandal" ("Infogate"), a complex affair that included many unauthorized expenditures by the Department of Information such as the secret funding of the *Citizen*, an English-language newspaper that articulated government views.

The *verlig* ("enlightened") Botha soon began to warn Whites that they must "adapt or die." This vague phrase seemed to mean that Whites should accept relaxation of some aspects of petty apartheid,[7] the upgrading of the living standards of comparatively middle-class Blacks, and the opening of certain categories of skilled labor to Africans, except in areas controlled by strong White unions.

At the same time South Africa was experiencing pressure from abroad for multinational corporations operating there to adopt one of the four "codes of conduct": the Sullivan (USA), that of the European Economic Community, the Urban Foundation, or the Canadian government. Pioneered by Leon Sullivan, a Baptist minister who had become a director of General Motors, the codes focused on desegregation of facilities, equal pay for equal work, training, hiring practices, improving the quality of life outside the work site, and recognition of trade unions.

In 1978 South African exports to the United States increased dramatically, from $553.7 million for the first six months of 1977 to $944.7 million for the same period the following year.⁸ Worldwide "stagflation" and uncertainty in the oil market sent the value of net gold output up 38.2 percent that year.⁹

During 1979 and 1980 talk of "change" proliferated. Yet it seemed to be more rhetoric than reality. Even the relaxation of petty apartheid was spotty and inconsistent—only a few hotels (luxury-type) were opened to Blacks, for example, and most Whites considered toilets too sacred to share with "non-Europeans." More significantly, it became clear that even the *verligte* leaders had no desire to share power. All the change they envisioned lay within the grand policy of separate development.

Fundamental to the "new" approach was a comprehensive national strategy designed to unite White and Black "moderates" in a combined military and socio-economic assault on a common enemy, "Marxism." The goal was to maintain internal stability by avoiding the political threat of massive unemployment and giving middle-class Blacks a stake in the status quo. A President's Council consisting of nominated leaders of the White, Colored, Asian, and even the small Chinese sectors was proposed. Although urban Africans would not be allowed to participate in the council or have their own parliament, they would exercise "self-determination" in the homelands and through urban community councils. The new linking would occur within a far-reaching regional constellation of southern African states, all of which were heavily dependent on South Africa for food, machinery, and expertise.

Concerted attempts were made to induce Black leaders to serve on community councils, but most of them refused to do so. Then after an outcry, because Africans would not be included in the President's Council, Colored and Asian leaders refused to participate in the body. The government then announced that Africans would have their own separate Black Council, which would maintain contact with the President's Council. Black leaders rejected this too.

Debate continued on various constitutional proposals along federal, confederal, or consociational lines. The opposition Progressive Federal Party (the "Progs") took the position that any constitution must be negotiated with *all* ethnic groups. It supported natural pluralism based on voluntary rather than enforced association, and regarded the African as a fellow citizen, with political rights. (Whether the latter was tantamount to "one person, one vote" was a question subjected to inconclusive debate.)

In any case, it became clear that Botha was shifting power away from Parliament and party caucus toward his own cabinet machine. The "security planning budget" increased tenfold in 1980.¹⁰

Internal strains were compounded by the unfolding of more chapters in the "Infogate" scandal, clashes between *verkrampte* hardliners and more liberal *verligte*, a shortage of skilled labor, and the emergence of new Black political groups. Acts of sabotage increased: the ANC's daring coordinated explosions of costly SASOL plants made some White South Africans feel that "the Rhodesia story" was moving close to home.

Yet the threat of future urban warfare seemed unreal in comparison with the golden present: the boom that swept the country as gold prices shot up. Other commodities rose to new highs. Between 1979 and 1980 sugar, for example, more than quadrupled in price.

At the same time that Whites were enjoying almost unparalleled prosperity, African rents were hiked by the landlord (the government) in some urban areas (in Soweto the increase was expected to be 75 percent by 1981). The cost of bread, the poor person's staple, rose 25 percent.

In 1979 Black unemployment (excluding the impoverished homelands) rose to an estimated 25 percent—the result of an escalating birthrate, an increasingly capital-intensive economy, and the small number of Black training programs.[11] After substantial pay increases during the early 1970s, it was clear that since then Black wages had fallen in terms of purchasing power.

Forced removals of "surplus" workers to the homelands accelerated. As one economist put it, "the diseconomies of growth were shifted to the homelands." In 1980 the worst drought in a century hit the country. Hundreds of emaciated Africans in the homelands wasted away and died. Although Blacks were eager to upgrade their skills, the government sponsored only a few training programs, and continued to recruit European labor for the openings wanted by many Blacks.

The Riekert and Wiehahn Commissions

Most devastating for Africans were the recommendations by the Riekert and Wiehahn Commissions, which supposedly had been set up to "liberalize" the system. The Wiehahn Commission's purpose was to investigate legislation pertaining to labor. It will be recalled that although Black unions were not recognized by the government, and strikes by Blacks were a criminal offense, strike actions had persisted since 1972.

In the face of mounting international pressures, the Commission decided that recognition of unions and removal of racial discrimination in employment would be preferable to sanctions. Its principal recommendations were that job reservation be abolished and that Black unions be registered—recommendations that the government accepted. However, it retained many weapons.

Registration depends on government's approval; the unions are company unions and "parallel" unions beholden to management rather than workers; the procedure for settling industrial disputes is cumbersome; political activities are prohibited; mixed unions are tabooed. Anyone involved in a dispute risks being arrested for riotous assembly, conspiracy, terrorism, or breach of contract. Any worker dismissed can be endorsed back to the homelands. The new job reservation policy is also hedged with conditions providing safeguards for individual and group interests, and stabilizing existing work reservation determinations.

Behind the recommendations of the one-man Riekert Commission was the fact that for decades all Black employment was channeled through the state labor bureaus, operating under a maze of intricate laws that have been a source of despair for White employers. Despite elaborate pass controls, thousands of Blacks defied a system that divided South Africa into ethnically based nation states, treating the majority of its Black citizens as foreigners. Finding the risk of incarceration—or even the reality of a few months a year in prison—preferable to near starvation in the homelands, they had been working illegally in "White" areas.

Instead of easing the restrictions, Riekert's recommendations strengthened them, for he saw control of the rate of urban in-migrations as an absolutely essential "social security" measure. Hence influx control is strengthened by making availability of housing and employment the criteria for residence. A threat of dismissal becomes a threat of deportation.

The weight of control was shifted from the worker to the lawbreaking employer, subject to a fine of 500 rands ($600 in 1981) for each offense. At the same time it fueled Black anger, suffering, and a desperate resort to crime as a means of survival.

Both the Wiehahn and Riekert reports were politically designed to separate the African "haves" from the "have-nots." Their recommendations emerge from the awareness that, because of the process of mechanization that was turning most White workers into supervisory personnel or white-collar wage earners, the future lies with Black labor. Entrepreneurs had been warning that the shortage of skilled workers was a bottleneck to growth. Hence the commission's recommendations to upgrade the status of those Africans allowed in "White" areas through improved housing, education, and training programs. The recommendations become a device to neutralize growing political unrest by offering carrots to a privileged few, using more efficient sticks. A new "grand design" unfolds: neo-apartheid.

The University of Cape Town's South African Labor and Development Research Unit criticized the new dispensation as an expansion of state control over the industrial relations system, and many Black unions denounced it. Nor did the tactic succeed, for in 1980, particularly, there was a tremendous upsurge in work stoppages and boycotts. The most salient feature of these actions was the degree of solidarity shown by the strikers and other workers. They were risking dismissal, imprisonment, and even deportation for the sake of a common goal.

Workers had come to recognize the Achilles' heel in the government's policy of rapid economic growth. Black political leaders were beginning to cultivate links with unions. It is in the labor field that Black militants see their major hope.

Notes

1. T. R. H. Davenport, *South Africa: A Modern History* (London: Macmillan, 1978), p. 291.

2. For the complete text of Mandela's speech see Donald Woods, *Biko* (New York: Paddington, 1978), pp. 23–29.

3. W. A. de Klerk, *The Puritans in Africa* (London: Rex Collins, 1975), p. 304.

4. Davenport, *South Africa,* p. 294.

5. Ibid., p. 310.

6. Loraine Gordon et al., eds., *A Survey of Race Relations in South Africa, 1978* (Johannesburg: SAIRR, 1979), p. 3.

7. "Petty apartheid" refers to laws pertaining to segregation of sports, eating and toilet facilities, park benches, post offices, and the like, but not to fundamentals such as equal wages, marriage rights, residential rights, and suffrage.

8. Gordon, *Survey of Race Relations, 1978,* p. 149.

9. Simon Jenkins, "The Great Evasion: South Africa, A Survey," *Economist* 275 (June 21, 1980): 8.

10. Jenkins, "The Great Evasion," p. 16.

11. Loraine Gordon et al., eds., *A Survey of Race Relations in South Africa, 1979* (Johannesburg: SAIRR, 1980), p. 197.

CHAPTER SIX

The Christian Institute and
the Renaissance of Black Consciousness

In the early 1960s there was only scattered protest from the churches against the repression that followed Sharpeville. The major crucible of Christian challenge to apartheid was a small, dedicated, action-oriented group—the interdenominational and interracial Christian Institute.

By the early 1970s the initiative for change had begun to shift to Black consciousness groups, many of which the Institute helped to foster. This was accompanied by the indigenization of churches, as Blacks began to assume leadership positions in multiracial churches belonging to the South African Council of Churches and within the Council itself.

The Christian Institute was formed in 1963 after a series of dramatic confrontations between progressive and conservative DRC leaders that followed the signing of the Cottesloe Statement. The report from the Cottesloe Consultation, convened by the World Council of Churches (WCC) nine months after Sharpeville to discuss Christian responsibility in race relations, reflected a compromise between the three Afrikaans churches (the NHK, and the Cape and Transvaal DRC synods) and the five English-speaking churches represented.

Unity and equality of the races were affirmed in terms vague enough to be compatible with separate development. Nevertheless, the conference did declare, for example, that persons had the right to own land wherever they lived and to participate in government. Furthermore, the compromise threatened to draw the isolated South Africans into closer contact with the precepts of the international church.[1]

The effect on Prime Minister Verwoerd was electric. Summoning the DRC theologians to order, he stressed that they had been unduly influenced by the "liberal" WCC and that they must remember the high purpose of apartheid. They would have to recant. And recant most of them did. The two DRC synods at the Consultation also withdrew from the WCC.

In addition, the establishment felt threatened by the publication in 1961 of

Delayed Action, in which eleven Dutch Reformed theologians refuted on biblical and moral grounds all arguments for apartheid,[2] and then called for radical change in government policies.

The high hopes for ecumenical cooperation between the DRC and the English-speaking churches were dashed. It now seemed that the only solution lay in a new kind of ecumenical thrust not tied to denominational structures. Thus the Christian Institute came into being, under the leadership of C. F. Beyers Naudé, a key figure in the DRC delegation at Cottesloe. He had been a member of the inner circle of the Broederbond, Moderator of the Southern Transvaal Regional Synod, and leading candidate for the office of Moderator of the General Synod—a post for many years second in influence only to that of the Prime Minister. (For many years Prime Minister Vorster's brother, J. D. "Koot" Vorster, was Moderator.) Naudé's position helped to signal the extent to which he was striking at the heart of South Africa's civil religion.

Like most Whites, Naudé was brought up in comfortable circumstances, cushioned from any real contact with Africans, Indians, or Coloreds. His crisis had begun a few years earlier when White missionaries working among non-Whites in Johannesburg brought back reports of bitterness toward White persons and the church that they represented. Naudé did not believe them until he went out to the locations himself and began to listen. And he listened on repeated visits. At the same time, he explored the Bible more deeply. Yet only gradually did he understand the extent to which the DRC faith he espoused was a justification of White privilege.

After founding the Christian Institute, Naudé was told by his church that he could not retain his posts in both church and institute. Sadly, he made the anguished decision to resign as Moderator, and faced the challenge of an embattled new life.

The DRC barred its members from using the Institute; those who did so suffered social ostracism. When Naudé tried to participate in the burial service following his mother's funeral, he was shouldered away from the graveside.

The first activities of the Christian Institute focused on formation of nationwide Bible study groups, using study guides and the Institute's journal *Pro Veritate* to challenge Christians to rediscover the biblical message. Study fellowships also exposed some South Africans to developments in the church in Europe and North America.

At the beginning, many members of the Christian Institute were Afrikaners—men such as Prof. A. S. Geyser, who was tried for heresy by the Hervormde Kerk for cooperating with Naudé in founding the Institute, and Dr. Ben Engelbrecht, a professor of divinity at the University of Witwatersrand. The struggle in the 1960s to influence the Dutch Reformed churches came to nought, however, and the Institute turned increasingly to emphasizing its ecumenical ministry.

A primary goal was to help Christians identify with the poor and seek a redistribution of power through widespread participation in decision-making at every level of society, not least in the churches. The Institute was firmly committed to nonviolent change and to peace—but not the false peace of avoiding conflict.[3]

Its statement of principles recognized that all fundamental problems of the world were to be found to some degree in South Africa. Although Christ is Lord of human society, declared the Institute, "in southern Africa some people acknowledge the lordship of other gods: the supreme importance of race, apartheid, Christian nationalism, denominationalism, and a self-centered piety." Christians must come to see that "southern Africa is a sick society because of its alienation, and doomed to die unless it is healed."[4]

Resurgence of Black Consciousness

The ecumenical thrust encountered a major obstacle: the resolute indifference of most English-speaking South Africans. Hence the Institute made another major reorientation—it began to encourage the resurgence of Black consciousness. Gone now was the old liberal illusion that change could come solely from education and moral appeals directed to the privileged. Rather, Black initiatives would be crucial in pressing for change.

The Institute was responding to the renewal of Black consciousness in the late 1960s, after the years of dormancy following the "Treason Trials." Students at the new university colleges for "non-White" students had become increasingly resentful over the fact that their student bodies were not allowed to affiliate with the largely White National Union of South African Students (NUSAS), although some students did become individual members.

To Blacks, there was a contradiction between principle and practice in NUSAS: though preaching the ideal of nonracism, members of the organization were unable to live out their ideals. At a national conference in 1967, for example, the African delegates were given separate accommodation in an African township. Although this was not the fault of NUSAS, to many Black students it was another instance of White domination of the multiracial organization. Their feeling is expressed in the words of one African: "What is the use of a Black man talking about the erosion of freedom in South Africa? We have no freedom."[5]

In any event, NUSAS had been unable to bring about any real change, African students insisted. The time had come for Blacks to do things for themselves. It did not help Africans to see several quiet Black faces at a multiracial conference that ultimately concentrated on what White students believed to be the needs of Blacks. Whites and Blacks simply lived in different worlds.

Impetus for a new direction came from the University Christian Movement (UCM), founded in 1967 by a White Methodist minister, Basil Moore, to open fresh avenues of contact between the races. Within eighteen months there was a Black majority at its sessions and a caucus had emerged that was interested in radical writings from the United States, particularly Black theology as a vehicle for examining the Scriptures and the predicament of the oppressed. Although many students considered UCM too religiously oriented to be relevant to their socio-economic situation, it was through this caucus that Black theology was introduced to South Africa and that Black consciousness gained impetus.

It was this caucus, too, that launched a dynamic new organization, the all-Black South African Students Organization (SASO). Its formation spelled the disruption of the traditional alignment of South African students—NUSAS representing English-speaking campuses, and the Afrikaanse Studente Bond (ASB) representing the Afrikaans-language universities supporting apartheid.

SASO was born at a conference in 1969, under the leadership of Steve Biko. Gradually a consensus evolved that Black students must unite now to face their problems, and to promote community awareness, achievement, and pride.[6] In the words of Barney Pityana, second president of SASO, the first step was: "to make the Black man see himself, to pump life into his empty shell, to infuse him with dignity, to remind him of his complicity in the crime of allowing himself to be misused and therefore letting evil reign supreme in the country of his birth. . . . This means that Blacks must build themselves into a position of nondependence upon Whites. They must work toward a self-sufficient political, social, and economic unit. . . . Black man, you are on your own!"[7] Many White liberals and NUSAS members of course saw this as an ominous sign of counterracism. To them Steve Biko replied, "It isn't a negative hating thing. It's a positive Black self-confidence thing involving no hatred of anyone, not even the Nats—only of what they represent today."[8]

At a meeting in December 1971, a new umbrella organization was conceived. The Black People's Convention (BPC) drew together students, church and ministerial organizations—notably the African Independent Churches Association (AICA)—social and cultural groups like the YWCA, and a few politicians, survivors of the old ANC.

The aims of the BPC included emancipation of Blacks from psychological and physical oppression, creation of a just and humanitarian society, and reorientation of theology to make it more relevant to the aspirations of Blacks. The term "Black" was to embrace all groups suffering repression and exploitation—Africans, Coloreds and Asians. White liberals were not welcomed as immediate collaborators, but were encouraged to direct their efforts at reforming White South Africans.

It is interesting that angry young political leaders such as Steve Biko were concerned with Black theology (which can be described as a theological study of disinheritance and liberation, from the perspective of people oppressed because of their color).[9] Biko, it will be recalled, had attended both Lovedale and Marianhill. He declared:

Black theology seeks to relate God and Christ once more to the Black man and his daily problems. It wants to describe Christ as a fighting God and not a passive God. . . . Blacks have had enough experience as objects of racism not to want to reverse the tables. . . . In time we shall be able to bestow upon South Africa the greatest gift possible—a more human face.[10]

The quest for an indigenous theology included the search for continuity with African traditional religions. Many Blacks had become convinced that while using modern technology, human beings should still live in harmony with nature, and that communal values involving the sharing of land usage rights and accumulated wealth should be emphasized.

Instead of a "Black problem," they declared, there was really a "White problem," for Whites had not responded to the essential challenge of the Gospels: to identify with the poor. African communalism was an alternative to both capitalism and communism. Thus Black theology was recognized as much more than the awakening of Black nationalism—it was to be the basis for a revival of Christian witness in lethargic churches.

In many ways, then, the Christian Institute encouraged Black initiatives. It also joined the South African Council of Churches (SACC), which had changed its name from the Christian Council of South Africa in 1968 and also had begun to move increasingly toward a Black orientation.

Spro-cas and Further Projects

Gradually the activities of the Institute expanded. In 1969, a year after the SACC had published a strong condemnation of apartheid entitled *Message to the People of South Africa,* the Christian Institute and the SACC cosponsored a follow-up program, the Study Project on Christianity in Apartheid Society (Spro-cas). Its six commissions, consisting of dedicated scholars, examined the following issues: education; processes of social change; power, privilege, and poverty; apartheid and the church; law and justice; political alternatives to apartheid. The commission on alternatives suggested a vigorous campaign of improved education for Blacks, literacy programs, new tax structures, recognition of African trade unions, the phasing out of migratory labor, and federal structures with strong organs of local government and proportional representation.

In 1972 a new program, Spro-cas II, was launched. Emphasizing action, it embraced programs in labor, education, and social issues, and represented a turning-point in the Christian Institute's involvement in the struggle of Blacks.

Spro-cas was responsible for launching one of the most important Black consciousness groups, the Black Community Programs (BCP). In 1971 a seasoned Black social worker, Bennie Khoapa, was invited to join Spro-cas, where he worked out a plan for a service organization that would help make Blacks themselves agents of the change they were seeking.

In 1972, after getting a go-ahead from Spro-cas, Khoapa hired several persons, including Steve Biko (a Spro-cas staff member), and the BCP began founding clinics run by Black personnel, literacy campaigns, an urban youth movement, and a church leaders project to reorient the churches toward the needs of Blacks. In cooperation with SASO, it also encouraged Black trade unions.

To complement the BCP, the Christian Institute set up a Program for Social Change to help Whites prepare for inevitable change. The BCP was successful in raising the consciousness of its constituency; the PSC (often criticized by Whites as "socialist") was not.

Recognizing the numerical importance of the independent churches, their search for continuity within African traditions, and their isolation as Black introspective communities divorced from the Christian mainstream, the Christian Institute encouraged the formation of the African Independent Churches Association.[11] Then, in response to the great need for formal training of ministers, it helped the AICA to finance and staff the Theological College for Independent Churches. Unfortunately, the wide range of independent churches, and acrimony among their charismatic leaders, made it impossible for the Institute to carry on the delicate task of maintaining the college. In 1974 the AICA elected a new board of management and then joined the SACC.

The Christian Institute also encouraged a reform movement within the NGK "daughter" churches—namely, the Coloreds' Sendingkerk, the Africans' Nederduitse Gereformeerde Kerk in Afrika (NGKA), and the Indians' Reformed Church in Africa (RCA)—in all of which younger ministers were beginning to voice discontent with a synod under the control of White pastors serving as missionaries. Several ministers of these churches were active public supporters of the Institute.

In 1974 an increasing number of NGKA ministers took an interest in the Institute, and in 1975 that church voted to eliminate the category of missionary, and drop the condescending term "daughter church."[12] The DRC was asked to open its doors to Black ministers so that racism might be dissolved and the two churches stand side by side. Then the NGKA joined the South African Council of Churches, from which the DRC had withdrawn in 1961.

The influence of the Christian Insitute was felt in other ways. For example, in 1973 Anglican, Methodist, Roman Catholic, and Presbyterian laypersons and clergy—all members of the Institute—made a pilgrimage from East London to Cape Town to draw attention to the decimation of African family life under the migratory labor system. Another example involved the tension generated when a Black caucus in the Anglican church succeeded in replacing the old unequal basis of representation—parishes—by one based on the number of communicants. For a moment it seemed that Whites might charge the majority Blacks with reverse racism. But this threat was avoided because the key individuals working for change had experienced the fellowship of the Christian Insitute.

After the 1972 unrest on Black campuses led to the expulsion of student leaders, White students demonstrated at English-language universities. They were particularly vociferous at the University of Cape Town. In the following days Christian Institute members who had demonstrated were severely harassed. The Cape regional director, the Rev. Theo Kotzé, and his family were prey to a volley of telephone threats, and their home was shot at and assaulted by firebombs. A church was burned down and two attempts were made to set fire to the Insitute's Ecumenical Center. Automobile bolts were loosened and steering wheels mysteriously collapsed.

Harassment of all organizations working against apartheid intensified. Letters were opened, phones tapped, and the security police (BOSS, Bureau of State Security) made surprise visits, designed to intimidate. Informers were placed in critical positions and subtle threats were made against highly vulnerable Blacks.

Beginning of the End

The Schlebusch Commission, appointed in 1972 to investigate NUSAS, UCM, SAIRR, and the Christian Institute, summoned many Spro-cas and Institute staff members to appear before it. As a matter of conscience, they refused to testify, but offered to appear to explain the reasons for their civil disobedience: this was a political not a judicial commission, and it refused to reveal evidence or permit cross-examination of witnesses.

The passports of Naudé, Kotzé, Dot Cleminshaw, and Nikki Westcott were seized or withdrawn. Several members were sentenced to prison and fined. Two Blacks—BCP director Bennie Khoapa, and Manas Buthelezi, director of the Christian Institute in Natal—were banned for five years under the Suppression of Communism Act. Offices of *Pro Veritate* were broken into, Spro-cas offices were searched, *A Taste of Power* (the final Spro-cas report) was banned, and charges were laid against the directors of Ravan Press (then affiliated with the Christian Institute) for publishing subversive literature.

In 1975, after the Commission's report, the Christian Institute was declared an "affected organization" and barred from receiving funds from abroad. Thus most of its financial support was abruptly cut off. As a result of these pressures, White membership declined somewhat. Yet Black support rose sharply, and the "hard core" who remained with the Institute increased their financial contributions and felt strengthened in purpose.

It is important to note that this was a period of increasing repression of any group influenced by Black consciousness. In 1974, for example, land and buildings belonging to the Federal Theological Seminary (FEDSEM) were expropriated by the government. It had been formed in 1961 by Anglicans, Presbyterians, Methodists, and Congregationalists as an interdenominational training center for Black candidates. (Although the churches were against segregated seminaries in principle, South African law gave them little choice if such a seminary was to be residential.) It was built on land donated by the Church of Scotland, near the (Black) Fort Hare University in Alice. There it not only developed good theological education, but also helped to stimulate Black theological thinking.

Students at Fort Hare found at FEDSEM a window on the world concerned about helping Blacks fight racism. FEDSEM thus became an important center of support for SASO. It was a situation that the government could not tolerate. In 1971 the rector of Fort Hare, the head of a notably conservative and paternalistic White administration of a school for Black students, offered to buy the FEDSEM site, and three years later it was expropriated.[13]

In 1974, at the SACC annual conference, Beyers Naudé seconded a controversial resolution supporting the right to conscientious objection. Even after the Christian Institute was declared an affected organization (1975), he and his colleagues continued to take risks. Shortly after the Soweto disturbance, for example, the Institute published *Is South Africa a Police State?*, a dispassionate account of all political trials, detentions, and bannings over the previous several years.

The response was predictable: liberal English-language papers published descriptions of the document, but the government snapped back with biting criticism. It also briefly imprisoned Beyers Naudé, carrying out a sentence imposed three years earlier, after he had declined to give evidence before the Schlebusch-Le Grange Commission. In the spring of 1977, the Institute put out a second report, *Torture in South Africa?* Excerpts were published in the local and foreign press.

Faced with a volley of pressures from many quarters in the wake of Soweto, the government retaliated. On October 19, 1977, it shut down the Christian Institute and seventeen other groups openly working for liberation of Blacks (including BPC, BCP, SASO, the Black Women's Federation, the Union of Black Journalists, and the Soweto Students Representative Council). *Pro Veritate* was ordered to cease publication (as was *The World*, the leading Black daily). Beyers Naudé was banned—barred from speaking publicly, being quoted in the press, meeting with more than one person at a time (except members of his family), and traveling beyond the magisterial district of Johannesburg.

In Retrospect

How great was the influence of the Christian Institute? Its increasingly radical views, which challenged not only deeply ingrained racial prejudices but the elitist political system, the dehumanizing patterns of labor, and the consumer definition of "happiness" that formed the foundations of the

Whites' affluent lifestyle, could hardly be expected to appeal to the average White parishioner.

Nevertheless, the Institute exercised a seminal influence quite disproportionate to its small membership. It provided resources and a supportive community to Christians who were willing to "stand up and be counted." Moreover, says Walshe, it served as a center of dissemination of ideas at a time when African political organizations had been systematically repressed. Although not responsible for the resurgence of Black nationalism, which had a dynamic of its own, it offered a language of protest and renewed optimism about shaping the course of history. This bolstered the confidence of Black leaders in a variety of organizations and produced ferment in church structures.[14]

On a theological level, the Institute had an impact in southern Africa similar to that of liberation theology in Latin America, which challenges Christians to accept the scriptural injunction to work with and to *be* with the poor.

Some members had also begun to seek a synthesis with Marxist analysis, and found themselves wrestling with profound questions, such as: Can moral consciousness transform class conflict into societal consensus for equalitarian justice? Can Christians put themselves at the cutting edge of social evolution, activating protests and working with movements for justice, yet rouse compassion and limit the violence inherent in change that threatens the power of elites?[15]

Throughout its history, the Christian Institute leadership adhered to a nonviolent philosophy. Even when the World Council of Churches in 1970 established the Program to Combat Racism, which included grants (for nonmilitary purposes) to freedom fighters, the Institute (as well as the SACC) dissociated itself from this decision, rejecting it on the grounds that the program might encourage violence. Yet government spokesmen persisted in condemning the Institute for supporting revolutionary violence.

Although it is true that in 1977 two embittered ex-Christian Institute members challenged pacifism when they set up the so-called Christian Institute in Exile (in Holland), they had no authority to speak for the Institute itself. Their stance flatly contradicted the continuing commitment of Beyers Naudé and other leaders in South Africa to nonviolence. In 1979 the Holland office was closed by Theo Kotzé, former director of the Cape branch of the Institute.

There can be little doubt that Minister of Police Jimmy Kruger understood that the threat posed by the Christian Institute had nothing to do with the danger of armed struggle. Nonviolence can also be a threat too—indeed, more so—in that it rests not on military weapons, which can be seized, but on ideas and ideals, which cannot be captured.

The real threat posed by the Christian Institute lay not in its call for some reforms, but in its call for truly radical change—at the roots of society. The Institute challenged men and women to share resources, to redistribute power through change in political and economic structures, to give up "the South African way of life," and even to accept a lower standard of living.

Notes

1. Elfriede Strassberger, *Ecumenism in South Africa: 1936 –1960* (Johannesburg: SACC, 1974), p. 225.

2. Peter Walshe, "The Christian Institute and African Nationalism," *Journal of Church and State* (Autumn 1977): 460.

3. Ibid., p. 461.

4. "The Christian Principles for which the Christian Institute Stands in Southern Africa" (Johannesburg: Christian Institute, n.d.).

5. Donald Woods, *Biko* (New York: Paddington, 1978), p. 32.

6. Muriel Horrell, ed., *A Survey of Race Relations, 1970* (Johannesburg: SAIRR, 1971), p. 245.

7. Woods, *Biko,* pp. 34–35.

8. Ibid., p. 55.

9. Muriel Horrell, et al., eds., *A Survey of Race Relations, 1971* (Johannesburg: SAIRR, 1972).

10. Steve Biko, "Black Consciousness and the Quest for a True Humanity," in *Essays in Black Theology,* ed. M. Mothlabi (Johannesburg: Project of the United Christian Movement, 1972), pp. 22–27.

11. Walshe, "The Christian Institute and African Nationalism," p. 468.

12. The Reformed Church in Holland (Gereformeerde Kerken van Nederland), which came out in support of South African liberation forces, now refers to the NGKA as "sister church." The declaration of support from the GKN immediately provoked a reaction from the White NGK in South Africa, resulting in a complete break from the "mother church" in Holland. This means that the Reformed Church in Holland (GKN) is now allied with the World Council of Churches "against" South Africa.

13. In 1979 a new FEDSEM opened at Edendale, near Pietermaritzburg; in opposition to government policy, it is nonracial.

14. Walshe, "Christian Institute and African Nationalism," pp. 477–79.

15. Ibid., p. 478.

CHAPTER SEVEN

The South African Council of Churches

In the 1960s the South African Council of Churches (SACC), together with the Christian Institute, became an instrument of prophetic leadership. By the late 1970s Blacks had finally assumed executive positions in the SACC, a development that confirmed the view of many Afrikaners that the organization was a "Black power base." It also served to project an image of the SACC as a "revolutionary" group linked to the hated World Council of Churches (WCC).

Today, as the foremost ecumenical agency grouping the "anti-apartheid" churches, the SACC finds itself in continual clashes with the government. The latter obviously regards the SACC as a serious threat, but at the same time fears taking direct action against it. Instead, the government has confined itself to harassment, banning, and imprisonment of individual staff members. Despite such overwhelming pressures, the men and women serving the SACC continue to take great risks in the manifestation of their faith in a Christian society.

The Council is the principal large organization where Blacks and Whites can get together and speak openly to each other. For Whites, it is one of the few places where they can become more familiar with Black opinions and experiences. For Blacks it is almost the only forum where they can air their aspirations and frustrations. The SACC is also a vivid example of ecumenism at work.

The Council traces its roots back to 1904, when the Dutch Reformed and English-speaking churches founded the South African General Missionary Conference (GMC). This event prepared the way for South African participation in the international and interdenominational missionary gathering at Edinburgh in 1910, a great milestone in the history of missions and ecumenism. Although the GMC acknowledged the interests of the native races and the need to influence legislation on their behalf, it focused far more on proclamation, education, and medical aid than on any activity that could be construed as "political."

In 1936 the GMC was reorganized into the Christian Council of South Africa (CCSA), a stronger body with more executive powers—a change representing the switch from missions to established churches. The fact that the Council—which grouped twenty-nine churches and missionary organizations representing all the major Protestant traditions—included some of the Dutch Reformed churches soon led to major conflicts over racial policies. In 1939 the DRC left the Council because of its "English" character and its attitudes on racial matters.[1]

During the following years the Christian Council moved somewhat gingerly toward stronger stands. In 1942 it convened a conference on Christian reconstruction in South Africa at the (Black) University of Fort Hare, and in a general atmosphere of optimism began discussions on bridging the gulf between the racial groups.

By 1949, at a similar conference at Rosettenville, the mood had changed to one of apprehension, for institutionalized apartheid had arrived.[2] Out of this meeting grew a booklet entitled "Race—What Does the Bible Say?" in which it was clearly stated that "spiritual unity in the church cannot remain spiritual. . . . To the church, there is committed the task of extending its pattern of unity to the world."[3]

Among other things, the conference asserted that the franchise should be accorded to all capable of exercising it, and that every child should have the opportunity of receiving the best education that the community could give. Despite the somewhat paternalist tone, the affirmations were a direct attack on the unfolding of apartheid.

For most of the history of the CCSA, the position of general secretary was a part-time job, except for the period from 1958 to 1961 when the Rev. Arthur Blaxall held the position.[4]

Partly because the Christian Council was rather ineffectual, the Christian Institute took on in the early 1960s many responsibilities that the Council might have assumed. In 1967, however, when Anglican Bishop Bill Burnett became head of the Council, its headquarters were moved from Cape Town to Johannesburg and the organization expanded its work. In 1968 its name was changed to the South African Council of Churches, a move that reflected the fact that indigenous churches, not missionary societies, now made up the overwhelming majority of the members.

During the 1970s the SACC grew rapidly. Much of this growth can be attributed to the dynamic leadership and vision of a young White Methodist layman, John Rees, who became general secretary in 1970. In the first five years of his office, the number of full-time divisional directors rose from two to thirteen and the full-time staff from ten to over forty.

The budget expanded, for Rees displayed a remarkable ability to raise funds from organizations within South Africa. (Nevertheless, the SACC has had to rely on overseas churches and foundations as its major source of support, because the country's churches, with their large Black majorities, are poor by Western standards, and simply do not have the funds to finance both their own programs and those of ecumenical organizations. The need for overseas support became even more crucial as the SACC came increasingly under fire from the government.)

The Blackening of the SACC

When Rees took over, Blacks made up 85 percent of the membership and 90 percent of the observer churches in the SACC. Yet Whites tended to retain positions of authority—in the churches and in the Council.

Rees determined to change this. Radical new policies were instituted: equal salaries were paid to Black and White council staff, toilets were desegregated, and every White administrator was given a Black secretary and every Black administrator a White secretary. Blacks moved into senior positions: by the end of 1975, seven out of thirteen full-time directors were Black. At the first national conference that Rees attended as general secretary, delegates elected their first Black president, the Rev. August Habelgaarn. (Since then, the Rev. E. E. Mahabane and Ds.[5] Sam Buti of the NGKA—both Black—have served in this capacity, an honorary one.)

Even more significant was the "blackening" of SACC membership. The process began in the late 1960s when a number of new churches that had originated as missions handed over their work to local Christians. These churches then began joining the SACC.

The first such group was that of the Lutherans. Although numerically strong, they had never played an important role in South African church life, partly because they had been under the control of conservative missionaries. The situation changed when the missions merged their work, the churches became autonomous bodies under indigenous leadership, and eight of them joined the SACC. They brought into the organization a powerful new voice, embodied in such figures as the Rev. Habelgaarn and Dr. Manas Buthelezi, a leading exponent of Black theology who served several times on the SACC executive.

The second significant group was that of the African independent churches. Although two of them had been associated with the Christian Council since 1936, the breakthrough came in 1971 when the African Independent Churches' Association (AICA) was accepted into SACC membership and was followed by other groupings. As a result, the number of churches in association with the SACC rose to fifteen hundred. More individual independent churches joined during the years that followed.

A third group was that of the NGK "daughter" churches, all of which had observer status in the Council by 1974.[6]

Throughout this period, Black consciousness and Black theology played an important, if somewhat indefinable, role. One effect was that between 1971 and 1977 the number of Blacks in top positions increased a hundredfold. Blacks also felt more free to vent their frustrations in churches and organizations like the SACC, and there were some traumatic moments of Black/White confrontation. At first the Whites found this threatening. By 1973, however, the director of SACC's Justice and Reconciliation Division was writing of Black consciousness: "This needs to be encouraged and supported by the churches." In 1975 the SACC also commended a statement by Black ministers that read, "We offer ourselves to the White man as bridge builders into the future. . . . We do not judge Whites, knowing that for both of us there is the new commandment that we love one another, no matter what the past injury, hurt, misunderstanding, and oppression."[7]

In that same year there were moves at the NGK umbrella synod for the three Dutch Reformed "daughter" churches to join the SACC as full members. In the end the Sendingkerk and the RCA did not follow through, probably because the majority of their clergy were still White missionaries from the "mother" NGK. The Black NGKA, however, formed a militant caucus, and agreed that in the future all White ministers in their church must become NGKA members and cease to be "missionaries" who kept their membership in the White NGK. The delegates also voted to take full membership in the SACC.

The ceremony celebrating the NGKA's admission on July 22, 1975, represented an historic breakthrough of the ecumenical movement into the NGK family of churches. Moreover, a "daughter" of the church so closely linked with the National Party had asserted her independence, and was entering a community of peers. The assembly vibrated with excitement as some one hundred fifty White and Black delegates rose to sing "*Nkosi sikelel Afrika*— God Bless Africa."[8]

Conflicts with the Government

The publication by the SACC of *Message to the People of South Africa* in 1968 alarmed a great many Whites. Prime Minister Vorster himself warned any clerics who were planning to "do the kind of thing here in South Africa that Martin Luther King did in America" to "cut it out, cut it out immediately, for the cloak you carry will not protect you if you try to do this in South Africa."[9]

Why the uproar? The thrust of the *Message* was that the unity of humanity within the church could not be divorced from what was happening in society, and that apartheid denied the work of Christ. It declared that apartheid was not just a political policy, but an ideological substitute for the gospel, determining all human relations in a way that contradicted Christian belief. For many it had become a false faith offering happiness and peace for the community and for the individual. Hence Christians were "under an obligation to live in accordance with the Christian understanding of man and of community, even if this be contrary to some of the customs and laws of the country."[10]

The *Message* also raised a challenge: what alternatives could be pursued? In response, small "Obedience to God" groups were formed in which Christian Institute members played a vital role. Many participants came to the conclusion that the church must put its own house in order.

Out of this concern emerged a report jointly prepared by the Christian Institute and the SACC, *Apartheid and the Church*. The report described how denominationalism, segregation, discrimination, and paternalism undermined the witness of the church, and made specific recommendations, such as simplicity of lifestyle, symbolic acts against racial discrimination and equalization of salaries for ministers irrespective of race.

WCC's Program to Combat Racism

During the 1950s and '60s worldwide Christian concern about apartheid grew rapidly. In 1969 the World Council of Churches, meeting in England, sponsored a consultation on racism that concluded that force might be resorted to by Christians in order to dislodge entrenched injustice. It also proposed a Program to Combat Racism (PCR). Although the SACC recognized that the social order in South Africa was largely based on structural violence, it objected to sanctioning counterviolence to change the situation.

In September 1970 the PCR dropped a bombshell. Without consulting or even informing the SACC, it set up a Special Fund of grants to "oppressed racial groups and organizations supporting the victims of racial injustice."[11] Obviously, liberation movements such as the Patriotic Front in neighboring Rhodesia and the South West People's Organization (SWAPO) in South-West Africa/Namibia would be included.

South African church members learned about the decision when it was splashed across the front pages of newspapers. The fact that this was only one project of the PCR, that the grants were made for humanitarian purposes (such as medical assistance), and that the WCC never sanctioned violence (expressing "solidarity with" rather than "support for" movements dedicated to violent change), was lost on most South African Whites, who saw the WCC as a purveyor of guns instead of Bibles.[12] (In 1980 the PCR program amounted to only 5 percent of the WCC annual budget.)

Leaders of SACC member churches held a series of meetings where they expressed support for the other work of the PCR, but objected to grants made by the Special Fund to liberation movements using violence. To Vorster, however, churches that supported the PCR in any way were anti-South African and wedded to revolution. They must get out of the WCC or else! Eventually, he allowed the member churches to request a consultation with the WCC on the subject of the grants, but set up such restrictions on the agenda and location that the consultation never took place. On the other hand, the churches remained in the WCC.

The political situation had changed dramatically since the Cottesloe Consultation ten years before. By 1970 a Black armed struggle was growing throughout southern Africa, chiefly against the White minority governments in Mozambique, Angola, and Rhodesia, but inevitably aimed at South Africa as well. By 1970, too, WCC leaders had begun to despair of the churches' power to change the direction of South Africa. They felt that the liberation movements were legitimate expressions of political revolt and, though their methods might be questioned, the justice of their cause was clear. This did not mean that the WCC espoused violence, but that it did not foresee the advent of real change except through pressure from beyond South Africa. Moreover, the liberation movements included many Black members of South African churches, and these people needed humanitarian aid.[13]

The grants continued, and each year the debate was renewed with an intensity that people outside South Africa find difficult to understand. For Black Christians, without whose participation some of the churches might have withdrawn from the WCC, the real issue was not membership in the world body, but rather, how real was the commitment by their churches to the struggle against racism? In any event, the WCC stand awakened South African churches to the fact that time for change was running out.[14]

Although the government hesitated to take direct action against the SACC, it found other ways to harass the organization. In 1974 Methodist minister Fred Shaw formed the right-wing Christian League. The group, a counterpart of the Catholic Defense League, had the avowed purpose of warding off a Black Marxist takeover of the Republic of South Africa (RSA), and persuading South African churches to withdraw from the WCC. Methodist leaders not only denounced the group constantly but established a committee to investigate Shaw's conduct.

After years of speculation that the organization acted as a government front, the Minister of Foreign Affairs admitted that the group had received funds from the former Department of Information. It was also revealed that the league had received funds from American financier John McGoff, alleged to have been given over ten million dollars to support his attempt to take control of the *Washington Star.*

The Issue of Conscientious Objection

The next head-on collision with the government occurred over the right to conscientious objection. The issue exploded at the SACC annual conference in 1974. That the meeting was held in a Black area—Hammanskraal, north of Pretoria—and that the site was the Catholic St. Peter's Seminary (although Catholics had only observer status in the SACC)—underlined both the trend toward ecumenism and the growing strength of the Black majorities in the churches.

The conference took place during a tense period of southern African history. The war in Mozambique had ended and a Black regime was in power there. South African Blacks were anticipating an end to apartheid in their own country. The civil war in Angola had reached a peak and RSA troops were fighting there (a fact unknown to most South Africans). Guerrilla warfare in Rhodesia and Namibia was escalating. Military training in South Africa was mounting and the defense budget was soaring. The clash of ideologies had intensified; it was a time for taking sides.

Small wonder, then, that a conference resolution supporting conscientious objection made headlines and brought down the wrath of the government.

The preamble asserted that "Christians are not automatically obliged to engage in violence and war," and that this was particularly true in South Africa, a fundamentally unjust society in which primary institutionalized violence had provoked the counterviolence of the freedom fighters. Clause 2, the most crucial, declared: "The Conference . . . calls on its member churches to consider. . . whether Christ's call to take up the Cross and follow Him in identifying with the oppressed does not, in our situation, involve becoming conscientious objectors."[15]

The resolution sparked hours of heated debate, but was finally passed. Outside the SACC, criticism began to seethe. Opponents ignored the fact that the statement explicitly deplored violence as a means to solve problems, and thus did not justify the Black use of violence. Even many liberal newspapers and politicians, as well as some church leaders and congregations from SACC member churches, rejected it. The large multiracial churches and many Black churches issued strong statements of support, however.

The government introduced a bill providing harsh penalties for anyone attempting to persuade someone else to avoid military service. This evoked such criticism that in a rare about-face the government eased the penalties somewhat, and has never invoked the measure against anyone.[16]

Although the resolution is popularly known as the "conscientious objection resolution," this is a misnomer. There is virtually no pacifist tradition in South Africa. Indeed, it is not a strictly pacifist statement. The Hammanskraal resolution advocated "selective conscientious objection"—objection to a war, not on principle, but on grounds that the objector does not believe a particular war to be justified (a position like that of many young Americans during the Vietnam War). The argument was that Christians may take up arms only in a just war, and defense of a basically unjust society could not fill the definition of a just war.

Behind this lay the implicit recognition that South Africa was already in a civil war. Some Black delegates at the conference had sons and relatives in the militant arm of liberation movements.

In any case, the resolution stimulated the multiracial churches to conclude that conscientious objection is a valid Christian option. A 1977 statement by the Catholic bishops described this position: "We defend the right of every individual to follow his own conscience, the right therefore to conscientious objection both on grounds of universal pacifism and on the grounds that he believes the war to be unjust."[17]

Despite the wrath of the vast majority of the White population, the resolution brought a tide of support from Blacks, and united the multiracial churches in a new way. The SACC emerged stronger than ever from the worst ordeal it had ever experienced.

Foreign Investments, Civil Disobedience, Education Programs

In late 1976 John Rees announced that he intended to resign in hopes that a Black would succeed him, and in February 1978 Anglican Bishop Desmond

Mpilo Tutu became the first African genei..l secretary of the SACC.

A few months later, at its 1978 conference, the SACC demonstrated its increasing concern with political affairs by paying special attention to the controversial issue of investments by overseas firms. Instead of calling for a moratorium on or a withdrawal of foreign capital, it laid down minimum criteria for investments. These included asking all businesses operating in South Africa to negotiate with Black trade unions, to extend the right of family life to all workers (thus phasing out the migrant labor system), and to pressure the government to make it possible for workers to enjoy stable family life near their workplaces.

These guidelines followed a more comprehensive list of investment criteria sent out by the SACC national conference to church bodies overseas. The list included nonsegregation of all eating, comfort, and work facilities; equal pay and fair employment practices; programs to train Blacks for supervisory and technical positions; recognition of trade unions; introduction of labor-intensive industry; a voluntary 2 percent self-tax on gross profit, to go to education for Blacks; and refusal to invest in the manufacture of armaments.

The theme of the 1979 Conference was "The Church and the Alternative Society." In his wide-ranging speech, general secretary Desmond Tutu attacked many aspects of the political order and explained that his reason for refusing to serve on a government committee on urban Africans was that the preconditions for meaningful dialogue had not been met—namely, abolition of pass laws and Bantu education, abandonment of removals and resettlement of people, and a national constitutional convention that would include all racial groups. American civil rights leader Jesse Jackson also addressed the gathering, and to much applause declared that Blacks were in a state of slavery in South Africa.

The most dramatic statements concerned civil disobedience. Lutheran Bishop Manas Buthelezi asserted that the time for pious resolutions had passed and that now action must be the objective. Dr. Allan Boesak of the N. G. Sendingkerk stirred the house by calling for a massive civil disobedience campaign. The conference resolved that churches should withdraw from cooperation with the state as far as possible "in all those areas in the ordering of our society where the law violates the justice of God." Specifically, it recommended that churches reject the legal restrictions that racial laws imposed on clergymen licensed as marriage officers. The SACC's Justice and Reconciliation Division was instructed to examine other strategies of resistance.[18]

Such resolutions represent one element of the "horizontal" dimension of SACC work—declaration of church opposition to institutionalized injustice. The other two elements are education of White members to the moral implications of apartheid, and mobilization of the resources of the Black majority by means of education and self-help projects. They are facets of the broader objective of convincing advocates of change at home and abroad that they have an ally in the multiracial churches.

SACC Internal Structuring

Today the national headquarters of the SACC is lodged in Diakonia House (Johannesburg), an ecumenical center that includes offices of the Anglicans (CPSA), the Evangelical Lutheran Church of South Africa (ELCSA), and other groups. It is a bustling, friendly place. Blacks and Whites pore over reports together, confer informally in the halls, or gather for tea-breaks—a rare picture of racial camaraderie in the land of apartheid.

The SACC comprises over a dozen divisions and special funds, including: Theological Education (provides better training for Black ministers); African Bursary Fund (arranges scholarships for promising children in rural areas); Ecumenical News Services (publishes *Ecunews, Kairos*, and occasional books and pamphlets); Mission and Evangelism (produces a wide variety of media, including audiovisual aids, for promoting the gospel); Ombudsman's Office (helps to educate the poor in wise purchasing and outwitting exploiters); Inter-Church Aid (provides home industry work for wives of migrant laborers, develops self-help agricultural projects of all kinds, and generally applies appropriate technology and the use of small tools and machines that individuals can make and repair themselves); Asingeni Relief Fund (makes funeral arrangements, and provides medical aid and legal defense for persons deemed to be wrongfully arrested; it is reported that seven out of ten Asingeni "clients" are released as innocent because the fund provides defense); Dependents' Conference (performs the important and sensitive task of aiding ex-political prisoners to involve themselves in self-help projects, and of helping families of the imprisoned with small grants for their support and education). Both the Asingeni and the Dependents' Conference are constantly attacked by the government, which considers them abettors of treason.

Space permits only three of the other divisions to be described here.

Justice and Reconciliation:
Interviews with Wolfram Kistner and Tom Manthata

The Justice and Reconciliation Division is involved in some of the most controversial work of the Council. The division's overburdened director, Wolfram Kistner, is a thin, raw-boned, blue-eyed man with an almost humble manner. To those who know and work with him, however, he is a man of unusual intellect and power. In our own meeting with him we were also struck by his vision and his grasp of the international dimensions of South African problems. He explained, "Actually, the entire Council is involved with justice and reconciliation. Our division is *conscienticizing* both South Africans and people abroad. For instance, we place special emphasis on conscienticizing others about the homelands, migrant labor problems, and resettlement—issues that people don't like to think about. We try to make them aware of the terrible suffering that resettled people experience. Ideological justifications are used to make people blind to the suffering. The word 'homeland' itself has an ideological significance.

"People outside the RSA need to see through this, to realize that the authorities are not concerned with giving Blacks a home where they can develop their full potential, but to have reserves of cheap labor and keep Blacks from participating in decisions affecting their lives.

"Others fall prey to the 'national security ideology.' So part of our work has been setting up a Study Commission on Faith and Ideology."

Kistner was one of the few South Africans we met who spontaneously talked of nonviolent action, which he saw as refusal of cooperation with a system that practices violence and exploitation. The Justice and Reconciliation Division, he pointed out, was trying to stimulate nonviolent courses of action in different parts of the country.

In an address to the 1979 SACC Conference, Kistner had spoken of strategies of nonviolent resistance and suggested an example by posing a question: should churches continue to apply to the state for recognition of ministers as marriage officers if they know that the economy depends on migrant labor and that official policy does not allow many married people and their children to live together as families? He said, "Some people at the conference, such as Hendrik van der Merwe, a Quaker, wanted to play down confrontation and emphasize the positive by affirming the fellowship of all South Africans. I found it necessary to develop the resistance aspect as well. It implies a preparedness to suffer. And I found it very significant that a charismatic—Bruce Evans, the Anglican bishop of Grahamstown—spoke of being prepared to go to prison."

In Kistner's opinion, "obligatory resistance" included resistance to any rearrangement of the system that did not fundamentally change existing power structures. Although the churches could not commit their members to any strategy of opposition, they had an obligation to provide information so that their members could recognize the ethical challenges. At the same time, the churches had an obligation to insist on concern for the opponent, for people engaged in maintaining a system of oppression have destroyed their own freedom and become captives of the system themselves.

When we asked whether the chances of achieving fundamental change by nonviolent action seemed favorable, Kistner shook his head. "No. Still, I believe it has a long-term conscientization value, particularly in alerting Whites to the injustice that happens before their own eyes and partly with their own collusion.

"We have to conscienticize on an international level as well. Overseas churches are usually willing to contribute funds to support change here, but they often fail to realize that fundamental change here is impossible without their contribution to fundamental change in their own situation, where forces support oppressive South African policies.

"The multinational corporations have an independent power that is not controlled by national states. A new international order has become a necessity for this. The church should sensitize its members' consciences to their global responsibility."

Kistner's assistant is a young Black Catholic named Tom Manthata. A solidly built man of medium height, with watchful eyes and a somewhat detached manner, he seemed slightly reserved at our first meeting. He has good reason to be wary of strangers, we learned. Because he was a leader in SASO, Manthata was detained three times, once in solitary confinement for eighteen months. He was also brutally tortured.

He declines to talk about these experiences, but a close colleague says that he is a threat to the Afrikaner police because he is absolutely unbreakable. He infuriates them by taunting them openly: "So this is your great culture?" Moreover, he flouts their warnings by continuing to organize people in Soweto. An important member of the Committee of Ten, Manthata is widely known as "the brains" in the Black Consciousness Movement, a movement that seems able to survive bannings, imprisonment, and torture.

At our second meeting, Manthata was much more outgoing and expansive. His task at Justice and Reconciliation, he explained, was to restore the personality of Black workers in Christian terms and to awaken their creativity. "The worker needs protection. If he can't find it from unions, shouldn't he get it from the churches? He needs to realize his worth as a human being; he needs an opportunity to do service in the love of God.

"The clergy are ignorant of industrial laws. In fact, to discuss them can be an offense under the Terrorism Act. Also, when people are contracted into industrial areas, they lose contact with their churches at home, and ministers in the city usually fail to reach out to them. So our task is to conduct seminars on labor relations with clergy who minister mainly to Blacks. When these clergymen are aware of what is expected of them, what they must know, what delays equality at the industrial relations level, they begin to relate to their parishioners in a new way."

Manthata was bitter about the Wiehahn and Riekert reports, which he saw as an effort to shift responsibility to the White unions for policing Black "illegal" workers. "In effect, the government is saying: 'Now it's your duty to see that your rights are not encroached on by Blacks.' And it's tied in with civil defense. 'You are careless—check on these people,' is the message. So every White becomes a policeman."

"Yet you remain optimistic?" we asked.

"In the long run, yes. Once Blacks are conscious of the system and how it works, they can act. In a sense we try to see how we can reach gut reactions. So that your need to redeem your soul becomes a gut reaction."

South Africa is not only a racist, but a sexist society. Paradoxically, it has produced a number of extraordinary women. Among the Whites might be mentioned writers Olive Schreiner and Nadine Gordimer; political activists Helen Suzman, Helen Joseph, and Ruth First; and political analysts Muriel Horrell, Ellen Hellman, and Jennifer Davis.

In the past two decades several Black women have achieved a certain prominence—among them Indian sociologist Fatima Meer, Indian ANC lawyer Phyllis Naidoo, union leader Lucy Mvubelo, and activist Winnie Mandela, wife of ANC leader Nelson Mandela. Today a growing number of Black women are taking leading parts in the struggle for liberation.

Some of them have been involved in work for the SACC: Sally Motlans (wife of Ntatho Motlana, chairman of the Soweto Committee of Ten), as vice-president of the SACC; Sophie Mazibuko as an assistant field director for the Dependents' Conference; Anne Rathebe as director of the African Bursary Fund; Bernadette Mosala as head of the Home and Family Life Division; Deborah Mabiletsa as director of the Women's Division.

Home and Family Life: Interview with Bernadette Mosala

The Home and Family Life Division uses conferences, seminars, courses, and publications to explore the potential richness of the family. In working toward that goal it tackles concrete problems such as migrant labor, divorce, illegitimacy, lack of accommodation, unemployment, and the generation gap. More recently the division became increasingly concerned with youth work, health education, and the appalling conditions of hostel dwellers.

Bernadette Mosala, the division's head, was a high-school teacher for seventeen years before John Rees convinced her to take over the administration of Inter-Church Aid, a position from which she rose to become administrator of the whole Council. She is a heavy-set woman, with short graying hair, large eyes framed by gold-rimmed glasses, and a lined forehead that seems to express both weariness and determination.

When we first met, in 1978, she was lying in a hospital room suffering from a recurrence of pernicious anemia, and could scarcely communicate with us. The following year, when we met in her office at SACC headquarters, she described her illness as the result of imprisonment (together with her husband Leonard, a member of the Committee of Ten) after the 1976 disturbances. The story of that experience was a long one, but she seemed willing to share some of it with us, and in the end we spent more time talking about it than about her present work. She said, "The police wanted to know what went on at the SACC, and how John Rees worked. Then, as they moved me from one interrogator to another, I gradually saw that they linked me with some students I'd once met for a few minutes, and knew absolutely nothing about. They wouldn't believe me. They had a hang-up that at the Council we were channeling money to students to make bombs! And they'd shout: 'Don't say "South African Council of Churches"—say "South African Council of Communists!"'

"My husband had the colonels for interrogators. Mine were the niggling little men who are jealous of your education, and in many ways are the worst. 'Bloody old woman, we're going to break you!,' those little men used to scream. They smacked me. They starved me. They'd bring food, let a dog eat it before my eyes, and then give me the empty plate.

"Sometimes they made me kneel eight hours on the stone floor. Other times, they'd make me squat for hours—I couldn't let my legs give way. Once they interrogated me for twenty-six hours without stopping. I lost my sense of day and night.

"After I was released, I couldn't work for a very long time, I was so ill. Leonard was called to Minister of Justice Jimmy Kruger, who said, 'Tell her to go back to the classroom. If she returns to the Council, she'll be banned for five years.' "

"And what happened?" we asked.

She smiled. "Leonard simply replied, 'I can't tell her to chicken out. Nor have I ever wanted her to be a carbon copy of me. She makes her own decisions.' In the end I went back to the Council. Much later, Kruger was dropped from his job—imagine my relief! I've had no real hassles. But one never knows what will happen. In a country like this, one never knows."

Women's Division: Interview with Deborah Mabiletsa

The Women's Division focuses on problems of domestics, who represent 60 percent of actively employed Black women and are the most exploited group of African workers. They have no contracts, no unemployment compensation, no disability benefits, and no other rights covered by legislation. Their wages are low and their working hours long. Although domestics take these jobs as a last resort, the employment situation is so precarious that ten women line up for every job available.[19]

In South Africa the law decrees that "live-in" Black domestics occupy one-room huts behind the employer's house. They are not permitted to have either their husbands or their children with them. Under the best circumstances, mothers may visit their children, who usually live with relatives, once every week or two. (One Christmas a scandal broke out in the press when it was discovered that several White employers had allowed their servants to keep their children over the holidays.) Cut off from their families and friends, these women become lonely. To help fill this void and meet other needs, the Women's Division has set up services that can be incorporated into the work of parish churches.

Deborah Mabiletsa presides over the Women's Division. She is a self-made woman with broad experience in education, social work, and political activities. She is an imposing woman: stocky, with a vibrant voice, a ready laugh, and a manner that reflects self-confidence. After a warm welcome into her office, she began telling us about the three-pronged approach to the program.

The Domestic Workers Employment Project (DWEP), a joint program of the SACC and the SAIRR, created "centers of concern" where volunteers teach reading, writing, driving, sewing, cooking, first aid, and typing, she explained. "Most of these skills enable domestics to plead for better wages and conditions. No longer can employers say, 'You're just ignorant—you deserve no more.' There are also group discussions and counseling services. Our women come to feel they belong to a support group, even though it *is* a secondary group that can never replace their own family."

The division also organizes seminars, conferences, and courses to help develop the leadership potential of women in the African independent churches. Another important area is that of raising the legal status of the South African Black woman, through conferences that expose her minor status and explore realistic alternatives.

Mrs. Mabiletsa spoke with some passion about the plight of the Black woman. "Before she marries she's under the custody of her father or brother or uncle. Then custody switches to her husband. To seal a contract, a woman must find a male relative to underwrite it.

"In the independent churches, women have special problems accruing from illiteracy and lack of training. Yet they're doing a great deal for church development and, to my mind, they're doing it better because they are not so involved as men in power struggles. At our last conference we agreed to form a women's union among the independent churches. We're moving! Actually, these churches already have a number of women bishops who preach from the pulpit. In this respect they're ahead of the traditional churches."

She responded easily to our questions about her own background. "I was born in Alexandra Township, one of Jo-burg's worst ghettos, and there were five children in the family. My father always supported my desire to go to secondary school, though my uncles, like most Black men at the time, couldn't see why he should invest in educating a *daughter*. Then my father died. My mother, a domestic, somehow managed to scrimp and borrow enough to send me to Inanda Seminary, a Congregational secondary school.

"An American, Dr. Lavinia Scott, was the principal, and she used to tell me, 'If you are ambitious, the sky's the limit!' She got a White family in the States to sponsor me so that I could go on to teacher's training. I loved that woman—she was one of the significant persons in my life."

During the five years Mrs. Mabiletsa was teaching, the Bantu Education Act began placing more restrictions on African education. She left the field to begin social work training, and eventually became the first African director of a family welfare agency, Entokozweni. In 1973 she resigned in order to come to the SACC.

Since then she has been active in many spheres. She has taken part in many conferences on race relations in South Africa and has traveled to the United States twice—to study social group work at the University of Pennsylvania, and to attend the twenty-fifth anniversary of the Supreme Court school desegregation decision. She also studied marriage counseling for a year in Melbourne, Australia.

In 1976, after Indian sociologist-activist Fatima Meer was banned, Mrs. Mabiletsa became president of the Black Women's Federation, and remained president until it was banned in October 1977.

That same year she became active in Women for Peace, an interracial group that sprang up after the 1976 riots, and has been cochaired by Mrs. Harry Oppenheimer and Mrs. Cecil Cillier, the wives of two prominent South African industrialists. "But the White women, well intentioned as they were, found it hard to take real action," she sighed. "I'd say, 'What do you want to do to *prevent* further crises?' They were afraid to move. So I withdrew from the group. I'd given it credibility."

In 1978 she attended a conference in Freiberg, Germany, convened by the Arnold Bergstraesser Institute to bring South African leaders into a dialogue about their future. "It was depressing," she told us. "The Nationalists insisted that they'd sink or swim with separate development, that power-sharing would come over their dead bodies. To which I responded, 'Don't you want to avoid that embarrassment?' "

As she leaned back in her chair and laughed, we were struck again by the ease with which she seemed to move between two worlds. Her past activities, and even the fact that she was wearing a rosy African turban and a shirt embroidered in an African design, suggested the pride she took in her Black heritage. At the same time, she possessed a sophisticated knowledge of Western social work concepts, a command of English superior to that of most people for whom it was a first language, and a first-name familiarity with prominent American and European political activists.

By South African Black standards, Deborah Mabiletsa and her lawyer husband Martin have enjoyed fame and fortune. But they have paid a heavy price, we learned. For many years her husband had been active with the PAC. Robert Sobukwe, and later Steve Biko, had frequented their home. Martin had never engaged in violence, however. A few days after the Soweto uprisings, he went to the police to intervene on behalf of some students. The police beat him up and interned him for two days. Nevertheless, he continued to act as defense lawyer for students involved in the riots. A few months later the authorities tried to link him with an assassination plot about which he knew nothing. Deborah continued, "My husband fled to Swaziland. But the Swazi authorities, who were cooperating with the South African police, also detained him. Fortunately, he escaped to London. The police here questioned me too—eight or ten of them fired questions at me for hours. They did not beat me, but the bombardment of their insults was cruel and humiliating.

"I lived in a state of apprehension for my husband for a very long time. I felt terribly alone. I *could* have become bitter. It's my children who have become bitter. 'How can you drink tea with Whites?' they ask. I tell them about the Christian doctrine, which is nonracial. I explain that some Whites agonize about the situation. That even though the church hasn't really been relevant to our problems, some Christians are working for justice. That by the time they're my age, they'll be living in a free society. 'Above all,' I say, 'you must keep hope.'

"But the tragedy of the Bantu Education Act is that young people today haven't had the chance to go to school and work with Whites that we did. They're far more isolated from Whites—and more militant."

For a moment, a look of despair crossed her face. "It's become difficult to communicate with my own children. They can't believe in God, unless it's a Black God. They think we are passive, and that the time for dialogue is over. If they're in the living room with their friends and I pass near, they become quiet, as if to say 'This one must not hear.' All of this leaves me lonely."

Interview with Margaret Nash

The SACC has offices in every province except the Orange Free State. They are usually tiny affairs, staffed by overburdened officers who perform a wide variety of tasks.

Dr. Margaret Nash, for example, is Ecumenical Education Officer for the Cape Western branch, a position that includes traveling, writing, speaking, and visiting a host of projects. A prolific writer, she has authored a book, *Ecumenical Movements in the 1960s*, as well as dozens of pithy, well-documented pamphlets and articles on subjects ranging from foreign investment to unemployment, housing, urban-industrial mission, and terrorism. A later booklet, "Black Uprooting from White South Africa," was on the pass/migrancy/resettlement constellation—a subject that must have been extremely embarrassing to the Nationalist government. The booklet was banned in early 1980.

With her short blond curly hair, vivid blue eyes, quick movements, and incisive way of talking, she emanates a spirit of energy. Like many of the actively concerned Whites we met in South Africa, Margaret lives in a small home with no servants—a home that does not fit into the stereotype that all Whites dwell in luxury. Yet she is nagged by the thought that she still enjoys a life of relative privilege, and tells herself that she must become more willing to share.

In the 1960s she joined the Christian Institute. She recalled, "In many ways the time after the Christian Institute was declared an 'affected organization' were the best days of all. We managed to continue our programs, and often got thirty people for weekend seminars, in spite of being prohibited from receiving funds from abroad. It was a paradox—or a miracle—for, although some South Africans withdrew from the Institute it was then that we began to get more financial support from inside the country. We decentralized and learned we could do without a lot of things, like the shiny paper for *Pro Veritate*. We became more of a confessional church. The spirit of fellowship was beautiful."

One night Margaret took us to visit the Crossroads community, a squatter camp near Cape Town where Black workers had been living illegally with their wives and children. For months government authorities had been threatening to bulldoze the shanties in the same way they had demolished similar communities in the past. Already hundreds of Crossroads residents had been harassed and taken to court; dozens had been brutally beaten in night raids. The men legally in this "White" area were to be sent back to single-sex hostels in Black townships; wives, children, and "illegal" men would be given train tickets to their homeland, the Transkei.

As we drove to Crossroads, Margaret, who had published several booklets on the housing crisis in Cape Town, pointed out that the city was desperately short of houses. "Black squatters have helped to solve the problem by creating, out of nothing and with their own hands, some kind of shelter so that they could live with their families. Instead of welcoming this, the government destroys their homes!"

The authorities' rationale was that the Cape is a preference area for Colored labor. Actually, the policy did not enjoy the support of the Colored community, Margaret told us. Behind the move, of course, was the Whites' fear that without such harsh controls Blacks would become a majority there. Efforts to preserve the community had attracted international attention, and the movement enjoyed the support of many groups within South Africa. Some leaders saw it as part of a campaign against apartheid itself.

Unlike government-built townships, Crossroads had an astonishing vitality and communal spirit, Margaret explained. None of the homes had electricity, and most were built of corrugated iron, unmatched shingles, and packing-case boards. Yet the interiors were unusually immaculate. Crossroads also had a very low crime rate, partly because it had created its own home guard. As Margaret talked, we thought of an article in the *South African Outlook* by Sister Benigna, who had been coordinating self-help projects at Crossroads:

> A short drive through one or other of the main "roads" in the evening—around seven in summer and five in winter—is something of a treat: vegetable stalls and cooked-meat counters are set up, merry music from transistors, people laughing, enjoying one another's company, doing business, discussing problems, meeting girlfriends and boyfriends—it's a regular carnival, but a daily affair.
>
> Mornings and afternoons project the rhythms of carrying water, washing clothes, and cooking—all in the context of community support, amidst the hardships and struggle of shack living and low wages. But once it's dark—*come here* to discover the true meaning of domestic peace! Each little shack aglow with its candle or paraffin lamp—and the family and some friends sitting around in the glow and shadows, sharing, discussing, laughing, talking, eating and drinking, while here and there one church or another has gathered to sing or pray, and all neighbors get full benefit of the sermon.
>
> Meantime the Committee of Crossroads is probably having a meeting by candlelight, up at the school, discussing community problems— of arrests, demolitions, rental arrears, threats on account of extensions made to houses, and the endless problems which beset any community of migrant families in the Cape.[20]

Our car stopped at the Noxolo Community Center. It had begun as the Noxolo (Peace) School two years earlier, when community residents themselves had decided that their school was grossly overcrowded, and had proceeded to find teachers and collect school fees. Later they had even built a new complex with their own hands. It was used not only for primary school pupils, but also as a night school for adults and a place for students to prepare for exams qualifying them to enter the university.

We arrived in a cold rain, and waded through mud and huge puddles to the school. Several Xhosa women in turbans and long skirts welcomed us shyly, shaking hands and giving their names. Then they pointed to the murals on the outside walls: colorful scenes of trees, birds, flowers, and an African village. After chatting a while with the Black and White women in the hall, we moved to a nearby church, which community members had constructed themselves. A few Black men, then more, filed in behind and took seats on the "male" side of the church.

After a hymn sung in Xhosa, the White Anglican bishop launched into the Lord's Prayer and a sermon in English, translated by a Xhosa woman. The sermon, which emphasized that we are all part of one family, God's, was followed by a prayer for the families *and* a prayer for the authorities, that their hearts might be changed. After more hymns sung passionately in Xhosa, a Black priest preached a sermon in that language.

As we all filed out, everyone took a place in the "receiving line" headed by the clergymen and began shaking hands with those still filing out. Unlike the Whites, the Blacks marched out and seized our hands. Then, in a jubilant mood, they began dancing, a step to one side, a step to the other. Caught in their clasp, we too danced back and forth, losing ourselves in the rhythm. All of us were caught in the fleeting—yet timeless—joy of community.

Afterwards, we remembered Sister Benigna's words, "Are these people a burden to us? No. They are our healing, our cure for much that is sick in our society. We *need* the Crossroads people. We can't let them go."

As the SACC moves further into the 1980s, what kinds of confrontation may occur with the government?

If the authorities decide to clamp down on the Council, they have several options. They could ban the organization entirely, cut off its overseas funding, ban its leaders one by one, or continue to defame it.

All these options carry risk for the government. Banning the SACC would rouse great opposition, particularly from Blacks who form the vast majority in the member churches. Blocking overseas funds would stir up international opposition, something that the Nationalists want very much to avoid (despite their pretense that international public opinion is of no concern to them).

Banning individual leaders would also provoke outcries around the world, for many of them have international stature. The ongoing campaign to malign the Council may be the easiest route, but such efforts have often been ham-handed. For example, long before the Christian League's support from the government was exposed, many people suspected the link, partly because the League's accusations against the SACC seemed bombastic even to many Nationalists.

The new element in the long church-state struggle in South Africa is that the SACC has begun taking the initiative.

Notes

1. Elfriede Strassberger, *Ecumenism in South Africa: 1936 –1960* (Johannesburg: SACC, 1974), p. 160.

2. John W. de Gruchy, *The Church Struggle in South Africa* (Grand Rapids: Eerdmans, 1979), p. 53.

3. Ibid., p. 56.

4. After the ANC and PAC were banned, Blaxall became involved as the "bag man" for a fund to aid families of political prisoners. The government prosecuted him; he was found guilty, and was deported to England. The fund was not very different from the SACC's controversial Asingeni Fund, except that Blaxall administered his fund personally. Blaxall was a pacifist and at that time the South African representative of IFOR.

5. "Ds." is the abbreviation used in South Africa for the Afrikaans *dominee* (Dutch, *domine*; English, *dominie*), i.e., "clergyman," "pastor." The "s" of the abbreviation comes from the Latin *dominus*.

6. David Thomas, *Councils in the Ecumenical Movement: South Africa, 1904–1975* (Johannesburg, SACC, 1979), pp. 64–65.

7. Ibid., p. 68.

8. Ibid., Prelude.

9. Ibid., p. 9.

10. de Gruchy, *Church Struggle,* p. 120.

11. Thomas, *Councils in the Ecumenical Movement,* p. 72.

12. Ibid.

13. Ibid., pp. 73–74.

14. Ibid., p. 75.

15. Ibid., p. 89.

16. Ibid., p. 90.

17. Occasional Papers No. 5, "Declaration of Commitment" (Pretoria: SACBC, 1977).

18. *Ecunews* 24/79 (August 3, 1979): 19–28.

19. Jacklyn Cock took a random sample of domestics in the Eastern Cape during 1978 and 1979. Of 225 households polled, wages ranged from 4 to 60 rands per month (the rand equaled approximately $1.20 over that period). Three-quarters of the domestics earned below 30 rands per month. Says Cock: "There are no laws stipulating the minimum wages, hours of work, or other conditions of service" (Jacklyn Cock, *Maids and Madams* [Johannesburg: Ravan, 1979]).

20. Sister Benigna, "Inside Crossroads," *South African Outlook* (February 1978), p. 28.

CHAPTER EIGHT

The Anglicans

It is three o'clock on a Sunday afternoon in Johannesburg and a racially mixed congregation has gathered for a service in St. Mary's, the Anglican Cathedral. The voices of the hymn-singers seem to soar to the ceiling, with a deep-throated, moving intensity. As you walk down the aisle, you realize that the "multi-racial" throng consists of Blacks with only a sprinkling of Whites.

Most of the Blacks are women—domestics who occupy a separate one-room shack in the backyard of their White employers' home, and have been given the afternoon off in order to worship. Sedately clad in skirts or dresses, medium-heeled shoes, and knitted caps or turbans, they turn their weary yet animated faces toward the altar.

A tall, thin, gaunt-looking canon in a flowing white chasuble faces the congregation. Flanked by two Black servers clothed in surplices, he begins the sermon. Imperious in his stance, austere in his gaze, he seems to embody the remote "White father" preaching to his flock. Indeed, he is speaking of remote times, when Jesus talked with his disciples about certain laws, among them the law that Jews might mix socially only with Jews. "And Jesus said, 'That law you may not obey,'" declares the canon. Solemnly, one Black assistant repeats the pronouncement in Sotho; the other follows in Zulu.

You begin to realize that the raw-boned, bushy-browed cleric is speaking in parables. Indeed, by the end of the sermon all metaphor has slipped away. "Many in South Africa now are seeking freedom," he asserts, his face still impassive. "Many are oppressing their brothers. . . . Let us pray for those in detention, and for their families. Let us pray for the souls of those who oppress their brothers."

That scene in the cathedral illustrates some of the paradoxes and conflicts in the Church of the Province of South Africa (CPSA). On the one hand, the church proclaims that its worship is open to persons of all races. On the other hand, this is hard to implement on the parish level because most parishioners attend churches in their neighorhoods, which are segregated, and because of resistance from Whites. (At St. Mary's most Whites attend the morning service.)

105

Secondly, although Anglicans have tried to help Blacks up the ecclesiastical ladder, Whites still hold most of the top positions. In 1980, for example, the highest ranking CPSA office holder, the archbishop of Cape Town, was a White, Bill Burnett. Only one of the ten diocesan bishops and four of the ten suffragan bishops in South Africa were Black.

Thirdly, while the CPSA has continued in the forefront of opposition to apartheid, most of the opposition—when not in the form of prophetic statements of courageous individuals who may suffer for them—remains at the level of pious synodal resolutions.

The tradition of protest against apartheid that crescendoed in the 1950s under the leadership of Geoffrey Clayton, Ambrose Reeves, Michael Scott, and Trevor Huddleston was reinforced in 1968 when Bill Burnett, then head of the South African Council of Churches, spearheaded the SACC's *Message to the People of South Africa*. Since then CPSA has also vigorously supported the right of conscientious objection. It has described laws providing for detentions, bannings, and imprisonment without trial as forms of "violence against freedoms of the individual and an attack on the dignity of mankind" that "lead to counterviolence against the state imposing such laws." It has appealed for a fully representative national convention to draft a new constitution and asked dioceses to increase their efforts to make multiracial life a reality within the church so that its members could be prepared for inevitable changes in South African society.[1]

In order to identify areas of racism within the Church itself, the CPSA synod created a Human Relations and Reconciliation Program early in the 1970s, with "challenge groups" on both the diocesan and provincial (nationwide) levels. The purpose was not only to improve the race relations record of the Anglican church, but also to demonstrate that change could be brought about without resorting to violence. Hence it was a response to the World Council of Churches' Program to Combat Racism and the WCC's assumption that change in South Africa would have to come through increased pressure from external forces.

The groups did not seem to have found a positive and convincing alternative to the WCC program. However, on the provincial level, the challenge group brought about proportional Black-White representation on committees and commissions, substantial progress toward parity in Black-White wage structures, greater prominence to local languages, and some progress in spreading wealth from the rich to the poor dioceses.[2]

The gap between resolutions at the top and practice at the grassroots is as evident in the CPSA as in other churches. In the prickly field of education, for example, the Anglican bishops gave their support as long ago as 1976 to Catholic initiatives to integrate church schools. By early 1979 all the independent private schools linked with the Anglican Church in the Johannesburg diocese had accepted the principle of no racial bar. Yet in early 1980 only one school had actually accepted Blacks—two pupils.

As Father David Bruno put it in a conversation with us, "The church has little power at the parish level. It is really laypersons who run our private schools. Some of them murmur, 'Well, we really shouldn't move till the government says it's OK.' Others reject Black applicants as not capable enough, not able to hold their own with Whites. This becomes a vicious circle, of course—a very vicious one.

"As for local church structures, they are dominated by Whites. The synod recommends that more Blacks be in office, but White parishioners vote for a White, and a great many Blacks do too. Whites say that Blacks lack a time sense and a sense of duty, that they fail to show up for meetings, or do not stick to formal rules of order.

"Right now we are having an election for a new president of the Mothers' Union, which is largely Black, since the White women have a separate organization called the Anglican Women's Fellowship. Two Blacks and a White woman have been nominated for the presidency of the Union, and already Whites are saying 'Blacks wouldn't be able to cope; they lack initiative.' There may be some truth in this, but it's a reflection of narrow Western values about organization. In any case, these values can be learned.

"Also, at these meetings Blacks have to communicate in English, which at best is their second language, and more often a third.

"My feeling is, 'All right, Blacks *will* make mistakes. We have to expect a period of a little disorder. But the goal is worth it.' "

Despite such obstacles, Anglicans have made real progress in tidying up their own backyard. All three Anglican theological colleges are now integrated. The CPSA has also set up a special fund to help promising Black clergy go to the United States, Canada, or Britain for further training.

There are difficulties in training a Black leader in the church, points out Canon Michael J. D. Carmichael, Provincial Executive Officer of the CPSA and former principal of St. Bede's, a Black theological college. "It may take nine years from the time you spot him to the time that he has completed his university degree and his theological training. And then he still needs time for practical experience before he is ready for leadership. But the results are good. My own successor at St. Bede's, a Black, is an old student of the college. He is also a member of the Anglican Consultative Council, and as a member of the Executive participated in the 1978 Lambeth Conference [the worldwide conference of Anglican bishops]."

Another "home" area in which Anglicans have made steps forward is that of Black-White stipends. Equality between Black and White stipends was achieved by 1973, by assessing greater contributions from richer parishes. According to recent planning, parity between richer and poorer dioceses will be realized by 1985.

In 1979 the denomination also recognized African customary union as a valid form of marriage—a significant step toward what might become genuine acceptance of African culture. Anglicans have also sponsored training programs in community development work and many self-help projects in which Black parishioners learn gardening, carpentry, sewing, basket-making, and other skills.

Courageous Leaders

Behind these impulses for change stand strong leaders. Among the Whites are Bruce Evans, Bishop of Port Elizabeth, who emphasizes that the church must regain its prophetic ministry; Bill Burnett, Archbishop of Cape Town, who has declared that the denial of justice to disenfranchised South Africans is so gross as to make the South African way of life indefensible; and Timothy Bavin, Bishop of Johannesburg, who was arrested, found guilty, and fined for helping to lead a march sponsored by Johannesburg clergy (mostly SACC members) to protest the detention of the Rev. John Thorne, who was supporting the 1980 Colored school boycott.

Perhaps the most courageous White Anglican leader of all is a priest who continually defies the state, and does so not only in words but in actions. David Russell has worked for many years with outcasts of South African society—first with Blacks uprooted from their homes and sent back to desolate "homelands," and later with migrant workers on the Cape.

In early 1977, when authorities were demolishing the homes of squatters in the Modderdam community on the Cape, and protesters were gathering for nonviolent resistance, Russell and two social workers did what no one else dared to do: they threw themselves before an oncoming bulldozer. It stopped. The bulldozing, however, continued until the last shanty was destroyed. Undaunted, Russell continued his work.

In October 1977 he was banned. He broke his banning orders several times—for example, by returning to the Crossroads community. In his defense, Russell testified, "I admit . . . I left my home to hold a small prayer service for a sick member of our congregation. My crime is that I went out after 6:00 P.M. to pray for someone in need."

In December 1979 he broke bounds by attending the Anglican synod, forewarning the authorities (in Gandhian fashion) of his plans. The move accentuated their dilemma, for they do not seem eager for church-state confrontations.

Russell was later sentenced to twelve months in prison, but was released, pending an appeal.

Prominent among Anglican Black leaders is Alphaeus Zulu, who was made the first Black suffragan bishop, in 1960, later became bishop of Zululand, and still later a president of the WCC. Since retirement he has been Speaker of the KwaZulu Legislative Assembly. Another is Sabelo Ntwasa, a priest who directed the Black theology project of the University Christian Movement, edited *Black Theology in South Africa,* and for his activities was banned and detained. But there can be little doubt that the most outstanding

Black Anglican leader is Desmond Tutu, the plucky, magnetic bishop who became the first African general secretary of the South African Council of Churches.

A Portrait of Bishop Tutu

As mentioned before, John Rees announced in late 1976 that he intended to resign as head of the SACC, in hopes that a Black would be named to succeed him. In February 1978 Bishop Tutu was named to fill the position.[3] The move was a significant step not only for the South African church, but also for South African society. The process of choosing an African executive was long and agonizing, for it was imperative that he be acceptable to the White constituency, yet not an "Uncle Tom" who would fail to articulate the needs of Black Christians.

The fiery bishop lost no time in establishing himself as a man who would "speak truth to power." In the first twelve months of office, he declared himself on a wide variety of controversial issues. He attacked the homeland policy, supported the ordination of women and the right to conscientious objection, and hotly defended the banned Christian Institute against Minister of Police Jimmy Kruger's accusations that it favored violent revolution. Bishop Tutu condemned both the violence of racist institutional structures and that of guerrillas, and at the same time asked Anglicans not to abandon those who were fighting for human rights even if the struggle became violent.

When a commentator from the government-controlled South African Broadcasting Corporation engaged the new SACC head in a television "dialogue" that brimmed with attacks on the WCC's Program to Combat Racism and the SACC's Asingeni Fund and Dependents' Conference, Tutu fended off the attacks with spirited observations about the double standard of morality in South African society.

Despite the Bishop's forays into the political arena, he has maintained his reputation as a man of deep piety; amid the demanding tasks of his position, he prays several hours daily.

Desmond Mpilo Tutu was born in 1931 in Klerksdorp, in the Transvaal; obtained a teacher's diploma at Pretoria Bantu Normal College in 1953; taught for three years; got his ordination training at St. Peter's Theological College, Johannesburg; and became a priest in 1961. A year later Tutu, his wife, Leah, and their three children were sent to London so that he could further his studies.

Tutu worked as a part-time curate at a church in Surrey, obtained a Bachelor's degree in Divinity (with honors) and a Master's in Theology from London University, returned to South Africa in 1966, and taught theology in South Africa and Lesotho. After another stint in England, this time as Assistant Director of the Theological Education Fund of the World Council of Churches, he became Dean of Johannesburg, then Bishop of Lesotho. After taking up leadership of the SACC in 1978, he traveled widely in Europe and the United States. In 1979 he received the prestigious Honorary Doctorate of Laws from Harvard University.

Inasmuch as Bishop Tutu has been the constant subject of attacks by Whites, it was somewhat surprising to discover in our first interview with him at SACC headquarters that he is extraordinarily sensitive to the predicament of his White colleagues. "The Council is incredibly fortunate in the kind of people it's gathered round itself. Some staff members do leave because of the strain, for it takes an unbelievable kind of commitment to withstand the pressures from our society. I underline especially those of our staff who are White. They're caught in the crossfire—they're looked at as people who've 'sold the pass.' When they have to go overseas, they're clobbered as White South Africans who must be enjoying the spoils of the system. Their anguish is great."

As he leaned forward in his chair, we sensed the energy in his solidly-built, lithe body. He is short, yet gives the impression of being a big man. He has a high forehead, long nose, short cropped hair peppered with gray, and lively black eyes framed by gold spectacles. He speaks with his hands—indeed, his whole body seems always in movement.

That day he was wearing the traditional white clerical collar, silver pectoral cross, and purple shirt, with carefully pressed tweed trousers; somehow there was a certain debonair quality in his attire and his manner. We remembered that Bishop Tutu has a reputation as a prankster, a prelate who brought a spirit of merriment to the august body of bishops meeting at the decennial Lambeth Conference in 1978 in England.

He continued, "Here at the Council we're a living example of a community in which Black-White relations contradict the spirit of apartheid, a place where persons of different races, cultures, and sexes work well together. We have tensions, but they're not racial tensions—they arise from the fact that people are people. Here I don't have the awareness that I'm talking to a European—he's just my colleague.

"But the Council is very vulnerable. If you read the press, you'll see that by innuendo the government is trying to prepare the climate for the public to accept action against the Council. The government is out to get the Asingeni Fund and the Dependent's Conference, especially. The authorities and the White community by and large believe that assistance to detainees, and even a little meager support to their families, is aiding and abetting them in their nefarious activities!

"To withstand these attacks we need unity. But many churches don't give overt support to Council statements. For instance, I had to issue a statement denying that the Christian Institute—now banned, so it couldn't speak for itself—promoted violence. We thought other church leaders would step in too. At least they could have said, 'Yes, that's what the Council says, and it's true.' Thus far, almost all of them have hesitated to take even that little step.

Many church leaders *are* courageous. But we're getting into a position where the government picks us off one by one."

As the Bishop talked of the need for unity, we recalled that he himself had been a pivotal figure in a clash between rival factions in the Black liberation movement. At the funeral of PAC leader Mangaliso Robert Sobukwe in March 1978, large numbers of militant youth had demanded that Chief Gatsha Buthelezi, who was scheduled to address the gathering, leave immediately. As the Chief left, he was stoned by a crowd that surged toward him. One of his two bodyguards fired eleven blank shots and prevented Buthelezi from being stabbed in the back. Later the Chief declared that he had information that the banned Black People's Convention and South African Students Organization were responsible for using the youths for "political thuggery," and that the Black Consciousness Movement was creating Black disunity by staging an international attack on him and his Inkatha movement. He also attacked Tutu for supporting the youths' actions.

When we asked Bishop Tutu about the incident, he shook his head and let out a long sigh. "All that I said at the funeral was said without condoning the action those young people took. I tried to quiet them down, but at the same time I did express my understanding of their feelings. They represent a widely held view—opposition to the Bantustan policy. They reject Bantu education, Bantu councils, all the paraphernalia that go with the policy. They see the Chief as a collaborator. That incident was a nasty thing to happen to anybody. But I believe that if the Chief were to step out of the Bantustan policy, he would be acknowledged by all Blacks as their leader. God has given him leadership qualities. And I've been trying to set up a meeting for rapprochement. But the Chief refused to meet with me.

"As for the Council, we see ourselves as existing to work for justice and peace and reconciliation. In that order. There's no use of crying 'Peace, peace!' where there is no peace."

"Speaking of peace, perhaps you could clarify your position regarding violence and nonviolence," we asked.

He answered promptly, "I am a man of peace, but not a pacifist. Clearly the Christian Church is not entirely pacifist—I need only refer to the position of Western Christendom during the struggle against Nazism. The idea of a 'just war' is very much alive. How could I commend nonviolence to Blacks who know that resistance movements in Europe were praised to the skies, and who hear similar movements condemned because they are Black? Blacks are victims of *structural* violence in this country, victims of police brutality, of a cruel pass system that divides families. You know what I mean?"

"Yes, except that we'd have to be Black to *really* know what you mean."

He smiled appreciatively, and continued, "When people ask whether I support the Program to Combat Racism to give humanitarian aid to the Patriotic Front and to SWAPO, I point out that neither I nor the SACC support the granting of these funds. I have *condemned* acts of violence by those in this country we call terrorists. But I also condemn the violence of South African troops when they shoot down innocent women and children and refugees in Angola and Namibia. There's a selective morality operating in South Africa. Let us condemn *all* violence."

"Have there been violent threats on your life?," we asked.

"Well, yes." The phone rang, and he bounced to his feet. "Hal-lo! Eh?" He launched into a rapid conversation in English. Then he set down the phone, summoned his secretary, and began an even more animated dialogue with her in a mixture of English and Xhosa, the language whose "clicks" non-Xhosa find so mysterious. "My friends—". He turned to us, his arms spread wide in a gesture of helplessness. "I must fly; I am called to a meeting. Please excuse me."

On our return trip, he greeted us as if we were old friends. Coming out of his office into the waiting room, he shook hands warmly and asked, "Can you wait till the man I'm talking with comes to a full stop? He's at a semi-colon now."

As we settled into soft chairs in his comfortable but not luxuriously furnished office, we congratulated him on the honorary doctorate awarded at Harvard. He grinned. "It was fun. There were eleven of us getting honorary degrees, including Helmut Schmidt. It was a beautiful sunny day and thousands of people were there. They gave me a standing ovation."

We told him that this time we would like to know more about his personal life, and how he came to his calling.

He ran a hand through his hair, and began, "As you know, I was a teacher for four years. But when they introduced Bantu education, I knew I didn't want to have anything to do with that. I thought of the church. My grandfather had been minister for an independent church. And I'd been one of those who came under the spell of Trevor Huddleston. He was such a compassionate, loving, strong man. His white gown would get very grubby as he walked through the streets, with children streaming behind him. Children have a sixth sense for knowing who is good. And I used to sit on his lap. His speaking up for the oppressed showed me what a man of the church can do."

"Now that you're a top man of the church, what's a 'typical day' for you?" we asked.

He took off his spectacles, and rubbed the rims thoughtfully, "I'm up at 4:45. At 5:30 I take a run near my home in Soweto—I have to do something to combat this sedentary life. I leave home at 6:30. Five days a week I drive directly to the Cathedral downtown for eucharist at seven. By eight I'm in my office, for devotional readings and a quick look at the morning papers. Then there are staff prayers at 8:30. The rest of the day is full of meetings, interviews, conferences with my colleagues, occasionally formal luncheons. The staff knocks off at 4:30, but I stay. It gives me time for quiet—for reading and prayers. Unless there's a special meeting, I'm usually home at 6—having been away for nearly twelve hours. If no evening meetings are scheduled, I'm in bed at 10 or 11."

"This kind of life can't be easy for your wife."

"No, it's not. She'd like more family time. All of our four children are away now, however—two studying in Swaziland, one in Botswana, the other in England. And my wife was recently appointed a director of the South African Institute of Race Relations."

"But your wife worries about threats on your life?"

He replied, "They haven't been big threats, like those that others have suffered. Some have come by phone, others by letter.

"And then there were the rightists who somehow connected us with the shooting down of a Rhodesian plane by terrorists. They stormed into the corridor here at the Council. When I met them at the door, they threw thirty pieces of silver over my shoulder into the office and screamed 'Judas!' I can't call such incidents pleasant. And one can never know whether they'll get much worse in the future. We live in a volatile situation. Political thuggery is always around the corner.

"My wife and mother say, 'Why do you *talk* so much?' But I say, if it's my destiny to speak out, I'd rather be happy in prison, than unfree when I'm 'free.' I ask myself, 'What does Jesus Christ require of me?' I will do it, and say it, without looking over my shoulder.

"Besides, I have a tremendous sense of being supported by prayers, not for me alone. Whatever I say or accomplish is really due to the fact that so much is being done by others. So I have almost a physical sensation of support. It makes you happy to belong to this thing called the church.

"And it stretches around the world. Recently, for instance, I received a letter of support from a Lutheran pastor in Alaska. He knew details about the SACC and the situation. Letters like that make you realize that you belong to a fellowship that transcends time and space."

"Tell us what you think people in other parts of the world can do—especially Americans."

"Pray," he said quickly. "And be as conscious of the need for justice and liberation in the United States as here. Don't use South Africa as an excuse to hide your own problems. But we do need Americans. They can apply diplomatic pressure and economic pressure."

Although we knew that it was a treasonable offense for a South African to support divestment, we decided to probe a little. "For instance?"

He elaborated, "American corporations *could* radically reverse their investment policy. They could make substantial investments in Black education and training. They could look carefully at new investments. Multinationals do support a system of injustice, one that's inconsistent with Jesus Christ. These corporations *could* decide to continue here only if the Black labor force is decently housed, in *family* units and reasonably near the factories. They could make substantial investments in Black education and training. They could attack homeland policy, the population removals, the resettlement camps, the vicious new refinements of the pass laws. Multinationals have clout, but they don't use it."

He clenched his fists. Then, slowly, his hands relaxed, and he smiled. "You know, South Africa is not a one-commodity country. It has a sophisticated economy. When freedom comes, we can choose who our friends shall be. We'll ask, 'Which side were you on?' "

Shortly after this interview, Bishop Tutu elaborated on his views about foreign investment in public—thereby embroiling himself in open conflict with the state. On September 5, 1979, he declared in an interview on Danish television: "I find it rather disgraceful that Denmark is buying South African coal and increasing its dependence on South Africa."

Tutu knew that he was placing himself in triple jeopardy. The terms of Section 6 of the Terrorism Act are so wide that simply speaking of the withdrawal of foreign companies from South Africa could be considered terrorism. Also, the very existence of the SACC was threatened. Finally, he risked criticism from urban Blacks who feared that boycotts would endanger their jobs.

The initial apprehension of some Soweto leaders soon disappeared, however. Three weeks after the speech, when the Committee of Ten met to turn itself into the Soweto Civic Association, Bishop Tutu was wildly applauded when he told the crowd: "We want political participation, not petty dispensation. We want a completely integrated society." At the same meeting, Committee of Ten chairman Dr. Ntatho Motlana stressed that he was wholeheartedly in agreement on the matter of coal exports.

Moreover, numerous letters in the Black ecumenical weekly *Voice* indicated support for Tutu. One reader wrote: "The rate of unemployment will increase, but the rate of unemployment is already soaring. We are presently suffering for no purpose. But if it should be because of divestment, then it will be for a purpose."

It was evident to Tutu's friends that his speaking out was the result of long, anguished meditation. It was also precipitated by enthusiastic reception of Allan Boesak's proposal, at the 1979 SACC meeting, that the churches initiate programs of civil disobedience on a massive scale. Inasmuch as one reason that nonviolent resistance often foundered in the past was lack of coordination between national efforts and international forces, the role of Tutu—who travels widely in Europe and the United States—could be an important one. His action was something new. South African churches had never thrown down such a direct challenge to the government and the countries that directly support apartheid.

The response of the government demonstrated its fear of civil disobedience. In October, Tutu was summoned to a meeting with authorities. Later Minister of Police Louis Le Grange warned the SACC and "leftist ministers and spiritual leaders" to "cease and desist from irresponsible action and encouraging people to break the law."

Tutu retorted: "They plan to take action against the SACC and wish to prepare the public for that action. . . . We are tired of having threats leveled against us. Why don't they carry them out? . . . If they take on the SACC and the churches, let them know that they are taking on the church of Jesus Christ."

A special joint meeting of the SACC executive committee and heads of its member denominations issued a statement giving the bishop their full and unqualified backing. Later, as guest speaker at the annual conference of the Methodist Church of Southern Africa, Tutu declared: "I will do all I can to destroy this diabolical system, whatever the cost to me. I won't be stopped by anybody." At the same meeting a resolution was introduced to support people committing "acts of conscientious affirmation of fellowship in obedience to Christ, even when such acts may infringe present restrictions."

In March 1980 Tutu's passport was withdrawn. Yet he stuck to his guns. While refraining from advocating an outright boycott of South African products, he emphasized that he wanted other countries to exert diplomatic, political, and economic pressure to help achieve "desperately needed social change." The pass laws, homelands policy, forced removals, and resettlement projects are supported by foreign investments, he said. "Blacks are being hounded out of the urban areas to watch their children starve, and they will get desperate," he warned. After a trip to a resettlement camp in the Ciskei Tutu reported, "I met a little girl who lives with her widowed mother and sister. I asked whether her mother received a pension or any other grant, and she said, 'No!' 'Then how do you live?' I asked. 'We borrow food,' she replied. 'Have you ever returned food you borrowed?' 'No.' 'What happens if you can't borrow food?' 'We drink water to fill our stomachs.' This, in a country that exports food! That child will haunt me, and I cannot take it any longer."

Is this outspoken churchman politically ambitious? Tutu denies it. Yet many Black urban Africans do regard him as their political leader. The reality is that Bishop Tutu wields considerable power, for Africans take their Christianity seriously and do not recognize the western distinction between religion and politics. Moreover, in a country where apartheid permeates every aspect of a people's life, everything *is* politics.

Notes

1. *Ecunews* 12/79 (May 24, 1979).

2. Ernie Regehr, *Perceptions of Apartheid* (Scottdale, Pa.: Herald Press, 1979), p. 250.

3. A Colored Congregational minister, John Thorne, served as general secretary for four months in 1977. Both he and Ds. Sam Buti of the NGKA have served as SACC presidents, but the office is largely an honorary one.

CHAPTER NINE

The Methodists

The largest multiracial denomination in South Africa, the Methodist Church of Southern Africa (MCSA) has been in the forefront of opposition to apartheid and has made particular efforts to speak to a wide range of social issues.[1]

For example, the MCSA was the first denomination to go beyond support for mere power-sharing and come out for "one person, one vote" (Methodist Conference, 1978). It likewise rejected proposals for separate, ethnically-based parliaments. In 1979 the MCSA also became the first denomination to support the call for the release of imprisoned ANC leader Nelson Mandela. The Conference has also invited controversial figures such as SACC general secretary Desmond Tutu to address its meetings.

On the Conference level, the Methodists have also rejected the homelands policy, condemned the Prohibition of Mixed Marriages Act, urged increased giving to the SACC Dependents' Conference, and denounced government bannings of organizations, publications, and individuals. They have called on the government to create a national "relief scheme" for the unemployed and urged churches to give aid to those most severely affected by joblessness.

Yet many problems persist. The Conference has been nonracial since its inception. At lower echelons, the situation is different. Traditionally this church has been divided into racially defined "circuits"—groups of local churches that form a basic administrative unit within the church. In 1976 several districts began to desegregate circuits. However, many laypersons argued that Blacks and Whites had great differences in language, culture, and style of worship. The problems were real enough, others retorted, but they were problems that applied to individual congregations rather than to circuits.

As a result of this dissension, only a small percentage of the circuits were integrated by mid-1980. Those that took the step seem to have done so successfully. For example, the Rev. Austen Massey of the Christian Citizenship Department found a "magnificent and dedicated spirit" during a visit to the nonracial Empangeni circuit in the Natal Coast District. On the other hand, some Blacks point out that in the integrated circuits the superintendency usually remains in the hands of Whites.

116

As in other churches, there is a tremendous gap between leaders who are ready for change and the majority of White parishioners, who are not. One Methodist minister, Jimmy Palos, told us that when he wanted Coloreds in his circuit there was stubborn resistance from some Whites. "When you're dependent on your congregation economically and psychologically, it simply isn't easy to push change." For Palos, however, the event prompted him to join the SACC's Justice and Reconciliation Division.

Tony Saddington, a Methodist layman who once worked for the Christian Institute, points to the reluctance of most churchgoers to face the issue of institutional violence: "Whites—including Methodists—tend to avoid the issue by attacking instead the WCC grants to liberation movements."

To Alex Boraine, once President of the Methodist Conference, who left the ministry out of frustration and is now an articulate leader of the Progressive-Federal Party, the Methodists are no more to blame than other denominations. To him, the basic impediments are the fear and ignorance fostered by the Group Areas Act.

Considering the fear and inertia at the grass roots, it is significant that the Methodists have progressed in integrating church schools, and that in two cases they have appointed a resident Black minister to a predominantly White congregation. In one case it did not work out well; in the other, with some initial tensions, there was acceptance.

In 1978 the Methodist synod of the Eastern Transvaal and Swaziland district took a pioneer step by appealing to the rest of the Methodist Church in southern Africa to make rejection of apartheid a part of the confession of faith.

That same year the MCSA was shaken by a traumatic event: the decision of Chief Kaiser Matanzima, Prime Minister of the Transkei, to ban that church in his territory. Himself a Methodist, Matanzima charged that some Methodist clergy were opposed to the territory's independence and that this position derived from instructions of the World Council of Churches, which had openly opposed recognition of the Transkei. Despite pleas of the Rev. Abel Hendricks, president of the Conference, who told Matanzima that he had misinterpreted the recent debate, the Transkei government declared the MCSA an "undesirable organization" (i.e., banned from operating in the Transkei), and the Methodist Church of the Transkei (MCT) was established. MCSA property worth about $4 million was confiscated by the Matanzima government.

About one-third of the Methodist ministers in the Transkei openly opposed the new church and one of them was detained by the police. This has grieved Methodists in South Africa, for the church had its largest following among the Xhosa, and had been one of the first denominations to launch missionary work in the Transkei (then known as British Kaffraria).

That the Methodists have responded to a wide range of social issues is due in large part to good leadership. Among the Whites are Peter Storey, minister of the Central Methodist Church in Johannesburg and vice-president of the

SACC since 1977; Donald Veysie, president of the Methodist Conference from 1978 to 1979, and in 1980 named chairman of Durban-based Diakonia; and John Rees, the energetic layman who headed the SACC from 1970 to 1977, and then became director of the South African Institute of Race Relations.

Even more important, however, are the pressures exerted by the growing black leadership. In 1964 Methodists took a pioneering step by naming an African, Seth Mokitini, president of the Conference. Since then a number of Blacks have held that position, including Andrew Losaba, elected to the post in 1979, and Dr. Simon Gaubule, elected in 1980.

During the 1970s there were increasing calls for Africanization. To some this means chiefly increasing the proportion of Blacks in important posts. To others Africanization also means recognition of African customs. At a 1980 seminar on Africanization of the church held by the Black Methodist Consultation (a Black caucus within the church), the group's chairperson, the Rev. Stanley Mogoba, emphasized that many members in rural areas believe in both Christianity and their own traditional rituals and reverence for ancestors. He urged the Church to accept African customs and orientate them in relation to the gospel.[2]

What is the alternative? At a history-making conference on racism organized by the SACC earlier in 1980, Black representatives warned that "if after a period of twelve months there is no evidence of repentance shown in concrete action, the Black Christians will have no alternative but to witness to the gospel of Jesus Christ by becoming a confessional church." Reacting to that ultimatum, Losaba declared that there was still time for White Christians to change and thereby avoid the formation of a militant Black confessing church. "The ball is in the White man's court," he asserted. But he stressed that the most decisive action could come only from the lowest levels of the church.

The Rev. Mogoba put it somewhat differently. The Consultation had resolved that Blacks would not leave the church, he declared. "We expect the Whites, as a minority, to break away from the Methodist Church of Southern Africa if *they* find it necessary."

According to the Methodist newspaper *Dimension,* this threat of splitting the church down the middle may have the most far-reaching implications in the history of the church in southern Africa—far greater than the secession of the church in the Transkei. This development also calls attention to the fact that the spirit of Black separatism has become a problem in other multiracial churches.

Interview with Abel Hendricks

For the past decade, a Colored minister who identifies himself as a Black has moved quickly to the top as a Methodist leader. In 1975 and again in 1977, Abel Hendricks served as president of the Methodist Conference. In 1979 he made the inaugural address at the South African Christian Leadership Assembly (SACLA).

The first of the Federal Theological Seminary's alumni to occupy the Methodists' presidential chair, Hendricks also spent a year at Princeton University. His very first job was in a Potchefstroom shoe factory. In 1962, soon after being ordained, he was called to do pioneer work on the Cape Flats near Cape Town, where Coloreds were beginning to be dumped—first in hundreds, then in thousands—under Group Areas Act legislation.

He and his wife set up house in two rooms on the sandy wastes, and began reaching out to the outcasts. Working conditions were so poor that he had to do counseling in his car, their home was often bombarded by bricks thrown by persons who were venting their frustration with the system upon the new minister, and once he was stabbed while walking in the streets on a pastoral mission.

Today the Flats, though still desolate-looking, can boast at least one oasis: the Surrey Estate Methodist Care Center founded by Hendricks in his capacity as superintendent minister of the circuit that includes the Flats. Comprising self-help programs, day care for children and the elderly, a launderette, a used-clothes shop, dental and medical services, a worship center, and a counseling service, the center now involves five thousand persons (most of them Colored) in one or more of its programs.

At eight o'clock one morning Freda Hendricks, the Rev. Hendricks' attractive wife, met us at a nursery school in the Surrey Estate Center and led us to the manse. When we admired the well-tended green lawns and the spacious interior of their home, furnished in contemporary style, she smiled: "Yes it *is* rather different from the two rooms where we lived when we began working here."

As his wife brought in coffee, the Rev. Hendricks, a short, slender man with a trim pointed beard and lively black eyes, greeted us affably and immediately plunged into a discussion of his church. The Methodists had stood by their resolutions on labor, education, and the vote, he pointed out. They were also working for change within the church. Some Blacks were moving into important ecclesiastical positions. Most important of all, the Methodists were demonstrating that theirs was a *multi*racial church: "I was head in 1975 and 1977. In 1978 they chose a White. And now in 1979 it's a Black again—Andrew Losaba. Although they were the majority, Black delegates *could* have chosen a White. Blacks tend to look up to Whites and to vote for them—even when using a secret ballot. So you see, Whites must have supported Losaba too.

"This kind of thinking isn't new. When Methodists chose Seth Mokitini as the first Black president of the Conference in 1964, everybody thought that the Methodists would split. But he *was* accepted. Which proves that Whites are not beyond redemption!

"Another thing—during the 1977 general elections, when I was Conference president, I stated publicly that every voting White person takes along with him the destiny of five Blacks. Government officials complained that I told the electorate how to vote. So it was a major thing that the church allowed me to say this."

As the Rev. Hendricks went on, however, it became clear that he recognized many problems within the Methodist fold. The secession of the Transkei church pained him deeply; it demonstrated that Methodists, too, were subject to fears and power struggles. In the townships, he pointed out, Transkeian members of the South African Methodist Church who were working in the republic were being told to join the breakaway church; some had been threatened with the loss of Transkeian citizenship and property if they did not.

In South Africa proper, most of the church circuits were still not integrated. The common wage scale for Black and White ministers, on which the Conference had agreed a few years ago, had certain inequalities. White ministers were given more "perks" [fringe benefits], because some claimed that the cost of living was higher in White areas. Although exchanges of ministers between Black and White congregations did exist, they were hard to implement. In the end, "just a nucleus of radicals" really believed in the declared policy of the Conference, he had to admit.

"The challenge is to live according to the challenges of the New Testament, which of course is very difficult," he said. "In other parts of the world, the issues are blurred, but here they're clear-cut because the government *openly* declares racism as its policy."

There were also many difficulties in the Christian church at large, the Rev. Hendricks added. One that particularly concerned him was the need for greater clarity and amplification of the SACC resolution on noncooperation. "The trouble with the SACC is that it has no power to implement its recommendations. Another problem is that to achieve noncooperation with unjust laws, you have to have *total* noncooperation, action that comes from the people.

"Of course individuals *can* be effective. After I went to Crossroads and preached in support of the squatters, the authorities called me in. I told them I'd stand in my own defense and would not employ an attorney. The authorities withdrew the summons."

That Hendricks should have preached to African squatters threatened with eviction so that the government could implement a policy of preference for Cape Coloreds was particularly interesting to us. We were anxious to know why he called himself Black, inasmuch as many Coloreds seemed to distance themselves from Africans, and to hope for the greater power and privilege that the government was proposing to offer Coloreds in a three-tiered parliament.

He looked hard at us, closed his eyes for a moment, and then said slowly, "Shall I tell you a story? Before I entered the ministry, when I was a free-lance evangelist, I traveled from Potchefstroom to Klerksdorp for meetings, leaving in the late afternoon and returning the following morning at two o'clock.

At the Potchefstroom railway station, I'd leave my bicycle in the temporary storage room.

"One cold winter's morning I waited a long time, finally knocked softly on the door, then waited for more than an hour. The White railway policeman would not open the door. I summoned up all my courage, pushed open the door, presented my receipt, and in a cowering tone of voice asked for my bicycle. I could see that I had disturbed the young policeman's sleep. He came forward and struck me—right, left, and center—with a sound like the crack of a whip on oxen. I saw stars and was dazed.

"I walked all the way home—I could not get on to that cycle out of sheer humiliation, pain, and anger. The chill of the early Transvaal morning burned my face, and the fires of hatred burned in my soul.

"On my arrival home, I related the incident with deep feelings. In plain language my mother responded: 'You are as good as anybody else, and don't ever forget it. Carry yourself like a man. Respect everybody. God loves you.' She did not express sympathy. She told it like it is—I had to sink or swim.

"So you see, out of the challenge of her simple words a very bitter twenty-year-old made a crucial discovery: the Christ who adds new power to life. A power to love people whether they respond or not."

He looked out the window for a long moment and then added, "As a so-called Colored, I still feel in my body two major tensions—the fears of Whites and the aspirations of Blacks. Both hold the power to destroy—blind fear and blind aspiration are both destructive.

"Once, years ago, we did have integrated churches and schools; Africans—at least those on the Cape—could even own land and live more or less where they wanted. But since the Nationalists have begun their long series of discriminatory acts, how could I identify with Whites? It is deeply painful and yet gloriously meaningful to identify with Black suffering."

"How do you feel about the Colored political parties?" we asked.

"They are debating parties." He shrugged. "They have no power and can't even introduce legislation. The fact that the Colored Labor Party, which is more militant that the Freedom Party, gets the majority of our votes shows that we do identify with Blacks."

"Wouldn't the government's proposal of separate parliaments for Whites, Indians, and Coloreds give Colored persons some of the political power they lack?"

He grimaced, and said, "Parliaments excluding the African majority. That proposal is a dangerous divide-and-rule tactic. We need a common voters' roll for parliament. I'm a *South African*. No government can make me a 'Colored'! And majority rule would not necessarily squeeze out Whites. I, for one, wouldn't mind voting for you as a White, if you are capable. Yes, Indians and Coloreds are being wooed. And since they live nearer the Africans than the Whites do, a hate target can grow among Africans that will move from Whites to Coloreds and Indians. Very clever. The puppet show becomes more complex. But it is doomed to fail.

"From a Christian point of view too, it's unjust to ask for something for myself without asking for it for my brother. I can't support a migrant labor system or the idea of a Colored preference area—they are evil."

"Do you also identify with Black theology?"

"Well. . . ." He stroked his beard thoughtfully. "I don't believe that you can have a *Black* theology of redemption; Christ died for the whole world. I can't say I don't identify with Black theology, but it should never be construed to exclude Whites. Any theology that excludes any of God's creation should be questioned. I feel that I have a ministry to all South Africans, and that includes Whites."

"How do you see the future?"

He stared into his coffee cup, then set it down slowly. "Sometimes the government listens to us. But what we need is *legislation* for change. It must be accomplished by equal partners. I believe that there's still a volume of goodwill in South Africa. If it can be exploited, the transition may come with less pain.

"Our goal is not a negative one. We're not working for change in order to oppose the government, but to have a just and open society. Unless we *tackle* the issues together, we'll never *get* together. The primary task of the church, as I see it, is reconciliation. And we're working in this way not for the sake of integration, but for the salvation of South Africa."

Notes

1. We are indebted to the Rev. Abel Hendricks for taking the time from his pastoral duties in Bonteheuvel, near Cape Town, to talk with us. Other Methodists who contributed to this chapter were Alex Boraine, M.P., the Rev. Jimmy Palos, and Mr. John Rees. Some information was taken from *Dimension,* the monthly paper of the Methodist Church of Southern Africa, and from Ernie Regehr, *Perceptions of Apartheid* (Scottdale, Pa.: Herald Press).

2. At the annual conference in the fall of 1980, the Rev. Stanley Mogoba was elected secretary. The fact that Mogoba is a former Robben Island inmate and that he was chairman of the radical Black Methodist Consultation indicates a further strengthening of the BMC.

CHAPTER TEN

The Presbyterians

Since the early nineteenth century, when Scottish ministers were sometimes employed in Dutch Reformed congregations, the Presbyterian Church has enjoyed a close—if ambiguous—relationship with the DRC. Hence it has had a significance in the social and religious history of the country disproportionate to its numbers. In the last two decades, the Presbyterians have moved slowly toward becoming a more genuinely multiracial church, and a more united one.

We have seen how the Presbyterians became divided into four groups: the Presbyterian Church of Southern Africa (PCSA)—two-thirds White—and three Black churches, the Tsonga Presbyterian Church, the "Mzimba" Church (Presbyterian Church of Africa), and the Bantu Presbyterian Church (BPC; now called the Reformed Presbyterian Church). Such a situation is hardly conducive to a unified racial policy.

The PCSA has rejected the policy of homeland "independence," has stood for Black-White dialogue (especially during the unrest of 1976 and 1977), and has called on the government to support the rights of conscientious objectors. On some other issues, however, it has been more cautious than many other churches. For example, on the subject of investments the PCSA has supported study of the issue within the SACC, but emphasized exploring ways in which "creative pressures" might be exerted on companies in which the churches invest.[1]

This cautiousness is partly rooted in the Presbyterians' traditional links with the DRC, in the preponderance of White members, and in the fact that African and Colored congregations of the PCSA unite with the majority Whites only in presbyteries and at the General Assembly level, usually remaining divided at the congregational level.

A strong move, beginning in 1959, to unite the PCSA, BPC, and Tsonga Church eventually foundered in 1971, when the BPC opted out at the very last moment, and the Tsongas then followed suit. The result was severe disappointment to PCSA leaders who had persuaded their parishioners to commit themselves to a Black majority church—a big step in South Africa.

In 1979, however, a breakthrough occurred when the PCSA agreed to join with the United Congregational Church of Southern Africa (UCCSA)—a church 90 percent Black. Every congregation of the UCCSA was free to decide whether to join the union. The PCSA would join only if the majority of presbyteries ratify the decision. The Tsonga and Reformed Presbyterian Church may find it easier to join the union inasmuch as Blacks are a strong majority in the "umbrella" organization.

At the same time, Presbyterians have joined with Methodists, Anglicans, and Congregationalists in the Church Unity Commission, which proposes mutual recognition of members and ministers, joint ordination ceremonies, and ultimate unity.

Because it was agreed that united congregations could be formed before total union of the two denominations, a few Presbyterian clergymen have been moving ahead in their own way. Rob Robertson is perhaps the most outstanding example.

Portrait of Rob Robertson

Since the late 1950s Robertson has been a quiet pioneer in efforts to create a multiracial church at the grassroots level. Robertson is also one of the few leaders in South Africa to make an outspoken commitment to nonviolence. He puts his belief into practice by engaging in nonviolent action—and going to court to defend it.

In 1958 Robertson proposed that in each major center of the country at least one permanent multiracial congregation be set up, and in 1960 he launched the first, in a racially mixed area of East London. The North End Church became a close-knit group of Whites, Africans, and Coloreds. Since it was only a pilot project set up to prove that this could be done, and the participants had no wish to form another church, North End disbanded in 1970. Two mixed groups of members went to all-White churches, which thus became mixed and remained so.

In 1975 Robertson founded another multiracial church, St. Antony's, in Pageview, a Johannesburg Colored and Indian area now declared White. St. Antony's later became a united congregation of the PCSA and the UCCSA.

As we arrived for a return visit to St. Antony's one Sunday morning, children were racing down the slide under a palm tree in the courtyard. Nearby, their parents and others were chatting in animated groups. Many of the Whites were in blue jeans; most of the Africans, Indians, and Coloreds were in more conventional dress.

Near the entrance to the small, somewhat dilapidated-looking church stood Rob Robertson himself—a tall, spare man with high cheekbones, a small gray beard, and intense blue eyes circled with lines. Despite his gray hair, Robertson's agile step and quick smile conveyed youthfulness.

"Welcome back! . . . Say, Mary!"—as he beckoned to a Black parishioner —"Remember Jim and Marjorie?"

Mary led us inside. Children were handing out the programs. The interior had all the simplicity of the "primitive church": paint blisters flaking from the ceiling, rows of straight-backed cane chairs, a few flowers, pegboard walls decorated with posters, and a communion table consisting of an old table covered with an embroidered cloth.

Instead of formally calling the congregation to worship, the Rev. Robertson announced, "We're going to be a little experimental today. We'll be thinking of children—it's the International Year of the Child." He went on, "Too bad Bill couldn't make it today. . . . Anybody know how Vusi is doing? . . . Let's see now, what visitors do we have today? We're glad you came here while you're training in Johannesburg—how long are you going to be here, guys?"

As Robertson announced meetings and work parties (the latter to plaster and paint the church), more African and Colored families came in. Then we all raised our voices in a hymn. "Alleluia!" We rose and lifted our hands, and began twisting them back and forth. Many of the Black parishioners were swinging their hips, and gradually some of the Whites followed suit. The church echoed with light laughter and a chorus of alleluias.

The service became more solemn as Rob described a nonviolent action against the demolition of habitable dwellings in Pageview, homes in which Colored and Indian families had been living. "Several persons in this church have put up nearly a hundred posters that say 'Spare this house—people need it.' " Then the main program began. Two Black youngsters read the Scripture in Zulu. Then a mixed group of children acted out a brief play based on Christ's bidding "Let the Children Come unto Me."

A song about "Jesu," sung by Black youngsters in Sotho, was followed by "When It's Storming," a Swedish song translated into English. And as the children "rowed" back and forth, rocking their bodies and then making a rolling motion with their hands, the rest of us rowed along with them.

Then Rob gathered the youngsters around him and asked what they thought children needed. "To be guided," one ten-year-old Black boy responded promptly. Rob printed that on a flip chart. "To be happy," replied a White girl. "Books to read," answered another girl. "Love, friends," added two boys. "To play," announced another. "Nothing else?" asked Rob. Finally, one boy, a Black, said slowly, "Food."

Rob turned to the adults and asked what they thought children needed. "To experiment and explore, to share and give, discipline, language" came the answers, amid a good-natured free discussion.

Just before communion, Rob observed that some church members today felt that children should not have to wait until confirmation to share communion with their parents, and that perhaps they should all discuss this some time. Then he sat down on the middle chair of three facing the congregation, picked up the chalice, passed it to the Black woman beside him, received it back from her, sipped from it, and passed it on to the White woman on the other side. Then the two women passed communion to the rest of the congregation. On that day, the only acting elders were two young women.

The service drew to a close with hymns in Zulu, Sotho, Xhosa, and English. Many of us knew no African languages—but it did not seem to matter. When we came to "Africa Forward with God," Rob declared, "Let's sing this one loud and clear. We all know the refrain. So after the last stanza, let's close our books and *look* at each other—and sing to *each other*!"

An exuberant spirit took hold of the congregation. More than just a body of worshipers, we were a joyful community.

Afterward, we all joined together for tea behind the communion table. Two youths, one Black and one White, told us how they had become friends at the church, and of their work now on a "committee of concern" project, an alternative school in Soweto set up to prepare students for their diploma exams.

A retired White businessman engaged in Rob's campaign to save Indian and Colored houses spoke fervently of his five years at St. Antony's as a "blessing." The experience had opened his and his wife's eyes to a whole new world of relationships, and given fresh purpose to their lives. "Now when I see Black people I know around here, they wave, 'Hi, Martin!' That's practically unheard of in South Africa. But if we can't address each other by our Christian names, what's the use of having Christian names?"

The following Sunday we joined the Robertsons for simple lunch in their modestly furnished home. Our table companions included a Black parishioner who turned out to be an old friend of the family, a White woman deaconess, the Robertsons' three grown children, and Rob's wife, Gert.

A tall, dark, slender Scotswoman with a robust laugh, she seemed to be a real teammate for her husband. "Yes, the spirit here *is* a little different from that in other churches," she admitted. "In many White churches there's a reservoir of goodwill, certainly. So they'll say, 'Let's have an exchange with a Black church.' When the Black parishioners arrive, the Whites think naively that the Blacks will just respond quickly to 'How are you?' But Blacks today are proud. Some are even suspicious. Unless you make real efforts, they tend to stand around talking with other Blacks. So the Whites say afterward, 'See, it didn't work, did it?' And maybe they'll try again—a year later."

St. Antony's, we learned, is "different" in several ways. Not only are nearly half of the fifty-odd members African, Indian, or Colored, but all income groups are represented. A number of Catholics and members of other denominations attend fairly regularly, often becoming associate members. Over half of the congregation are men. A surprisingly large number are under thirty, and a fair sprinkling of all ages is represented. As one American minister observed, "St. Antony's is multi-everything."

We asked Rob to tell us more about his nonviolent campaigns to get better housing for Indians and Coloreds. For several years, we knew, traditional Indian townships in the Johannesburg area had been undergoing demolition so that new White developments could replace them. At the same time, some White areas had become almost deserted because of White emigration abroad and because the length of military service had been doubled. Hence many good houses were empty in White areas, while in Indian ghettos any kind of structure was inhabited. But Indians had been quietly moving into "White areas" and were usually welcomed by landlords, who not only wanted the money but also considered Indians very responsible tenants. When right-wingers publicized the situation, the authorities (who had been willing to see how this violation "sat" with Whites) reluctantly began evicting tenants.

One day an Indian family of eight living in a White neighborhood was dumped into the street. Having nowhere else to go, they decided to remain on the street in a tent. Robertson set up a tent beside them.

"I wanted the Naidu family to know there were some Whites who felt ashamed of what was done in their name," he explained to us. "I spent six weeks under a tent, and three nights under the stars. No, it wasn't good sleeping. People came to visit us late at night, passing motorists hurled insults at us, and there were ear-racking noises from the traffic. Women going home from work at 2:30 A.M. would come by singing and talking. Group Areas inspectors poked their heads in once after midnight."

A fascinating subplot in this drama was the offer of a Black man to let the Naidu family stay in his home in Soweto while he went to live in one of the crowded, squalid hostels. When the Black Good Samaritan heard that his proposal could not be accepted, he thrust a ten-rand note into the hands of the puzzled Mr. Naidu, pleading that he wanted to show his solidarity with the family.

In the sixth week, Group Areas officials, protected by police, confiscated the Naidus' tent and other belongings. Rob and the family continued living on the sidewalk for three nights with nothing at all for shelter.

Then Rob found a way: he rented a house in his own name, and invited the family to move in as his subtenants.

"The Naidus and I are now being prosecuted for allowing and taking up illegal occupation," said Rob cheerfully. "The case keeps getting remanded.

"Fortunately, evictions under the Group Areas Act in Johannesburg have stopped, at least temporarily. The government is bending its own policy by offering homes to these 'illegal' residents. There's no doubt that the patient endurance of the Naidus—and all the publicity they received—contributed to this softening of policy."

The government's action against Rob had not deterred him from becoming a member of ACTSTOP, a committee that was organizing appeals to the government to halt evictions of Indians until alternative housing was available. It had set up a "watch" of persons stationed with families threatened with eviction—a strategy that prevented several removals. Sympathetic stories in the newspapers and even on the government-controlled television made the authorities hesitant to force a confrontation.[2]

Rob's third nonviolent project was to form the Ad Hoc Committee on Pageview, to halt demolition of buildings in the area. Proceeding on Gandhian principles, the committee planned a three-stage campaign. It began with an appeal to the Minister of Community Development, surveys of the area, talks with residents, advising interested groups of their intention, and planning posters. When there was no positive response, the committee proceeded to inform the press, address meetings, and appeal again to the Minister.

In stage three, they prepared for action. The first action was that of putting posters on buildings about to be demolished. For this, Rob and several committee members, at the time of our visit, were soon to be arraigned. "That makes two court appearances in the future!" he grinned.

Part of Rob's work in the Justice and Reconciliation Division of the SACC involves coordinating and publicizing nonviolent activities in South Africa. One copy of the division's *Nonviolence News*, for example, described his own activities, a committee in Cape Town working to set up an ambulance unit as a practical example of alternative national service for conscientious objectors, a study program on learning nonviolence, a three-day conference on conflict resolution in southern Africa, and news of the Commission on Violence and Nonviolence.

Rob traces his concern for social justice to his parents. Although he grew up with playmates who abused "Kaffirs" and he was inclined to accept it, his mother, who was born in the multiracial society of Jamaica, helped make him aware of the subtle cruelty in their behavior. Later, his father, a chemistry professor and son of a minister, developed socialist views and formed a racially integrated club. There Rob, for the first time, saw Blacks drinking tea with Whites—a startling sight that "got me thinking."

After theological studies in Scotland, Rob gave up his old dream of becoming a missionary to China, for he realized that he could do far more in South Africa.

How did he come to his nonviolent stance? "My mother had pacifist leanings: four of her friends were killed in World War I. And from my reading of the Scriptures, I concluded that all Christians should be pacifists. Then I read Gandhi and King, and a Japanese writer, Kagawa." Later Rob became involved with the Christian Institute, partly because its head, Beyers Naudé, had a nonviolent orientation. A visit to Hiroshima in 1978 deepened his revulsion to warfare and fortified his determination to build a nonviolent witness in South Africa.

Rob worked at building that witness with the assistance of the International Fellowship of Reconciliation (IFOR), as its contact person in South Africa. Experienced nonviolent leaders such as Hildegard Goss-Mayr, Ulrich Henes, and Will Warren have come to South Africa to help train others in nonviolent action.

A few months after our visit Rob appeared in court charged with "malicious injury to property," arising from the poster campaign. He was convicted and fined 50 rands (without the option of imprisonment), which he refused to pay. A week later the sheriff and an assistant with a truck arrived to attach Rob's property; in preference to that, he paid the fine.

Rob has also worked on a multiracial church committee looking into alternative service for conscientious objectors. Increasing numbers of White youths—perhaps 10 percent of those called-up—are refusing to report for the draft. Many cite the injustice of fighting on the border against men who are Black and who feel that they have a duty to liberate the country from racial oppression.

Unlike many nonviolent activists today, Rob does not have a merely pragmatic approach to nonviolence. "I don't like the idea of *protest*—I think we should *appeal* to the authorities. Gandhi is right. Our approach should be done with love—we must try to convert the 'enemy.'"

Rob admits that often this cannot be done. Yet he can point to some modest successes—such as the fact that evictions under the Group Areas Act ceased after the ACTSTOP campaign and his prolonged demonstration with the Naidu family. Rob's innate gentleness and resilient good humor seem to have a certain power. When a rock was thrown through a window of the family dining room recently, he led his children through the front door in a vain search for the culprits. "When callers harass me on the phone, my answer is, 'Well, my friend, I'm going to say a prayer for you.' And almost always, the calls cease."

One Sunday afternoon some members of St. Antony's gathered for an informal service in Soweto, at the small four-room house of Grace Masuku. The walls were unfinished, each room boasted only a bare electric bulb hanging from the ceiling, and the tiny living room was unfurnished except for a row of wooden chairs, most of them borrowed, that lined the walls. Yet the stone floor was scrubbed and the house smelled faintly of soap.

The nine Whites in the party were greeted with handshakes and occasional hugs by Grace, her two sisters, a brother-in-law, and several children. Then more and more friends, neighbors, and relatives began to file in. Eventually thirty-one persons were jostling each other in the 9 by 20 foot room—the adults crowded together on chairs, the children sprawled on the floor.

After "Lead, Kindly Light" in Sotho and English, Rob introduced everyone whom he knew and asked others to tell a little about themselves. Then, following another hymn, Grace led the discussion—a sharing of her experiences in the schools of Soweto. As a grade-school teacher who had taught several years in that turbulent township, she was well qualified to make some observations about the progress since 1976: attendance was up, parents were cooperating with teachers as never before, and the size of classes was down from an average of about eighty to about sixty.

On the other hand, there were serious problems. School fees (ranging from approximately $6 in the first year to $60 in secondary school) were too high for most families. So few books were furnished by the government that five or six children had only one to share, and uniforms were far too expensive. Most classrooms had no heat or electricity during the winter—children were often asked to bring a lump of coal to class, but many could not; some pupils simply stayed away all winter. Youngsters who brought money to buy lunches at noontime generally ended up buying Coca Cola and "chips." A lively discussion ensued—the Whites agreeing that problems like "coke 'n' chip" lunches existed in their world too, but listening attentively to problems peculiar to Blacks. Whites and Blacks together came up with a few hopeful ideas—for example, parents or unemployed Soweto women should be sewing the uniforms.

Gradually almost everyone in the room participated in the discussion. "Are there any who haven't spoken, who'd like to say something?" asked Rob. Then one Soweto man pointed out, somewhat hesitantly, that the government spent over ten times as much on education for Whites as on education for Africans. The discussion became even more animated as Africans expressed their resentment, tempered by fatalistic acceptance of the system.

After another hymn, Rob led us in prayer. All the Blacks in the room, including the men, bowed their heads low, in a spirit of reverence that is somewhat rare among Whites. Even the youngsters on the floor bent far down and put both hands on their eyes (though one took a hand off one eye and took a long peek at us). All through the service, the children sat quietly, showing no restlessness whatever, but instead an eager interest in what was going on.

Then we all joined in a Zulu hymn, accompanied by a jubilant shaking and twisting of hands. And the service ended as we rose to sing:

> One man's hands can't tear a prison down.
> Two men's hands can't tear a prison down.
> But if two and two and fifty make a million,
> We'll see that day come round.

As Grace and her sisters brought in plates of cake and we began chatting in groups, we remembered an interracial service in a posh White Johannesburg suburb: the Whites had served coffee afterward in the handsome lounge, but almost without exception had made no overture to talk with their guests. What made the Soweto meeting different was not only that it had taken place in a home or that everyone had been encouraged to participate, but that the discussion had centered on a specific topic, one with meaning for both Whites and Blacks. It had offered an opportunity for Whites to learn first hand about life in Soweto, and it had occurred on the home grounds of the Blacks.

Most important of all, this was happening in small face-to-face groups. Perhaps this was an image of the primitive church. Perhaps it was also the face of the church of tomorrow.

Notes

1. Information on the Presbyterian Church in Southern Africa was taken from *The Christian Leader* (joint monthly paper of the Presbyterians and Congregationalists—discontinued in mid-1980); *Ecunews* and *Kairos* (periodicals of the SACC); John de Gruchy, *The Church Struggle in South Africa* (Grand Rapids: Eerdmans, 1979); and Ernie Regehr, *Perceptions of Apartheid* (Scottsdale, Pa.: Herald, 1979).

2. In 1980, with the rise in prosperity due to the high price of gold, the empty apartments in Johannesburg rapidly filled up. Extra pressure for living space was caused by an influx of White Rhodesians after the Mugabe regime took over the Zimbabwe government. The pressure to evict Coloreds and Indians increased enormously. ACTSTOP stepped in as advocate for those threatened with removal.

CHAPTER ELEVEN

The Congregationalists

The Congregational Church has not been so conspicuous as the Anglican or Methodist in opposing apartheid. In part this is due to its small size. In 1970 the United Congregational Church of Southern Africa (which includes Namibia, Botswana, Mozambique, Swaziland, and Zimbabwe as well as South Africa) numbered only 349,790 adherents (94 percent of whom were Colored or African).[1]

The Congregationalists' structuring also limits its political influence. The United Congregational Church of Southern Africa (UCCSA) consists of autonomous churches linked in a federation; its assembly can suggest but not direct policies of member congregations. Even the present federation—a merger of the Congregational Union of South Africa (the outgrowth of the London Missionary Society stations in the Cape Colony), the Bantu Congregational Church (the fruit of American Board Missionary work), and the London Missionary Society (principally concentrated in Botswana and Rhodesia)—was debated for many years before becoming a reality in 1967. The decentralized quality of the Congregationalists' structuring also helps to explain why they have moved only slowly toward unity with the Presbyterians.

Nevertheless, the Congregationalists have taken some pioneer steps. When the Rev. C. W. Hendrickse, a Colored, was named chairperson of the Congregational Union, in 1945, he became the first non-White to head a multiracial denomination. John Thorne, another Colored, was chairperson for the year 1968–1969. The first African, the Rev. Ben Ngidi, was named chairperson for 1970–1971. Since then a policy developed of rotating leadership fairly regularly between Whites, Coloreds, and Africans.

The Congregationalists also became the first denomination to choose a woman as chairperson, when Miss Emily Jane Solomon was appointed to their highest office in 1937. She remains the only woman to have penetrated the male stronghold at the uppermost level in any South African church. According to Briggs and Wing, "She fought for the franchise for women and for Africans, and was instrumental in helping to persuade the government of the day to give disfranchised Africans White representatives in the House of

Assembly, a mere remnant of what she had hoped to obtain for them."[2]

In recent years Congregationalists have trained many Blacks for leadership positions. Black laywomen, for example, have received a superior education at Inanda Seminary, a Congregational high school near Durban, and have gone on to become doctors, social workers, nurses, teachers, and community workers. Many Congregational ministers have been trained at the Black interdenominational Federal Theological Seminary. When Desmond van der Water, a Congregational student at the seminary, transferred to (White) Rhodes University, he set a pattern for nonracial theological training at the degree level.

Considering its small size and its decentralized character, the church of Albert Luthuli has produced a remarkable number of contemporary leaders. In addition to the three chairpersons noted above, outstanding African leaders include the Rev. Sam Arends, a Colored who was chairperson for the year 1978-1979; the Rev. Joshua Danisa, a Zimbabwean who held that post for the year 1979-1980; the Rev. Bekkie Dludla, activist member of the Diakonia Council in Durban; and Alan Hendrickse, prominent in the Colored Labor Party. Dr. Boganjalo Goba, who received his doctorate from the University of Chicago and later became principal of Albert Luthuli College, is an outspoken advocate of Black theology. It is his contention that Black theology will help to restore the fundamental biblical and African idea of a "dynamic community, a caring community, a caring concern that seeks to embrace all," within contemporary alienated society. Later he became more radicalized, calling for more Africanization—indeed, a total transformation of the churches.

John Thorne may be the most notable Black Congregationalist. In addition to chairing the UCCSA, he served temporarily as general secretary of the SACC in 1977. In 1980 it was his imprisonment for speaking out in support of the Coloreds' school boycott that sparked a dramatic interracial, interdenominational protest demonstration. The action was so successful that Thorne was released "like a hot potato" immediately afterward.

A number of Whites, too, have rendered outstanding service to the church. For example, the Rev. John de Gruchy, UCCSA chairperson for the year 1980-1981, came to the office after many years as lecturer in religious studies at the University of Cape Town and as Director of Communications and Studies at the SACC. The Rev. Joe Wing, several times secretary of the UCCSA and active in the SACC for many years, took a prominent role in the demonstration protesting Thorne's imprisonment.

As the power of Blacks in the UCCSA has grown, so too has its criticism of apartheid. In 1979 the annual Assembly expressed strong support for those who object to military service on either religious or moral grounds, and called on the Secretary of Defense to allow noncombatant duty for all sincere conscientious objectors as well as nonmilitary national service for those who refuse to serve at all in the defense forces.

The Assembly also rejected a resolution that would have implied criticism of the World Council of Churches' Program to Combat Racism. At the same time it urged change by nonviolent means and warned that a call to nonviolence by the church would be heeded only if it were accompanied by effective action to combat racism and injustice.

The government's labor policies, too, came under fire—especially the policy of making the Western Cape a "Colored Labor Preference area." The 1979 Assembly called on authorities to phase out the entire system of migrant labor and influx control. Among other things, the Assembly pointed out, the system forced employers to reduce the number of Africans in their service, separated workers from their families (thus fostering alcoholism, prostitution, homosexuality, and juvenile delinquency), prevented workers from leaving an objectionable employer for a better one, and fueled resentment among Africans toward Coloreds and Whites. The Assembly also sent down to the congregations a set of Christian labor principles for study and implementation, including four principles dealing with rights to unionize and strike.

A Visit with Unez Smuts

One of the most forceful voices in the South African Congregational Church today is that of a woman. When Unez Smuts was ordained, in 1959, she became the third woman minister in South Africa.

This outspoken critic of apartheid comes from a prominent Afrikaner family. Indeed, her forebears include Prime Minister Jan Smuts, the United Party leader whose policies prepared the way for the rise of Afrikaner nationalism.

The Methodist, Presbyterian, and even the NHK churches have followed the Congregational example by ordaining women. Female clergy in this conservative country remain few, however, even within Dr. Smut's own denomination. "In letters my fellow ministers still address me as 'Dear Brother!' " she laughs.

At our first meeting with her, she was wearing a jaunty white pants suit over a black shirt and clerical collar, an outfit that accentuated the trim, almost athletic quality of her diminutive figure. Despite her white hair, short and brushed back from her face, her intense hazel eyes and quick movements conveyed an abundance of energy.

That energy has made Unez Smuts something of a legend in Johannesburg. In the upper middle-class suburb of Atholl, she ministers to a congregation that includes Jews, Coloreds, and a few Africans. In addition, she directs seven home industries for the people of Soweto, operates a hospice for elderly handicapped Colored men, supervises a kindergarten on the church grounds, conducts a marriage and child guidance course, teaches handicapped and retarded children, trains Colored nursery teachers, runs a daily two-hour hot line, appears regularly on radio and television programs, conducts a faith-healing clinic every Friday, and supervises an imaginative feeding program that furnishes a million meals to hungry children during the winter months. She sleeps three hours a night and, when necessary, foregoes a night's sleep entirely.

Even as a child, Unez had strong feelings for the underdog, she confessed. "I used to play with Coloreds and Africans, our servants' children—and get thrashed for it. I remember interceding when a White boy beat a Black child. So the White boy beat *me*. And then I got thrashed again by my parents at home! But all this just made me more stubborn!" She cocked her head to one side and laughed. "My father belonged to the Dutch Reformed Church, but left it to become Presbyterian, like my mother," she went on. "They sent me to the Presbyterian Sunday school, but *I* insisted on going to a Methodist church—just to be different."

How did she come to the ministry? "Well, I always wanted to be something more than a housewife. At the age of eight I had an almost mystical experience in a classroom. I felt a sudden strange glory, as if God's presence was inside me, and something like a whisper, calling me to the ministry. Years later, at a Catholic convent where my parents sent me to become completely fluent in English, a sister asked everybody in the class what they wanted to be. When I said, 'minister,' she laughed."

By the age of twenty-six, however, Unez was in London, England, studying to be a teacher and a Methodist deaconess (a position equal to lay minister, representing the furthest a woman could go in the Methodist church at that time). Because her family had lost its money during the Depression, she worked as a cleaning woman from five until eight o'clock every morning before classes.

After a practicum in a poor section of London, then a position as deaconess at a Methodist church in Cape Town, she was called to preach one Sunday at a Congregational church. "When they asked me afterward if I'd like to join the Congregationalist fold, I began to realize that no other denomination offers so much freedom at the parish level. So I joined it. It was God's will.

"Then they asked me to take over St. Stephen's, in this well-to-do suburb. The church had six members, two rows of chairs, a whiskey box for a pulpit, and a rickety piano that played a handful of honky-tonk notes. We had no congregation, no furniture, nothing. But we did have the Lord, so then you're in the majority. Well, we renovated the church, and built a kindergarten—I had to be my own architect for that—and the sick began to be healed, and bring gifts, and ask what they could do. Soon they began to call me 'Padre'!

"From the beginning I didn't hesitate to preach that we Whites must answer for all the sins committed against dark-skinned persons. A few members did leave the church because they didn't like my views."

After the *Rand Daily Mail* ran a story on crippled children who were sleeping on concrete slabs in a Colored shantytown, Unez told her congregation that something had to be done. Within six weeks a simple hospice had been built, furnished with beds and blankets scrounged from manufacturers.

In 1977, when Unez heard of children in Colored schools who were fainting from hunger, she dreamed up Operation Christmas Pudding. "My congregation solicited dried fruit, flour, suet, brandy, stout, and spices from companies willing to offer the ingredients either free or at a substantial discount, delivered everything to a canning company willing to donate its services and, at the church, wrapped and labeled twenty-five thousand puddings. Then we 'picketed' liquor stores. When you've spent a fortune on booze at Christmas time, how can you say 'no' to buying a pudding for a poor child?"

Almost all the puddings were sold, and with the proceeds Unez was able to feed six thousand African and Colored children one meal every day during the cold months (April through October in South Africa), a lunch consisting of vitamin-and-mineral-enriched soup, together with two high-protein biscuits. In these schools attendance in winter has risen from 51 to 96 percent.

"When I was asked the date we were going to start the feeding program, I said 'April 6.' On April 5 we were bombed. Who was responsible? Some Whites were against the program. Others were against women activists. And there are even a few Blacks who believe that with full stomachs their people will be less revolutionary. We'll never know who did it. But no one was harmed."

Undaunted, Unez not only proceeded with her plans, but gradually expanded them. The operation that started as "Puds for Kids" became "Meds for Kids"—silver medallions the size of a penny with an embossed bear's head and the words "Bear me in mind." Girls buy them for their boyfriends, and vice versa. The program now feeds eight thousand children.

Her self-help projects in Soweto have also expanded. "One involves teaching women how to use donated scraps of material to make patchwork dresses, shirts, and spreads. Some are fantastically lovely! Now these women have a source of livelihood—and Soweto residents who couldn't have afforded new clothes can buy them cheaply. Other Black women make and sell school blouses—for White children. This means the women learn a new skill and the proceeds go to purchase materials to make school blouses for Black youngsters. We also supply wool, knitting needles, and patterns to help over a thousand children knit their own jerseys.

"Another self-help project for Soweto residents is raising their own vegetables, just as we've done on the grounds of St. Stephen's. If you trench down six feet, put in lots of junk like newspapers, then a layer of soil, and water, the seedlings will give you a yield in two months. It's late winter [August] and already we've harvested cauliflower and cabbage right here at the church!"

One of Unez's most ingenious promotions is the Easy Cooker. In Soweto many women leave home for domestic jobs as early as 4 or 5 A.M., and do not return until 7 or 8 at night. Even if the children go to school, they are left to roam the streets for long hours, unsupervised and malnourished. If these youngsters can at least look forward to one hot meal together as soon as their weary mothers return home at night, this helps in some small measure to bind the wounds in the family. The Easy Cooker consists of a carton lined with newspapers, tinfoil, and cushions made of newspapers. The mother starts a stew on a coal fire, places the boiling pot on a cushion, then puts another cushion on top; the stew (as well as scones and bread) will go on cooking for hours. And while the family eats dinner, the porridge for next morning's breakfast can begin simmering in the Cooker.

Unez could hardly be called a political radical, we realized, as we listened to her sermon one Sunday morning. In the small, well-appointed, flower-filled church of St. Stephen's, well-dressed Whites, five subdued-looking Coloreds and two Blacks listened attentively to their minister talk, in somewhat general terms, of the need for Christians to love one another. At the end, however, the Rev. Smuts became more emphatic: spiritual or racial pride, she declared, was sheer blasphemy.

Later we asked how she answered opponents who said that her projects were only acts of Christian charity, palliatives that did not get at the causes of the poverty and inequality in South African society. She said quietly, "I'm concerned about alleviating present suffering. I do what I can to make the lives of individuals more bearable. Also, some of the parishioners who get involved in these projects do come to see the basic injustices. For them it's an awakening. When I take people to Soweto, for the first time in their lives, many are shocked. Some have even left South Africa afterward. Of course, some just become more afraid. And others recoil—they can't get involved with *that*.

"Just the experience of interracial worship here is something, even though the Coloreds, and the African domestics—who come whenever their employers release them—don't have much in common with upper-class Whites. The Coloreds travel almost forty kilometers from their township, so you can see how much it means to them.

"It's true I don't get into demonstrations. I feel I can do more as an individual. For instance, in a sermon I once shook my fist about an iniquitous bill restricting Black employment still further. Some parishioners set up tables to send letters of complaint to Parliament. Maybe partly because of their action, the bill was subsequently dropped.

"I've had countless meetings with officials about the way they've closed down Colored schools held in garages, *ostensibly* because there wasn't one toilet for every ten children! I write letters to the Prime Minister about unemployment, housing, and the men's hostels, those dreadful places where contract workers have to live. Sometimes I talk of these things on the [government-run] radio, on one of those religious programs that are usually devoted to 'please be kind to Granny and the cat, especially the cat.'

"I've also managed to get a Colored choir on [government-run] TV. What a ruckus! But they sang so well that the radio booked them too. I even managed to use the all-African choir of Soweto's Baragwanath Hospital."

Fired by a spirit of independence all her life, Unez finds that functionaries of the church can be as frustrating as those of the government. "At the last assembly, they passed a resolution to look at problems of hunger. Because of my experience in feeding programs, I wrote a letter offering my assistance. They never acted on it. I also offered help on feeding programs to an Anglican bishop. He referred it to a committee. Period. Later I told him I'd read of the Acts of the Apostles, but not the Minutes or Committees of the Apostles!"

Unez's independent spirit was perhaps a factor in the decision by her congregation that instead of becoming part of the united UCCSA-PCSA church, St. Stephen's would remain an independent Congregational church. Many members of St. Stephen's look at the predominantly White PCSA as too pro-government, and believe that a united church would take away much of their autonomy and power in administering funds, thus curtailing the relief work they find so important in a time of increased tension.

During the past decade Unez has traveled overseas several times to address church groups on what they could do to help their brothers and sisters in southern Africa. In 1978 she was offered a job working for the United Nations as director of food-provision schemes around the world—a job that would have paid a "fantastic" salary, and would have released her from the tense world of South Africa. "My secretary called me a bloody fool to turn it down," she says wryly. "But my place is here."

"Padre" did not turn down the position because of optimism about South Africa. "Our national emblem should not be the springbok—but the ostrich! I'm afraid that time is running out, peaceful change is coming so slowly. Some of the best 'brains' in the country are leaving. Our congregation lost twenty-seven families in four months.

"Christianity is losing ground among Blacks," she adds. "The young regard religion as the downfall of their parents, because it didn't 'allow' them to fight. And when the church could speak out in a forceful way, it usually failed to do so. Today's atmosphere is becoming more tense."

Unez herself has been shot at three times. "Once they nearly got me another way—by dropping a brick from the top of a building. The only reason I'm here now is that I have a 'thing' about nails on the road. I saw one, moved out to pick it up, and the brick crashed down beside me. I was saved by God's will.

"An unknown caller banged on my door one night, too. I have a Siamese cat—if you know them, they're a cross between a lion and a cheetah—and it attacked the door with a roar. The caller left fast! Now I've put up a sign: 'Beware of wild animals.' There've been no further calls. We do live in exciting times."

That cat is Unez's only protection. She believes in nonviolence so strongly that she does not carry a gun, or even a police whistle. Nor does she own a dog.

When we asked Unez about her vision of the future, she shook her head. "Come the revolution, from the right *or* the left, I'd think Christian leaders would be the first to be lined against the wall."

"Then you might be one of them."

For a moment, as she gazed out over the park, a look of weariness passed over her lined face. Then she half-shrugged. "I know. But I'll just have to wait and see what God has in store for me."

Notes

1. Information on the United Congregational Church in Southern Africa is from *The Christian Leader* (joint monthly paper of the Congregationalists and Presbyterians—discontinued in mid-1980); *Ecunews* and *Kairos* (periodicals of the SACC); John de Gruchy, *The Church Struggle in South Africa* (Grand Rapids: Eerdmans, 1979); and Ernie Regehr, *Perceptions of Apartheid* (Scottsdale, Pa.: Herald, 1979).

2. D. Roy Briggs and Joseph Wing, *The Harvest and the Hope* (Johannesburg: United Congregational Church of Southern Africa, 1970), p. 292.

CHAPTER TWELVE

The Lutherans

In the past two decades Blacks have assumed a more militant stance in the Lutheran Church.

Until recently the Lutherans were slow in addressing themselves to the political and social issues in South Africa. One reason for this is the fragmentation emerging from the Lutheran tradition of official separation along racial lines. These churches differ from their Afrikaans counterparts, however, in that the Whites are a small minority, about 5 percent, and are not guided by the same nationalism that obsesses the Afrikaners. In the nineteenth century settler churches were created for Whites, whereas missionaries (German, Scandinavian, and American) set up separate mission churches for Blacks in the belief that conversion to Christianity should not alienate individuals from traditional contexts of family, clan, or tribe.[1]

In 1960 an important step in indigenization occurred: five missions united to become a regular church, the Evangelical Lutheran Church in Southern Africa, South Eastern Region (ELCSA-SER). Between 1959 and 1963 similar regional churches emerged out of missions.

In 1966 the Federation of Evangelical Lutheran Churches in Southern Africa (FELCSA) was formed, bringing the majority of Black and White Lutherans (including those in Zimbabwe and Namibia/South-West Africa) together on a council level. It consisted of seven missionary societies, thirteen churches, and some congregations.

In 1975 another kind of union occurred when the four regional churches—all of them Black, although some had White pastors—realized a long-standing dream and merged into one church, the Evangelical Lutheran Church of Southern Africa (ELCSA). These four churches became dioceses (the Cape/Orange Diocese, Northern Diocese, Southeastern Diocese, and Western Diocese), and a fifth, the Central Diocese, was formed to serve the Johannesburg-Pretoria area. ELCSA then became a member of the South African Council of Churches. Churches that belong to FELCSA but not to ELCSA include four White churches (those of the Cape, Transvaal, South-West Africa/Namibia, and Hermannsburg), as well as two Moravian churches (Moravian East and Moravian West), which are Colored. The four

White churches, together with two autonomous congregations, constitute the United Evangelical Lutheran Church in Southern Africa (UELCSA).

Although Whites fear being overwhelmed by the Black majority, a movement is growing to form one truly all-inclusive Lutheran Church in Southern Africa.

Because of this separation, it was not until 1963 that ELCSA-SER, the church in which American Lutheran missionaries were working, issued its first statement on race relations. Noting that non-Whites feel that they are victims of injustice under the present laws, the statement asked, "Can we defend a system that makes such laws the laws of the land?" ELCSA-SER also acknowledged that "there is apartheid in the Lutheran church."[2]

At the 1975 FELCSA meeting, delegates agreed in principle that their ultimate aim was to establish one Lutheran church in southern Africa. By that year, however, Blacks had become bold enough to underline some of the issues that divided them from Whites. At one point the Rev. A. W. Habelgaarn, a Cape Colored leader in the Moravian Church who was president of FELCSA that year (and in 1971 became the first Black president of the SACC), declared bluntly:

> In this situation, where we Blacks are simply not recognized as human beings, we are not trying to talk politics or put forward a political program. We want to act from a purely theological approach. But I can't preach to my people without understanding them in their contextual situation. . . . We can't ignore the fact that some of our young men are across the borders, and we have a responsibility to them.[3]

The conference also denounced the "alien principle"—that is, that the unity of the church is only a spiritual unity, and asserted that belonging to the one church "is not a problem of secondary importance, but belongs to the essence of the church." Delegates called for radical reconstruction of the South African political system in the light of biblical revelation.[4]

Concretely, what might this mean? Although the Black Lutheran churches in South Africa have not yet called for "one person, one vote," they have done so indirectly through the Lutheran World Federation (LWF). At its 1977 meeting in Dar es Salaam the LWF, including all South African delegates, called for universal suffrage in South Africa. They also declared that the situation in the Republic "constitutes a *status confessionis,*" thereby implying that the rejection of apartheid should become part of the confession of faith.[5]

In recent years FELCSA has evidenced in many ways its concern for preparing Lutherans for social change in southern Africa. One is a study program for member churches entitled "Christian Responsibility in a Changing Southern Africa." Another is the founding of the Mapumulo Institute, where ecumenical conferences are held.

In Namibia/South-West Africa, the territory over which South Africa has maintained illegal control for many decades, over 60 percent of the total population belongs to a Lutheran umbrella organization, the United Evangelical Lutheran Church of South West Africa (UELCSWA). The majority of its members are Black, and it has consistently identified with the independence struggle there. Members of the South West Africa People's Organization (SWAPO), the liberation force backed by most Blacks and hated as "terrorists" by most Whites, trust the Lutherans more than any other church. Its pastors work as chaplains in SWAPO and some of its leaders have engaged in consultations with SWAPO abroad. Most members of the Namibian DRC (the majority White church in the territory) distrust UELCSWA as a SWAPO "mouthpiece," while most Black Lutherans see the DRC as a "mouthpiece" of South Africa. Yet some observers feel that the Lutheran Church can play an extremely important mediating and moderating role in SWAPO as Namibia approaches independence.[6]

At a consultation of forty Lutheran theologians in Geneva in 1975, organized by FELCSA at the request of the Lutheran World Federation, the views of the church on Christian political involvement were stated clearly. "Christian responsibility includes politics," the conference asserted; ". . . political noninvolvement and indifference in a society of oppression and brutality is as much a sin as murder, for this contributes to the growth of unjust practices."[7]

The church's "Western theology" could not adequately deal with the situation in South Africa, the consultation declared, for it dealt only with "spiritual freedom," teaching conversion of the heart and obedience. "Black theology," on the other hand, "was a genuine and a positive expression of the ideas of Black Christians on God in the light of the word of God and their experience."

A Portrait of Manas Buthelezi

One of the foremost exponents of Black theology today is the head of the Central Diocese of the ELCSA, Bishop Manas Buthelezi.

What is Black theology? Dr. Buthelezi concedes that it is hard to define. Primarily, it is a contextual theology, he stresses—one that wrestles with the socio-political and economic situation. It seeks to root Christianity in African culture, and attempts to relate the kinship system—so important to Africans—to the biblical concept of "corporate personality."

It is also a reaction to the way Whites have dehumanized Blacks because of their color.

The fact that Africans, Indians, and Coloreds have been collectively referred to as "non-Whites" in official terminology suggests that they have the identity of nonpersons who exist only as negative shadows of Whites. In a theological sense this means that they were created in the

image of the White man and not of God. . . . The practical conse-
quence of this "non-White" theology has been the belief that "non-
Whites" can be satisfied with the "shadows" of things Whites take for
granted when it comes to their needs.[8]

In 1973 Dr. Buthelezi created a stir when he proposed six provocative theses
to the South African Congress on Mission and Evangelism. A central theme
was that the future of the Christian faith in South Africa depended largely on
how the gospel proved itself relevant to the existential problems of Blacks
inasmuch as South African Christendom was predominantly Black. Whites
had eroded the power of Christian love. Hence for the sake of the survival of
the Christian faith it was urgently necessary that Blacks step in to save the
situation. Indeed, it was time for Blacks to evangelize and humanize Whites.[9]

Born in 1935 in Mahlabatini, Zululand, Manas became a teacher at the age
of twenty-two. He became so involved with his students that he decided to
find a calling where he could help them shape themselves as integral people.
He chose the pastoral ministry.

Buthelezi became a minister and a distinguished scholar. He won his master's degree in theology at Yale University and his doctorate in theology at
Drew University. He has three honorary degrees, has taught theology in Germany and the United States, has been guest lecturer in several European
countries as well as South Africa, and has published many articles on Black
theology. He may well be the most traveled South African Black, having
visited sixteen countries on five continents.

In South Africa, Buthelezi has spoken before government commissions
and White businessmen's groups, urging them to improve Black education
and to recognize Black trade unions. In 1976, during the Soweto uprisings, he
was chairman of an umbrella body called the Black Parents Association
(BPA), which helped riot victims and their families arrange funerals, attempted to substitute dialogue for violence, and tried to persuade pupils to
return to their classes. All these activities were carried out despite the arrest of
the entire committee and bitter attacks from members of the puppet Urban
Bantu Council, some of whom urged that committee members' homes be
attacked and that the children who tried to prevent Soweto residents from
going to work be killed.[10] In the following year, the BPA paid out more than
$115,000 in aid, some of which came from Amnesty International and the
International Confederation of Free Trade Unions.[11]

In 1972 Buthelezi became head of the Christian Institute in Natal, and in
December 1973 was banned, probably for his activities in that capacity (reasons for banning are never given). Several months later a conservative news
magazine, *To The Point,* published a vicious smear on him. Then Dr. Buthelezi took an unprecedented action for a banned person—he sued the magazine for libel. At first, *To The Point* boldly stuck to its charge that Buthelezi
backed bloodshed in South Africa. But just before the case came to court, the
magazine did a somersault and admitted its claims were unfounded. Buthe-

lezi was awarded 13,000 rands [approximately $15,000] in damages. The editor, Dr. John Poorter (an ordained Baptist minister and an official in the South African Department of Information before taking charge of *To The Point*), risked going to prison for his refusal to comply with a court order to produce the notes on which the offending article—which he had written—had been based. Dr. Poorter was saved by Dr. Buthelezi himself, who refused to press charges because he did not want the editor to go to prison because of him.[12]

Something of this quality of concern for all human beings came across when we talked to Bishop Buthelezi in his offices at Diakonia House in the Braamfontein sector of Johannesburg. He is a handsome man, with a lean body, trim beard, serene eyes, and easy smile. His manner is gentle; he speaks slowly, observing you closely, and seems to be thinking things out as he talks.

"Since 1976 the churches have been meeting places for people working for change," he said. "But the situation *is* deteriorating, and race relations are worse than they were twenty years ago. It's hard to see hopeful outward signs—that is, signs based on what the government is doing. Our hope comes from inward signs. There's a new consciousness among Blacks today. We're convinced we shall overcome some day. Only if we're wiped out shall we lose that conviction."

"Do you have any hope of help from outside?" we asked.

He smiled, a bit ironically. "When the government says that 'in spite of criticism, people on the outside like our policy,' and then businessmen such as Henry Ford say 'we're here to stay,' what does it mean? That they do like our policy and they're strengthening apartheid. But if they can strengthen apartheid, then they have the power to weaken it. However, it is treason to speak of divestment. All I will say is, there are some who say that it is the only non-violent weapon left to us."

We changed the subject quickly. "You are related to Chief Gatsha Buthelezi?"

"He's my first cousin. But we do not agree on many things," he replied, somewhat abruptly.

"Can you tell us how you got into Black theology?"

He stroked his nose with his finger, and leaned back in his chair. "Well, Black consciousness and Black theology started as topics of debate in the United States—there's no doubt about that. When I was in the States, between 1963 and 1968, my studies included Black theology, but for me it wasn't much more than a matter of intellectual curiosity.

"After I returned home, in 1968, groups of students—many of them members of the University Christian Movement—invited me to speak on Black theology. For instance, I remember listening to Biko tell theology students why SASO had broken with NUSAS. It was an inspiring address! So *I* was inspired—I was challenged to think in a new direction. And I found this approach close to what I'd studied at Drew."

He leaned forward, his elbows on the desk and his chin in his hands. "I find it *exciting* to do theology where the action is. The situation prescribes what you are doing. This atmosphere of hate and polarization prescribes what theology does. As new things emerge, you have to experience what is happening."

"What is your church doing, then?"

"Well, the Lutherans have pressed for resolutions, but their actions *are* rather disappointing at present. However, I'm afraid that the government squelches them. But to me, the more appropriate question is, 'What are *all* the churches doing?' Then you'd see that lots of things are happening—in terms of stands on conscientious objection, labor, expulsion of Africans to the 'homelands,' and many other issues. Our people are working together, not as Lutherans, but as Christians—they're cooperating with Protestants and Catholics. Individuals of all faiths are sticking their necks out. A number of our own pastors have been detained.

"As for me, my position means at present I'm mostly involved in church structure. I hope that's contributing to social change, because the church is one institution that is still functioning and is capable of mobilizing members. I believe that my work means I'm a facilitator, serving the needs of the people."

"You've said that when Blacks see their own blackness as a gift of God, Whites can be liberated from the urge to reject Blacks, because such a rejection will be rendered irrelevant. You've also said that today Blacks should evangelize and humanize Whites. That last thought, particularly, is provocative. Considering the way the situation is worsening, do you still believe this is possible?"

"I still believe that," he said slowly. "But such liberation may be a long time coming. Ultimately Blacks will have to evangelize and humanize Whites."

Notes

1. Ernie Regehr, *Perceptions of Apartheid* (Scottdale, Pa.: Herald, 1979), pp. 251–252.

2. Ibid., p. 252.

3. Ibid., p. 253.

4. Ibid., p. 254.

5. Ibid., p. 261.

6. Ibid., p. 254.

7. Ibid., p. 255.

8. John de Gruchy, *The Church Struggle in South Africa* (Grand Rapids: Eerdmans, 1979), p. 158.

9. Ibid., pp. 161–162.

10. Baruch Hirson, *Year of Fire, Year of Ash* (London: Zed, 1979), p. 198.

11. Loraine Gordon et al., eds., *Survey of Race Relations in South Africa, 1977* (Johannesburg: SAIRR, 1978), p. 33.

12. David Thomas, *Councils in the Ecumenical Movement: South Africa, 1904-1975* (Johannesburg: SACC, 1979), p. 19.

CHAPTER THIRTEEN

The Quakers

"I stay in South Africa because here I feel the working out of the Spirit. Here one can bear witness every day."—A South African Quaker.

With less than one hundred members, the Religious Society of Friends (Quakers) represents probably the tiniest multiracial Christian group in South Africa.[1] Yet the Friends exert an influence out of all proportion to their numbers. As Alex Boraine, a Progressive Federal Party leader and former president of the Methodist Church, has observed, "The small group of Quakers is fantastic. They do everything possible to bear witness."

That witness grows out of Friends' long tradition of pacifism and concern for social justice. Since George Fox founded Quakerism in England in 1652, its followers have believed that "there is that of God in every person." Thus it is intrinsically democratic, egalitarian, and nonexclusive.

Unlike Afrikaners, Quakers do not conceive of a deity who favors a chosen people. Unlike most other Christians, they do not worship according to a dogma or ritual. Among those Quakers following unprogrammed worship, members seek guidance from their individual lights through silent meditation in a corporate body called the "meeting." Out of this gathering of the meeting some vocal ministry often develops. Because there is no minister, all members feel a responsibility. From time to time a member rises to share some thought, some seed for meditation, with others there. Out of this approach—individual and mystical, yet based on community—has come the concern for others so often expressed in social action. Most (though not all) Quakers adhere to the Friends' Peace Testimony, which opposes war of any kind. This pacifist position follows from the belief that if God is present in the spirit of every person, then by everyone's inner lights we can settle differences through peaceful methods of reconciliation. Conscientious objection to war is a value following from the belief in the universality of the Inner Light.

In Britain and America Quakers have been in the forefront of struggles to free slaves, crusades for women's rights, and movements for humane prison conditions. In World Wars I and II, the Vietnam War, and other conflicts, they have also established a worldwide reputation for assistance to victims on both sides of the battleline.

146

Afrikaners are hard put to disparage Quakers. One of the great heroines of Afrikaner history was Emily Hobhouse, an English nurse who exposed brutalities in British concentration camps during the Anglo-Boer War. She had worked closely with English Quakers who were providing aid in the camps. Moreover, after the Boer War a group of Quakers arranged to get back two hundred family Bibles from British soldiers who had stolen them from Afrikaner homes they had burned. The Bibles had extensive family trees written down in them and were infinitely precious to the Boers. Their return was never forgotten.

Nevertheless, Quakers have made Nationalists extremely uncomfortable. Quakers believe in mixed worship (although in practice very few Blacks come to the predominantly White meetings). Many have also been very active in working at the causes of oppression.

To some of their Quaker counterparts abroad, South African Friends are not committed enough to strong action to dismantle apartheid—action such as withdrawal of foreign investments. Most South African Quakers believe that boycotts and divestment would not be successful, and would only polarize the situation further. The divergence in viewpoints stems from a variety of causes, one of them being the difference in attitude toward nonviolence.

As Gene Sharp has pointed out, there are at least six types of principled nonviolence. South African Friends tend to believe in a type traditionally associated with Quakerism, "active reconciliation." This refers not only to outward actions, but to personal reconciliation and improvement of one's own life before attempting to change others. Although seeking to accomplish positive changes in social policy, adherents of this approach never use coercion—even nonviolent coercion. Rather, they seek to convince their opponent through positive action of goodwill.[2]

Some activist American Quakers (themselves a product of a more pragmatic and secular society) feel that they have moved beyond this type of nonviolence, because they are concerned with radical social change—that is, change at the *radices*, the roots. Hence they believe not only in conciliation, but in nonviolent confrontation, direct action such as sit-down strikes, seizures of plants, and boycotts, all within the overall search for a nonexploitive society.[3] It is difficult to categorize such an approach, but it seems to be a blend of those that Sharp calls *satyagraha* ("insistence on truth"), referring to Gandhian strategies, and "nonviolent revolution." By no means do all American Quakers fit this description, however. There is a great variety of viewpoints even among activists, many are not activists at all, and some are not even pacifists. It is also true that some South African Quakers are basically conservative, willing to work to ease the plight of the unfortunate through "good works," but less eager to remove the structural causes of injustice and violence.

Yet the fact remains that South African Friends do exert influence out of proportion to their numbers. Since their membership is so small, the Society itself does not often take action as a body. In a statement, Quakers have said of their work: "Probably of greatest value is the practical service toward improvement of racial relations given by individual members—either in their professional capacity, through voluntary service of an individual nature, or in cooperation with various agencies at work."[4]

As a corporate body, Quakers express their social concern primarily through Quaker Service, which has offices in Johannesburg and Cape Town. In Johannesburg, Olive Gibson, an English social worker, heads the modest operation that includes a Black social worker, a Black translator/caseworker, and occasional White volunteers. Dozens of persons daily crowd into the tiny bare office, asking for jobs, financial assistance, help with family problems, and advice on how to deal with problems arising from struggles with cruel laws and a callous bureaucracy.

Despite the growth of unemployment, there is no dole for Blacks in South Africa. Categorical assistance for disability, sickness, old age pensions, children's maintenance, and workmens' compensation is available theoretically, but the maximum payment for Africans for either old age or disability benefits is equivalent to about $30 per month (compared with $110 for Whites). Also, so much red tape is involved that hundreds of thousands of eligible Blacks receive nothing at all. Unemployment compensation is even more difficult for them to obtain. More devastating still is the fact that all Africans illegally in "White" areas can receive no social assistance at all. The impoverished homelands can offer no relief; thousands of persons have been removed from White areas (particularly from rural areas where they have been displaced by mechanization) and resettled in temporary camps with little or no infrastructure.[5]

Quaker Service staff are dedicated to helping Blacks get full advantage of benefits due them—benefits that Blacks would feel helpless to collect without this expert assistance. The staff also try to find jobs for employable workers and refer others to self-help schemes operated by Blacks. Olive (who, unlike most White social workers, spends a great deal of time in volatile Soweto) believes that this drive for independence is one of the few encouraging signs in the generally dismal picture.

The Cape Western Branch of Quaker Service, in Cape Town, makes small grants to an unusually wide spectrum of programs, ranging from self-help centers in squatter communities to food programs and irrigation projects in the desolate homelands. Monthly Meetings are held in local parishes or congregations in support of projects concerned with religious instruction, education, self-help, and relief. Quaker Meetings have also supported families of political detainees and sent letters to authorities or the press expressing concern about infringement of rights.

As individuals, Friends often "speak truth to power" by publishing statements on controversial issues. South African Quakers are also noted for their extraordinary degree of involvement in volunteer work, to which some are committed full-time. Volunteers take food to detainees, help rural laborers build their own homes, assist families of unemployed men, lead handcraft classes, and engage in many other activities.

As members of other groups, Quakers have been represented (often in leadership positions) in organizations such as the SACC, the SAIRR, the Christian Institute, the Black Sash, National Council for Women, the Women's Movement for Peace, and many *ad hoc* committees.

Although most South Africans look askance at "liberated females," an unusually large number of Quaker women have taken leadership positions. Jennifer Kinghorn, for example, is a lawyer who has served as Clerk of the Transvaal Monthly Meeting and a member of the executive committee of the SACC. With three others, she also traveled to the United States to explore relations with American Quakers. Bunty Harmon Biggs is a British-born Quaker who has been almost a one-woman service committee in Pietermaritzburg. For example, she headed Kapugani, a group that managed to buy surplus food from South African farmers and then sell it to Africans for a fraction of what it would have cost in retail stores.

Rosemary Elliott, who has served as Clerk of the Southern Africa Yearly Meeting, was born in England and came to South Africa in 1954 after hearing Michael Scott describe his ministry in the land of apartheid. "I *knew* that God wanted me to go to South Africa to live," she says. For a year she did social work, and then, after marrying, moved to a citrus farm in the Port Elizabeth area, where she undertook voluntary relief work.

After Sharpeville, Rosemary struggled to form a small interracial group to "seek ways in which we could express our Christian faith more effectively in our lives." When the Christian Institute started, members of the group formed a close link with its leadership. Opposition from Whites to the group and to many other projects she has launched has proved enormously frustrating to Rosemary, who feels very much alone in the White community. "Then too, as soon as your group becomes slightly effective you're watched by the police," she says despairingly. "They go especially to the Blacks in the group, and ask so many questions about what goes on at meetings that the Blacks are afraid to come. We try to get into nonviolent action—but how is it possible in the South African context? Even the smallest project becomes absolutely exhausting."

One day, in an effort to help a Colored minister in prison, Rosemary walked alone into the Port Elizabeth police office responsible for the detention and torture of Steve Biko. "I had to go through a locked door, which they locked again behind me," she recalls. "I told the officer I'd come to say there was a great danger in suppressing people like Biko and my friend, who stood for peaceful change. He just stared at me, and muttered a few words. But I insisted on shaking his hand as I left. Later, I said to an African friend, 'It didn't do any good, did it?' But his answer was 'Unless someone speaks up like you, they'll think no one cares and do anything they like.'"

Nonmilitary Proposals for Conscientious Objectors

One of the most innovative projects in which Quakers have played leading roles is a plan for alternative service for conscientious objectors. It originated with Paul Hare, an American Quaker who chairs the sociology department of the University of Cape Town, is an authority on small groups, and has had long experience in nonviolent training and conflict resolution. In 1976, when the "unrest" spread to Cape Town, Hare and a small group of Quakers set up an ambulance service to transport injured Blacks. Later the ambulance was used for other purposes, including delivery of food, clothing, and relief supplies from White churches to families who had lost their homes. Quakers also arranged meetings between White politicians and bureaucrats, and spokespersons for the Black community to discuss basic improvements in community services.

More recently Hare joined Dr. James Moulder of Rhodes University and Dr. Francis Wilson of the University of Cape Town in advocating alternative types of public service for men who refuse on grounds of conscience to enter the military. Broadly speaking there seem to be three groups of conscientious objectors: those willing to serve in the Defence Force but unwilling to bear arms, those willing to work in civil service but not in the military, and those who object to serving the government in any capacity, including civil service and teaching in government schools for Blacks. Moulder and Wilson have suggested that such men work in a community service corps (which would not be confined to Whites) for disaster relief, fire fighting, hospital and prison work, or projects in education and agriculture. This could also help remove the misery and injustice that are the major causes of violence in South Africa, they point out.[6]

Hare and Unitarian Bob Steyn have made a more detailed proposal than that of Moulder and Wilson. Conscientious nonmilitarists would put in a longer period of service than that prescribed for military service, and their organization would be independent of the army. Their duties would include supplementation of existing organizations at times of natural disasters, working with potentially violent persons such as prisoners or mental patients, and acting creatively at times of strikes or mass protests. Orientation of the corpsmen would range from fire fighting to responding nonviolently to physical violence.

From time to time authorities have shown flickers of interest in both kinds of alternative service proposals, but in the end have rejected them. Hare's project, however, continues to receive growing support from English-speaking churches. For example, in 1979 the Congregationalists voted 500 rands ($600) to support it.

During the Coloreds' school boycott (originally nonviolent) in 1980, Hare played a dramatic role in preventing deaths and injuries. When the government put plainclothesmen in unmarked police vans, violence erupted among

youths who saw the police as *agents provocateurs*. As police activity accelerated, teachers and principals began to fear that the officers would enter the
schools. They asked the Quakers to intervene by communicating the Coloreds' feelings to the police commissioner.

Then a stone-throwing fifteen-year-old was entrapped: he was shot by
plainclothesmen who were crouched on the floor of their van, and shoved
into the gutter with the warning to his friends to "leave him alone and let him
die." Everyone realized that the funeral would be a setting for bloody rioting.
In response to appeals from school principals and other local leaders, Hare
put together a pamphlet on nonviolence with guidelines for marshals and tips
on how to be an observer. In a few days the marshals were given rudimentary
training. The police commissioner agreed to keep riot police out of sight. On
the funeral day, the marshals (all of them Black, because Whites would
hardly have been welcome) kept order while over twelve thousand students
marched for one hour, with no incidents—on the same street where police had
assaulted students a week before. At some distance the Quaker Ambulance
Service stood ready to help with injuries—injuries that never occurred. The
whole effort required intensive work, but as Hare observed, "If you can
perform like this, they will turn to you later for bigger things in times of
crisis."

Portrait of Hendrik van der Merwe

Another innovative project in which Quakers have played leading roles is
the Center for Intergroup Studies. Housed in the University of Cape Town
but independent of it, the Center seeks to promote greater understanding
among population groups in South Africa. It undertakes research (generally
geared to serve as a base for well-planned action), publishes books and other
documents, and conducts workshops with participants from outside the
Western Cape and overseas.

That this dialogue has depth was shown by the fact that in 1971 the Center
brought together leaders of the Afrikaanse Studentebond (ASB), the National Union of Students (NUSAS), and the South African Students Organization (SASO). Although SASO president Steve Biko lost no time in criticizing the White power structure and White liberals, all the groups discovered
more common ground than they had expected. Hendrik van der Merwe, the
Center's director and a leading figure in the Quakers' Cape Western Monthly
Meeting, maintained a sporadic friendship with Biko, and as chairman of
Quaker Service made financial contributions to some of Biko's Black Community Programs.

Another of the Center's major projects has been the Constructive Program, set up to further understanding of prejudice and provide practical
guidelines for overcoming racial and economic discrimination. It has
brought together persons who have never before been on the same platform.
Some of the most successful workshops have been conducted with high-

school students; others have included business and political leaders.

Van der Merwe is a remarkable man whose beliefs provide insights into the values of Quakers. His own evolution was unusual, for Van der Merwe is an Afrikaner. In South Africa, an Afrikaner who forsakes the dominant beliefs of his cultural group risks ostracism and almost inevitably suffers from a sense of isolation. This scholarly activist, who has earned a doctorate in sociology, traveled widely, and became an astute political analyst, grew up on a farm and did not even visit the nearest city (less than two hundred miles away) until he was sixteen. After graduation from high school, he became a farmer in his home district and then went to Rhodesia as a missionary of the Dutch Reformed Church. He returned from Rhodesia still convinced that God willed the separation of White and Black in both church and state, and he still refused to shake hands with a Black person.

"Back in South Africa," he recalled, "a fresh vision dawned upon me one day when my own elder brother casually referred to a Black female as a *vrou* ("woman") instead of using the normal derogatory word *meid* ("maid"). I asked him if he did not mean *meid* and he simply said, 'No—*vrou.*' Suddenly I realized we were all one people of one world. A new world opened for me. I saw myself as part of Africa. An Afrikaner became an African."

Van der Merwe's new outlook brought with it tensions with his church and his friends, and he longed for an association in which he could give expression to his personal convictions. Eventually, he did graduate study in sociology at the University of California (Los Angeles), where he and his wife, Marietje, became resident host and hostess at an international student center run by Quakers. This first encounter was the beginning of an involvement with the Society of Friends, one that ultimately led to his election as Clerk of the South Africa General Meeting (which in fact includes South Africa, Botswana, Lesotho, and Swaziland).

Like many other converts to a new faith, Van der Merwe is more ardent and articulate than most "birthright" Quakers. Aspects of Friends' faith that most appeal to him are their insistence on openness, their use of dialogue, their emphasis on conciliation, and their attempt to identify with both sides of a dispute.

On the one hand, in workshops and research studies Van der Merwe focuses on institutional violence. He recognizes the importance of Black consciousness, recruits Blacks for his staff, and encourages the training of leaders in the Black community.

On the other hand, he is deeply concerned about the violence committed by both Black and White extremists who have given up hope for a peaceful settlement. Too often, he says, liberation movements have become the victims of international power politics. Although he shares the sense of urgency of those who feel that everything they do should be aimed at immediate change, he cautions that working for change at all costs may destroy the future.

By the same token, he challenges unquestioning commitment to civil disobedience, which he sees as a negative act. "My plea is for a more positive response, which I would call *conscientious affirmation*. This does not necessarily require breaking any law; it requires affirmative demonstration of fellowship, love, tolerance, and a commitment to peace and justice. There is ample scope for such affirmation within the law."

Yet Van der Merwe admits that many laws are anachronistic. Some—such as the requirement for a permit to accommodate an African in a White home—he finds so morally objectionable that he refuses to obey them. "What I do emphasize," he says, "is the need for Friends—and others—to be conciliators and bridge builders."

"Bridge building" describes Van der Merwe's own role, not only at the Center and at Friends' meetings, but also in an arena few others can penetrate. Because he attended the University of Stellenbosch with present-day National Party leaders, shares their heritage, and maintains contacts with the Afrikaans community, Van der Merwe has entree to the decision-making elite. This is one aspect of his life that he cannot discuss freely. Yet it is clear that he has sown seeds that may bear fruit some day. The value of such quiet but intense dialogue can never be measured.

Notes

1. This chapter is based on extensive interviews with the following South African Quakers: H. W. van der Merwe and A. Paul Hare of the Cape Western monthly meeting; Raymond Cardoso, Elizabeth Taylor, David Thomas, Olive Gibson, and Jennifer Kinghorn of the Transvaal monthly meeting (Johannesburg); Rosemary Elliott of Addo. We are also indebted to Douglas Steere of Haverford College and Lewis Hoskins of Earlham College for their suggestions after reading the manuscript. Professor Hoskins, since 1959, has been the American vice-chairperson of a program called the United States-South Africa Leader Exchange Program. It was initiated and guided by him and Frank Loescher, a Philadelphia Quaker and professor of sociology, in cooperation with the Africa Institute and the American Friends Service Committee. It later became a privately funded, non-Quaker foundation. It has conducted symposiums and workshops, and arranged for exchanges of leaders in all professions between South Africa and the United States.

2. Gene Sharp, *Gandhi as a Political Strategist* (Boston: Porter/Sargent, 1979), pp. 207-9.

3. For an excellent discussion of the dilemma that Quakers face over the problem of confrontation, see Mike Yarrow, *Quaker Experiences in International Conciliation* (New Haven: Yale University Press, 1978), pp. 282-300.

4. "Annual Report, Quaker Service, 1978" (mimeographed).

5. See Marjorie Hope Young, "Social Work under Apartheid," *Social Work* (July 1980). The Black Sash has thoroughly documented the pass-migrancy-resettlement situation in its quarterly magazine *Black Sash*. In 1969 Fr. Cosmas Desmond exposed the beginnings of this resettlement scheme in his book *The Discarded People* (Harmondsworth: Penguin, 1969). For his efforts, which were also televised on BBC in England, he was banned for five years. He subsequently returned to his native land, where he now heads the British branch of Amnesty International in London.

6. Actually, the freedom to avoid military service for reasons of conscience is *not* guaranteed in RSA. All that is guaranteed is that a CO will get three years in detention barracks if he belongs to one of five small peace churches. He is usually (not always) given non-combatant service, but must wear the uniform. Men who do not so belong and refuse military service can be (and have been) imprisoned, and can be called up repeatedly until the age of 65.

CHAPTER FOURTEEN

The Roman Catholics

Although it was not until the 1940s and '50s that Roman Catholics became actively critical of South African state policy, by the 1970s the Catholic Church had become a major force in opposition to apartheid. It opened its schools to all races, began "blackening" its hierarchy, and supported the right of conscientious objection to war.

One reason for the Catholics' slowness in taking action is the fact that they constitute a minority church. Most White Catholics come from working-class backgrounds and are the children or grandchildren of Irish and Italian immigrants. (Since 1974, large numbers of Portuguese refugees from Angola and Mozambique have joined their ranks.) A lay leader in the ecumenical movement has observed that while most South African White Catholics do not place a high value on social change, they tend to respect authority, have a great deal of reverence for the church, and look to their leaders for guidance. Hence when the hierarchy decrees, for example, that Blacks will take higher positions in the church—assuming authority over Whites in some cases— White Catholics tend to go along with the decision. On the other hand, basic feelings of prejudice are slow to change.

In their 1977 Declaration of Commitment, the Catholic bishops vowed to speed up the promotion of Blacks, appoint Black priests to White parishes, give equal pay for equal work, and integrate Catholic institutions. Most of these changes are occurring slowly. Very few Black priests have taken charge of White parishes, and although equal stipends now exist in principle, White clergy receive more generous gifts from their White parishes.

Yet change is occurring. That Blacks have been assuming greater power is clear from the fact that, whereas in 1971 all of the bishops were White, by 1980 five out of twenty-nine were Black (African or Indian). These changes are largely due to the phenomenal rise of Black membership. In 1911 the church counted 24,000 Blacks and 25,000 Whites; in 1980 there were over one and a half million Blacks and 500,000 Whites.[1] (In only one decade, 1960 to 1970, the number of Black adherents rose 76 percent.[2])

To most far-sighted Roman Catholic leaders it is clear where the future of

154

Catholicism—indeed, of Christianity—in South Africa lies. Nevertheless, the power structure remains with the Whites.[3]

Change in the Catholic Church also depends on changes of attitude on the part of Whites in the hierarchy, who in turn have been responding to change in the world. The gradual "awakening" of a White archbishop may furnish some insight into this painful psychological and spiritual process.

Portrait of Denis Hurley

Denis Hurley, the six-foot tall, handsome, trim-figured archbishop of Durban, is known for his courageous stands on a great many issues. Unlike most members of the hierarchy, he is also likely to be out demonstrating—in protest against removal of Blacks from their homes at the Crossroads community, for example.

At the age of thirty-two, Hurley became the youngest president of the Southern African Catholic Bishops Conference, a post he held for eight years. Under him the conference began to issue a series of relatively forceful statements on race relations.

In the 1960s, after attending Vatican II, Hurley became more action-oriented and ecumenical. In 1965 he became national president of the South African Institute of Race Relations. Largely because of him, the Catholic Church took observer status in the South African Council of Churches. In the 1970s he urged that Catholic schools be opened to all races, that more Blacks assume leadership in the church, and that Catholics become actively involved in issues affecting migrant labor, pass laws, segregated residential areas, racially mixed marriages, and the basic right of families to live together.

In 1975 Hurley started a new venture, Diakonia, an interracial, interfaith communications center in Durban. Two years later he launched the Human Awareness Program, which, by working with change-oriented groups, aims to promote informed public opinion and foster a change of attitude toward sharing. At the same time, Hurley and other bishops became the object of a rightist hate campaign when they voiced support for the Young Christian Workers, a group that has pushed for basic rights for all workers—and has suffered persecution from the authorities.

We were fortunate enough to meet Archbishop Hurley on both our trips to South Africa. When we told him that we found his record to be an impressive one, he shook his head. "Speaking is easy—action is difficult."

We asked him to tell us about his own life. He spoke slowly. "It was an intellectual journey before an emotional one. I was born in Cape Town, subject to South African cultural values. Whites here have been brought up with the paternalist attitude that only the White man can run African activities. My intellectual interest grew out of studies at the Gregorian University in Rome, where I finished in 1940. Much was said there about the social teachings of the church, and especially Leo XIII's letter on the condition of workers and the evils of capitalism. Later, in South Africa, I began to talk on the 'native' problem. But my attitude was still basically academic.

"I was still isolated—nervous about getting involved in 'radical' activities. It wasn't till the late '50s that I saw one couldn't be authentic without knowing the *people* in the situation, and without taking sides. I was elected chairman of the Durban branch chapter of the South African Institute of Race Relations, and our big task was to save the land at Cato Manor for the Africans. We went on deputation to the city council—and lost. But I was becoming an activist, in a minor way. In the late '50s too—I forget the date—I attended a conference on racial affairs called by Anglican Bishop Ambrose Reeves. Many radicals were present. When a Black reporter commented, 'It *is* surprising for Catholic clergy to be "involved," ' it made me think.

"Then the Sharpeville massacre in 1960 stimulated me to do more with the Durban branch of Race Relations. But I was still mostly making speeches. It was through women—members of the Black Sash—that I learned about demonstrating. When an Indian was detained in Durban and committed 'suicide' from a prison window, we had a big demonstration here. I felt nervous the first day. Later I became intrigued by demonstrating—by the way people stared at me, taking a sneaky look, then ducking away."

In the late 1960s, Hurley went on, he was invited by Cosmas Desmond, a young Catholic priest, to see Limehill, a resettlement village of "discarded people." Black families were simply dumped in the bare veld, where there was nothing but a pile of folded tents and a water tank some distance away. "They even took a picture of me driving in a tent peg. More important, I was getting to know the people. They were dying, like flies, of an epidemic—especially the children. One afternoon, we counted ninety little graves. We sent their names to the Bantu Administration—which never answered the letter. I was realizing these people as beings who were suffering enormously. Also there was a certain excitement in taking action.

"One night in Milan, going over a speech I was to give in Germany, I suddenly realized that I *myself* was part of an oppressive people. They were oppressors, and I was one of them. It was a terrible feeling. It may seem strange that it took so long to realize, to *feel* this. But that is South Africa.

"That experience fired me with the desire to do something—to try changing attitudes. Though I often felt powerless, especially when the guerrilla movements began spreading through Mozambique and Angola, and then Soweto broke out. It looked as if violence would be the only outcome."

Diakonia and the Human Awareness Program emerged from Hurley's belief that social attitudes are the crux of the problem, and that carefully planned small group experience can change them. "It's true," Hurley conceded, "that the social attitudes that do most harm are those of the establishment. But I still feel that attitudes must change before political structures. It does take a war effort to change attitudes. Too often I feel utterly helpless to avoid a holocaust.

"But Christians must never yield to pessimism, no matter how 'correctly' the judgment is calculated. And the essential task of the church remains that of giving practical expression to Christian faith. The real test of hope is when the situation is hopeless."

Work of the Bishops Conference

The Southern Africa Catholic Bishops Conference (SACBC), with headquarters in Pretoria, represents thirty dioceses in South Africa, Botswana, Swaziland, Namibia, and Lesotho, as well as the independent "homeland" of the Transkei. To the Conference are attached a number of commissions concerned with subjects such as catechetics, liturgy, ecumenical contacts, education, social welfare, and justice and peace.[4] Some of these commissions have done notable work in race relations.

The Justice and Reconciliation Commission, for example, operates on a national, diocesan, and parish level, focusing on five levels of activity: (1) developing awareness of social and interracial justice, (2) assisting in programs in areas such as literacy work, rural development, urban training, and tutoring, (3) protests against social injustice, (4) examining the internal structures of the church to eliminate injustices there, and (5) attempting to persuade people to adopt a simple lifestyle constant with Christianity. The SACBC guidelines indicate that there should be a justice and reconciliation commission in each diocese. Unfortunately, there are only two full-time workers, Sister Brigid Rose in Cape Town and Louise Goemans in Durban, as well as a full-time secretary at SACBC headquarters in Pretoria.

A fairly new department in the SACBC is one called Church and Industry, composed of diocesan leaders who form lay committees of persons working in factories. These workers look into what is happening in their workplaces and organize for better labor conditions. Such groups, it is felt, can be more effective than most working priests, who have frequently been regarded as linked with management.

The body of Catholic believers also includes informal groups such as the Young Christian Workers (YCW), the Young Christian Students (YCS), and the Grail. All the leaders, and most of the members of YCW and YCS are Catholic. The Grail is an international lay Catholic women's organization. Grail women live in small communities. For several years they often worked in secular positions, but since realizing the need for women with their background within church structures, they have moved into more official positions. All the Grail women we met were well educated, thoughtful, committed people; several had felt "called" from their comfortable lives in Europe or America to work in South Africa. A small group of Black Grail women works in Soweto: one teacher, for example, runs youth clubs there.

In the past Grail members did a great deal of work with interracial groups, to stimulate dialogue between the races and discuss possible avenues of nonviolent action. These innocent-sounding activities have been infiltrated by informers, and half-veiled threats have been made on Black participants. In Port Elizabeth, a Molotov cocktail was thrown into the house where the Grail women were living. They were also harassed by calls at all times of the night. One voice, for example, purred into the phone: "I came this afternoon to kill you. Fortunately for you, you were out. Too bad. But I am a very patient killer." Although the women were frightened, their priest declared: "You can't move out." They stayed.

Catholics took a pioneering step in 1976 when they announced their intention of opening their schools to all races, in defiance of the law. The crucial decision had been reached after years of agonizing reflection, for as far back as 1951 the SACBC had declared that de facto segregation in church institutions could not be tolerated forever. By early 1976—two years after the crumbling of Portuguese colonialism in Mozambique and Angola—it was clear to the bishops that maintaining segregated schools rendered the church's teaching on social injustice invalid, and that it was a cause of acute resentment among Blacks. As Archbishop Hurley pointed out, there were dangers involved in establishing a policy of open schools: the state might close them down or White parents might withdraw their children. Yet the church must take this risk.

By the end of 1976 two "White" Catholic schools had admitted Black pupils with full knowledge of the authorities, who had apparently turned a blind eye to the situation (a typical illustration of how the South African government experiments with a new policy in order to see how it works). In 1977 a small number of Black children were admitted to thirty previously White Catholic schools, and the press seized on the story with a massive publicity campaign.

This set the Administrator of Education in the Transvaal hot on the heels of the schools, with threats to close them down. For months the two sides conducted a quiet dialogue on the issue, but the church remained firm on its stand to negotiate on implementation of policy, but not on principle. Since government officials were not eager for a showdown that would have international repercussions, the controversy simmered slowly until April 1978, when Party leaders (with the exception of those in the Transvaal) announced mild reforms, including the right of Blacks to send their children to private schools. By 1979 some government officials were even congratulating themselves in public about how well the new policy was working out. The hardline administrator of the Transvaal Province, who had obstructed the process in his area, was not reappointed to his powerful post.

Catholics moved slowly and cautiously, insisting that there be no lowering of educational standards for Black pupils. Since the state per capita expenditure for White pupils was over ten times that for African pupils, and the curriculum for "Bantu education" differed substantially from the White curriculum, inevitably Blacks felt inferior. Some persons feared that taking in less well prepared pupils would only reinforce White prejudices that Blacks *are* "inferior."

To the surprise of many observers, the new policy encountered no great obstacles in the schools or community. Almost no racial incidents were reported. Blacks have felt the opening of the schools to be a "gesture of substantial symbolic value," according to Archbishop Hurley. One survey showed that 85 percent of the parents of children at Catholic schools in Johannesburg were delighted with the prospect that their children would now have the opportunity of breaking down racial barriers. Very few withdrew their children.

Sister Margaret, a nun teaching at Holy Rosary convent school in Port Elizabeth, reported that the project of integrating the school had been exciting for everyone. The staff opened themselves to the African aspects of South African history and to the riches of differing languages and cultures. White pupils learned that their Black classmates were basically "no different." Said one White girl:

> The martyr I had hoped to be has faded. I no longer only love my fellow pupils because I am a Christian; I like them because they are people I can talk and laugh with. I am getting to know them better each day, and don't take any extra care to be kind, helpful, or friendly. It is a most wonderful and beautiful experience. I hope that it carries on throughout my life.[5]

Another development has been the belated participation of Catholics in ecumenical ventures. The Catholic Church has observer status in the SACC, and some Catholics work in various offices of the organization.

The chief organizer of Durban's interfaith, interracial Diakonia was a White layman, Paddy Kearney. Later he shared that responsibility with a Black coorganizer, Thami Dumisa. Diakonia represents eight member churches and its interracial staff, though small, has done some far-reaching work. It has published dramatic yet objective reports on the situation in the homelands, forceful statements on bannings and detentions, illustrated accounts of family life among Black migrant workers, and vivid descriptions of squatter camps. It has also sponsored workshops on a variety of topics ranging from conscientious objection to action that Christians can take to combat the rising unemployment among Blacks.

Diakonia is action-oriented: it has sponsored self-employment schemes, for example, organized deputations to the Durban city council to urge specific employment projects, and suggested ways that church buildings might be shared, or used to provide facilities in Black townships.

In the last decade the Catholic hierarchy has spoken out more decisively on conditions among migrant laborers, the need for simpler lifestyles among both laity and clergy, and the duty of the church to demonstrate its solidarity with the poor and deprived.

Although the Catholic Church has moved forward, a great many problems lie ahead. From the right has come a White backlash, most evident in the Catholic Defense League, a lily-White organization similar to McCarthyite groups in the United States during the 1950s. The SACBC has unequivocally criticized the League's attacks on bishops, its endeavors to influence overseas opinion, and its tactics of equating concern for social justice with communism. Such a stand has few parallels in the Catholic world, for in general the church has been reluctant to disown rightist elements in its own ranks.

From progressives—especially those who are Black—has come insistence on Africanization of the church. To them the fact that 85 percent of the bishops and 90 percent of the clergy are White in a church over 75 percent Black, is proof of latent paternalism, even racism. South Africa also relies heavily on White foreign-born "expatriates" for filling religious vocations, they point out. These persons are often deeply dedicated, yet a vast "experience gap" separates them from Africans.

Progressives are acutely aware too that in other African nations the process of indigenization has gone much further. Seventy-five percent of the Catholic bishops, and ten of the twelve cardinals on the continent are African.

The sheer weight of demographic change also spells future shifts in the relative power of Whites and persons of color. In his best-selling *The Coming of the Third Church,*[6] Swiss theologian Walbert Bühlmann points out that whereas in 1960 51.5 percent of Catholics lived in North America and Europe, and 48.5 percent in Africa, Latin America, Asia, and Oceania, by A.D. 2000 the proportion will change radically. In that year only 30 percent of Catholics will be living in North America and Europe; 70 percent will be citizens of the Third World. And the Third Church, says Bühlmann, is flourishing, especially in countries where the demographic explosion is massive (as in Latin America) and in those where the number of newly baptized is greater (as in Africa).

Bühlmann spent several weeks in South Africa in 1979, and we had the opportunity for a long conversation with him. The Black priests he had talked to felt that they were not fully accepted, and that the hierarchy rarely asked their advice, he confided. This was a tragic state of affairs, especially in light of the fact that it was so difficult to get Blacks to take up priestly vocations.

To Bühlmann, the best way to promote the gospel was by means of "basic Christian communities"—small groups of laypersons who gather, with or without the help of a priest, to study the Bible, relate a passage of Scripture to their own lives, and decide what they can do to act on the gospel. In the Latin American countries such groups are viewed by many bishops as the principal impetus for evangelization and social change in the coming decade, and more than a hundred thousand basic communities are said to be active there.

In Africa, said Bühlmann, they have scarcely begun. However, a number have sprung up in Angola and Mozambique in spite of—or because of—the fact that Marxists have taken control of many church institutions. In South Africa, said Bühlmann, two basic Christian communities are functioning, in an informal way. The Lumku Missiological Institute, for instance, is promoting gospel neighborhood groups, and in East London an interracial interdenominational community is flourishing.

A model for the future, Bühlmann felt, would be to create five to ten basic communities in every parish. Such communities should be multiracial and even interdenominational whenever possible. Already thousands of them across the world were being led by married leaders who did the real work. Bühlmann looked forward to the day when married persons could be ordained to the priesthood, in order to give to the many basic Christian communities the chance to have the eucharistic celebration.

Interview with Peter Butelezi

One of the most significant signs of moving toward Africanization was the appointment of the first Black South African Archbishop in 1978. Peter Fanyana John Butelezi is no radical, however. Since taking office, he has seemed anxious to pursue a noncontroversial approach. Whites tend to be pleased. Many Blacks, however, are impatient. One African priest, for example, says "Butelezi's an organization man. He is *White*."

The position, of course, is an onerous one, made doubly difficult by the fact that he was appointed to Bloemfontein, the capital of the Orange Free State, "the heart of Afrikanerdom." Even today, a great many Afrikaners retain a traditional suspicion of Catholics.

Butelezi was born in 1930, received his primary education at a mission school in the impoverished township of Alexandra, joined the Oblates of Mary Immaculate, and was ordained a priest in Rome in 1957. After several teaching and administrative posts, he became Auxiliary Bishop of Johannesburg in 1972. A scholar, Butelezi speaks twelve languages.

Today he lives in an elegant mansion surrounded by stately trees, medleys of tropical flowers, and green lawns carefully tended by Black servants—in an exclusively White residential area. Indeed, his address is 9 Whites (*sic*) Road. He is served by a White secretary, and a German-born nun who refers deferentially to Butelezi as "His Grace."

Butelezi welcomed us warmly into his simple, functionally furnished office. He is a short, rotund man, with balding hair, large horn-rimmed glasses, and a perpetual smile. After an exchange of pleasantries, we asked why he thought he was chosen for this post. He laughed, a bit self-consciously: "I don't know—I wasn't consulted." Then, in his slow easy way, he added that he had done "a bit of pioneering work" by becoming, in 1972, the first Black bishop in an urban area. "Also, they realized they couldn't put just anybody in such a tense position—they didn't want him to crack up."

It *could* be stressful for a pioneer, he pointed out—to be the first Black archbishop, to be the first Black in this segregated suburb, to minister to White expatriate priests plagued by insecurity as Black Africans talk of autonomy. Yet he had faced no profound problems.

"What changes have you instituted here?"

"Changes?" He looked a little surprised at the question. "The big change is just my *being* here. Last Christmas I got a card from the State President. And from the Administrator of the Province. I'm a patron of the school of the Christian Brothers—which has only White children. I attend parent-teacher meetings in White schools. I run White parishes when priests are away.

"My presence is accepted by banks. White visitors bring me cake. White couples are coming with personal problems or problems in their children's marriages. I've even been asked to write a series of noncontroversial articles for a column called 'Weekend Thought' in the local English-language newspaper. It was an attempt to introduce me to the public and see how their readers would take it. Well, they've taken it very well."

"What changes would you *like* to see?" we asked. "Changes in education or labor conditions, for example?"

"Well," he answered slowly, "The schools are a complicated question. Catholics *have* opened their schools to Blacks. But even with Catholics it's a controversial issue. Some Blacks ask, 'Shouldn't we improve our present Black schools instead of putting a few Black pupils into private schools?' Others say, 'If our children go into these schools, won't this give them a White version of South African history?' It is a complicated question. As for labor, well, universities are doing research on this question. We must have the right information."

When we brought up Black theology, Butelezi showed little interest in the topic. It has its "positive points," he said, but some Whites felt it excluded them.

As for supporting the 1979 SACC resolution to refrain from cooperating with the state in areas where the law violates the justice demanded by God, it was "only a resolution—it must be discussed by the parish." Was he suggesting such discussion? "Well, that is difficult—one might do better to point out the *danger* inherent in continuing an unjust situation. Besides, it is illegal to resist in South Africa." Then suddenly he began to speak with more passion. "In America you are dealing with Christians. Here, with people who have no conscience. They would be prepared to kill five or six million people—even if it means suicide!"

Later we witnessed an elaborate ceremony in which Butelezi was given the pallium, in the modern cathedral of Bloemfontein. His address made no mention of suffering, or of hope for better race relations. He did not even refer to "Blacks." Such omissions Butelezi defends on the grounds that the Catholic Church is multiracial, and cannot think in terms of Blacks and Whites.

Most radical Blacks, of course, do not agree. On the other hand, many observers would call this a truly Catholic—and catholic—viewpoint. They would add that considering the "tense position" in which history has thrust Peter Butelezi, he may well be the right man at the right time, and one who will make a rough path easier for more revolutionary clerics to follow.

Interview with Stephen Naidoo

Butelezi's viewpoint is shared by many other South African clerics—among them Stephen Naidoo, an Indian who has become auxiliary bishop of the Archdiocese of Cape Town and vice-president of the SACBC.

Unlike many of his fellow South African Indians, Naidoo identifies himself as "Black." Actually, he is as dark as any African, for his forebears are Dravidians from southern India. He is a tall, well-built man with smooth skin and flashing, expressive eyes. His voice is gentle but it has a compelling quality. We sensed that this man, already widely respected among Protestants as well as Catholics, was destined to rise in the hierarchy.

Bishop Naidoo stressed that he experienced no problems in being accepted as a Black bishop. He did a great deal of public speaking before civic groups, in order to "build bridges." He also made a special point of going to a different parish each week in order to spend twenty-four hours with the priest; White as well as Black priests seemed to appreciate this. In the community, too, he had usually found a warm response. For example, after giving confirmation at a school for White girls, he had received a letter saying, "We love you, and want to give you all support possible." The girls did not have to write that letter, he pointed out.

The kind of change that Naidoo envisioned in the church was far from radical. Although he believed in the idea of basic communities of Christians working and sharing and forging links with communities, he felt that the leaders must have theological training. Because there was a shortage of vocations, the best way to accomplish this was to train deacons. He had "serious reservations," however, about ordaining women. He added, "We do need changes in the liturgy. For example, we should use indigenous languages more. And introducing African song would help Christians experience the reality that South African society is a multiracial one.

"In fact, we need to change the mentality of the people through cross-fertilization in various ways. I've thought a great deal about this, and I can't envision South Africa under a policy of separate development, or even the federation some liberals propose. The capitalist system that the Whites want to hold onto requires Black laborers, for example. I can't see any other kind of government but a unitary one. We'll need *real* labor unions, and the White factory-owner will have to learn to talk with his workers. This kind of understanding will bring about more sharing. And sharing materially, culturally, and spiritually will enable a South African liturgy to evolve."

Interview with Lebamang Sebidi

Lebamang Sebidi is not so sanguine that a "liturgy" can evolve so easily and peacefully. Together with a few other South African Catholic priests—

both Black and White—Sebidi is critical of the church's Western approach and its acceptance of the capitalist value system. Hence he sees Butelezi and Naidoo as "bureaucrats."

Sebidi's rebellion finally culminated in his leaving the priesthood—a rather common occurrence today. As Sebidi puts it, "I am just one among the legions. But I continue to be a practicing Catholic." Although the precipitating cause for his decision was a desire to marry, the latent cause was a long-simmering discontent with the institutional church.

For several years Sebidi was one of the leading priests at Regina Mundi, the Soweto cathedral (officially opened by Paul VI in 1963 when he was Cardinal Archbishop of Milan) that has been the scene of massive "prayer" meetings. Sebidi's quietly forceful manner and credibility with the young also led him to be invited into the Soweto Committee of Ten, the voice for Black demands in the volatile township. Three Catholics—Sebidi, young Black consciousness leader Tom Manthata, and Leonard Mosala, husband of SACC official Bernadette Mosala—have been serving on the Committee. Another Catholic, *Post* editor Percy Qoboza, has been called the Committee's "invisible godfather."

Born in 1939, Sebidi is a stocky, bearded man with an open manner, dry sense of humor, and bright eyes that seem to be sizing you up. When we met him in 1979, a few months before his decision to leave the priesthood, he was a course writer for the Theological Education by Extension College in Johannesburg.

We knew that from 1976 until late 1977 he had been rector of a major seminary, St. Peter's at Hammanskraal. The problems he incurred there with his all-White staff drove him to seek the support of Black priests. When the White staff sought the support of the hierarchy, almost 90 percent White, more Black-White confrontations followed. We asked him to tell us more about his troubles. He explained, "Over a year after my first conflicts with the White hierarchy, I helped form the Black Priests Solidarity Group. In October '77 all Black organizations were banned. The only organization left was the church. I'd become president of the solidarity group, and, together with several Protestant clergymen, we walked to John Vorster Square in our robes, carrying Bibles. We were charged under the Riotous Assemblies Act. Bibles are riotous here!

"A month later I was ousted from the rectorship. One bishop said candidly that they wanted a 'cultic clergy,' not a politically-minded one! A deeper cause for my removal is that South African Whites in both civil society and the church are domination crazy. 'Independent thinking' among Blacks goes against the grain of Whites: it contradicts their stereotyped image of a grinning Black, flat-footed and with big slappy hands. So one just has to 'think' and bang! You get it on the navel!"

Urged on by our questions, Sebidi expanded on the need for Africanization of the church. "In South Africa most Catholic priests are foreigners. Also, they can't even live in the Black areas they serve. If I say they don't understand Blacks, especially our feeling that there's little distinction between the 'religious' and the 'political,' it's not a criticism, but a statement of fact.

"These categorizations are Western. The whole church structure is Western. Like the need for money. They spend thousands of rands on hundreds of conferences, arguing about schools, evangelization, or what not—and far less on the *people*. I hardly need to comment on the investments and great tracts of land owned by the church.

"The African independent churches, which have grown so phenomenally in the past decades, get along without money. Most don't have a church building—or else they build it themselves. Ministers receive scarcely a stipend—they have regular jobs during the week. There's a far greater sense of belonging among members of these churches.

"We as Blacks don't have the resources to maintain an elaborate institution like the Catholic Church. So a subtle pressure is put upon us to make us dependent, and 'hold' us if we try to be recalcitrant."

The South African hierarchy has been criticized for not standing up strongly for expatriate priests expelled by the government, and we asked Sebidi to comment on this. He sighed, "Of course it *is* true that the church is in a bind, because a foreign priest needs to get permission from the government—every six months—to stay. But this demonstrates that we shouldn't be dependent on foreign clergy. And the great trouble with the Catholic Church is that it's more concerned with organization than with individuals."

Sebidi was particularly critical of training for young priests. "It's unreal. Training can take up to eight years! And they deliberately put St. Peter's [Seminary] hundreds of miles out in the bush. Seminarians can't integrate with the community when they return. It's like training a soldier in a hothouse. And why? Because of the celibacy rule. Which is nonsensical—for White or Black. When Cosmas Desmond married, he was judged on that single point. We lost an excellent man. They should be trained in Soweto or a big urban university. Actually, if the church changed on celibacy, that would change everything else."

"What else would you like to change in the church?" we asked.

"Women should definitely be allowed in the priesthood. And the church should engage in Marxist-Christian dialogue. Marxism makes a real critique of Christianity. It wouldn't exist if Christianity were what it should be. We always look at the atheistic element in Marxism, but it's not basic—it's something said in passing. The Latin American church has discovered this—and in the future Black theology will, too. Even though it's against the law to discuss Marxism!"

"And how do you see the future of Catholicism?"

"Basic communities!" Sebidi responded. "That's the church of tomorrow! Right now the form and rules of the church come from Rome, which is only a political structure. What do we need? Not conglomerations of individuals like the 'congregation' at Regina Mundi, but smaller groups of individuals whom we can call by name. We need spontaneity and latitude for incorporat-

ing African traditions. Some Blacks might want music and drums and dancing, like many African independent churches. But others might prefer guitars
or piano, for example. There are different levels of sophistication. In all of
this, there's a continual dynamism."

Labor Problems and the YCW

Catholic leaders are more and more aware that apartheid is rooted in racial
prejudice, but even more deeply in the tenacity of Whites to maintain political supremacy and economic privilege. The need for cheap labor leads to
exploitation and division. Paradoxically, this need renders true "apart-ness"
impossible, because the "South African way of life" depends on an abundance of docile cheap labor. For its part, the government is increasingly
aware that unity among Black workers could become its nemesis—hence its
suspicion of anything that could be construed as an independent labor movement.

Even the Young Christian Workers have been subject to persecution.
Within ten weeks in 1978, for example, thirty members of the group were
detained by South African authorities. In only four of the cases were charges
brought. After detentions ranging from one to over fifty days, the other
prisoners were released—with no apologies—probably in response to the solidarity demonstrations staged all over the world. The four brought to trial
were convicted on various charges of violence, charges considered so far-
fetched by the YCW and the youths' parents that they embarked on a long,
expensive appeal process.

The YCW is an international movement founded in Belgium in 1925 by
Father Joseph Cardijn for working-class youth. Using the formula "see-
judge-act," its members try to improve their own and their colleagues' working conditions.

In South Africa the YCW numbers less than a thousand members, con-
fines itself to youths sixteen to thirty, has received the pope's blessing, does
not preach revolution, and does not engage in labor organizing as such. Yet
the authorities perceive it as a threat. Why?

Although the YCW has not organized unions or advocated strikes, it does
attempt to make people aware of what is due them. For example, many
workers are afraid to stand up to employers who fail to send to the government that portion of their wages withheld for unemployment compensation.
YCW members (most of whom are African or Colored) inspire their co-
workers to confront the boss in such a situation. They might also encourage
maids to ask "madam" for a raise. Many YCW members later become active
in trade union or community work. In the words of Father Gerard de
Fleuriot, national YCW chaplain, "This is a youth movement, not a political
organization. Of course we do have a certain social vision. But to ask employers to apply the law—is this subversive?"

Interviews with Gerard de Fleuriot

On both our visits to South Africa, we met with Father Gerard in the run-down communal house he shares with several YCW members in a run-down fringe neighborhood of Durban. We had heard that de Fleuriot had been the object of verbal attacks from rightists, and that one of them had pointed a gun at the priest's head and fired. The assailant, however, was drunk, and had forgotten to load the weapon.

De Fleuriot shrugged off the incident when we asked him about it. And he struck us as a tough man. Although the lines of his forehead spelled weariness, his heavy build, muscular arms, square jaw, and clipped speech conveyed bulletproof determination.

In the same vein, he shrugged off the fact that he was born into an old aristocratic family on the formerly French island of Mauritius. De Fleuriot seemed more interested in talking about his struggle to build up the YCW since his arrival in South Africa, in 1968. During these years, we learned, he also engaged in running seminars on labor issues, editing a bulletin called *Church and Industry,* and writing articles, pamphlets, and a book on the social teachings of the church. As we listened to the accounts of his activities, and of the ongoing harassment he has suffered, we could begin to understand the constant strain of de Fleuriot's life.

He told us, "What makes the YCW different is that it focuses on small groups of six to eight persons, it's largely decentralized, and leadership comes from the workers themselves, not 'educated' leaders. Also we start with *life,* not an idea. 'What have you seen and experienced in your own situation?' we ask each other. We compare, then judge. Finally, *we act.* So the 'problem' of each group may be different.

"This year we are spending several months on a national issue—health. Health at home, at work, in the township. Last year, although the international solidarity campaign did result in the release of detainees, the noise we made inside the country scared off many members, and even more of their parents. The health issue, however, is so important that it's brought back old members and drawn new ones. We've also asked other organizations, like the Christian Life groups, and parish youth clubs, to join us.

"The health problem is staggering. Every year there are at least two thousand fatal accidents and three hundred thousand injuries at work out of a total working population of twelve or thirteen million. Many factories have filthy toilets. In some Black townships sewage disposal hardly exists."

One evening de Fleuriot took us to a YCW meeting in a tiny home in a Colored township of Durban. Four young men and two young women had gathered to share their experiences, in a discussion interspersed with laughter and occasional flirtatious glances. One youth was inhaling dangerous fumes at work, for example. Another cited lack of safety devices. Gradually, too, it became clear that some members were afraid of wearing a T-shirt proclaiming "We Want Healthy Working Conditions." When de Fleuriot asked if there was a parallel between putting on that T-shirt and putting on Christ, a lively religious discussion ensued.

Later Father Gerard observed, "We're training leaders to make use of Scripture. Christian theology is *explosive,* because of the demands it makes." Then he smiled slowly. "But it is also a security. Some of our leaders have successfully replied to interrogation—they've proved that what they did was Christian. Yes, *sometimes* that can even stop the courts and the security police."

Notes

1. Letter from Fr. Scholten, O.P., secretary general of the South African Catholic Bishops Conference. We should add that the Nationalist government restricted immigration of Roman Catholics in the sixties, especially Italians, Greeks, and Portuguese. With the fall of the Portuguese colonies of Mozambique and Angola, many White Portuguese colonialists fled to South Africa. Most live in ethnic ghettos and work at menial jobs. Immigration policy since 1950 in RSA was not unlike that of the United States in the 1920s when restrictions were placed on southern Europeans as well as other non-WASPS.

2. *South Africa Yearbook 1978* (Pretoria: Department of Information, 1979), p. 358.

3. The composition of the hierarchy in South Africa has lagged behind that of Zimbabwe, where Blacks have taken control. It was the Black archbishop of Salisbury who blessed the inaugural ceremonies of Prime Minister Robert Mugabe, a Marxist revolutionary and pious Catholic. For many years Black and White Rhodesian Catholics were highly critical of the White minority government, and they paid the price for it. The Mambo Press was bombed, for example, and American-born Sister Janice McLaughlin and Irish-born Donal Lamont, the bishop of Umtali, were exiled for their active identification with the liberation of Blacks.

4. Conversations with Archbishop Hurley of Durban and Father Scholten, secretary general of the SACBC, Pretoria.

5. *Star* (airmail, weekly ed.), May 26, 1979, p. 14.

6. Walbert Bühlmann, *The Coming of the Third Church: An Analysis of the Present and Future of the Church* (Maryknoll, N.Y.: Orbis Books, 1977).

CHAPTER FIFTEEN

The Dutch Reformed Churches

I—THE NGK

In the past decade a ferment has been growing in the Dutch Reformed churches. The most dramatic and visible movement has occurred in the "daughter churches" (now often called "sister churches")—the Nederduitse Gereformeerde Sendingkerk (NGSK; Dutch Reformed Mission Church, for Coloreds), the Nederduitse Gereformeerde Kerk in Afrika (NGKA, for Africans), and the Reformed Church in Africa (RCA, for Indians).[1]

Although change has been far less marked in the White "mother church," dynamic tension exists between *verligte* ("enlightened") and *verkrampte* ("closed-minded") leaders, reflecting the *verligte-verkrampte* cleavage in government circles. The latter are hard-liners on the issue of separate development. Generally speaking the *verligte* do not seek radical solutions; they tend to accept the framework of separate development, within which they hope to evolve a more humane treatment of the Blacks. More pragmatic than the *verkrampte,* they believe that negotiation and compromise are necessary, and are apt to favor abolition of the Immorality Act, the Prohibition of Mixed Marriages Act, and job reservation.

That the *verlig* element in the church has not been strong may prove tragic for the Afrikaners themselves. The White Nederduitse Gereformeerde Kerk (NGK; DRC, Dutch Reformed Church), with 42 percent of the White population, has enormous potential; if it were moved to take a truly active part in social change, change would come.

Such power, of course, rests on the importance of religion in Afrikaners' lives, and on the White NGK's close links to the state. It is ironic that the NGK criticizes the multiracial churches for violating Christian principles by involving themselves in politics, because it continually takes stands on political issues and engages in activities of a political nature. In the past the NGK has played a key role in winning acceptance for the view that there is no fundamental contradiction between Christian principles and apartheid. Today it carries on a steady campaign against the World Council of Churches as a "communist front organization," and publishes photos in *DRC Africa News* of "communist weapons" said to be recovered from "terrorists" who are "sponsored" by the WCC. It continued to attack the Christian Institute even after the Institute was banned.

NGK *verkrampte* use blatantly political arguments, as one did when he advised defeat of a synodal resolution that "might put the government in a very difficult position." Even more significant is the fact that 60 to 70 percent of the White NGK ministers are members of the Broederbond,[2] the secret society that has played such an instrumental role in Afrikaner politics. Perhaps the most telling example of church-state ties—one that shocked many NGK adherents themselves—was the secret donation by a government department of $180,000 to the NGK, which used the money to set up an "ecumenical affairs bureau."

The White NGK takes the official position that the New Testament accepts the fact of the diversity of peoples, which may give rise to a diversity of indigenous churches. However, this should be seen as a diversity within the one church. Hence the NGK is divided into ethnically oriented churches that are theoretically autonomous. They are linked together, however, in a Federal Council of NG churches with advisory powers.

Such a structure has helped to insulate Whites from hearing and understanding the aspirations of Africans, Indians, and Coloreds who share the same confession of faith. Even in the early 1970s the Afrikaans churches and the government confidently pointed to the membership of their "daughter" churches to support their contention that "our non-White peoples themselves want and appreciate apartheid." Ironically, that apartness has created its own contradiction: it has helped foment a concerted rebellion among the "daughters."

The White NGK is also isolated from the multiracial churches; in general it has spurned their initiatives to establish ecumenical contacts on a national level. (A few Afrikaans-speaking clerics join their English-speaking counterparts in local ministers' fraternals.)

Finally, the White NGK is isolated from the rest of the world. For example, the Afrikaners' obsessive hatred for the WCC is rooted in the sincere belief that as a bulwark of reformed Christianity, committed foes of atheistic communism, and agents of Western civilization on a continent seeking models of development, they should receive the thanks, rather than the wrath, of Western Christians.[3] In 1970 Dr. J. D. "Koot" Vorster, then Moderator of the NGK, told the church synod that the WCC was "not a church of God, but a church of the revolution." In an article in the *DRC Newsletter* Vorster declared that "in 1966 the Communist Party in the United States made a ten-year plan according to which 'A Church of World Brotherhood' would be brought into existence by 1970, as an integral part of a Soviet-oriented world government."[4]

The WCC is credited with introducing innocent South Africans to evil ideas, for most Afrikaners sincerely believe that it is not possible for honest Christians—unless they are misled by foreign agitators—to come to conclusions at variance with the official positions of the NGK and the government. "Liberalism" of almost any kind is considered subversive and evil.

Some, though by no means all, Afrikaners view Black theology as inspired by foreign elements. Thus the Schlebusch Commission asserted that "in the propaganda for a Black theology, the American social gospel is carried through to its logical conclusions."[5]

Even in the world fellowship of churches of its own faith, the NGK has persisted as a lone voice in the wilderness. At the 1972 Reformed Ecumenical Synod held in Sydney, Australia, the South African delegates of the NGK prepared a resolution approving the establishment of separate churches for different racial groups, but upholding the principle that no one may be excluded from worship on grounds of race. The synod deleted the first phrase, "the existence of different churches for different indigenous race groups must be accepted," on the grounds that this would constitute approval of apartheid in the churches, and replaced it with "even though different churches for different race groups may exist, no person may be excluded from worship on grounds of race."[6]

Ongoing tension with the "mother" Reformed Church in Holland culminated in the rupture of traditional ties. By 1974 conflict had broken out over the decision of the Dutch synod to support the WCC's Program to Combat Racism. That decision was not rescinded, and at its 1978 synod the South African NGK declared that it now regarded "the close bond which existed between us and the [Netherlands DRC] as severed."[7] All these differences illustrate a point made by Regehr: "The White Afrikaans Reformed churches are wrongly characterized as a conservative force; they are a *radical* force that rejects tradition, challenges the collective wisdom of the international church, and amends dogma to suit social and political conditions."[8]

Some Steps Forward

Despite these signs of intransigence and continuing cultural, ethnic, political, and spiritual isolation, the NGK has taken a few steps toward *verligtheid*. At its 1974 synod it officially rejected a theological rationale for racism. A report by the Landman Commission stressed that Scripture never used the term "race" in its modern scientific sense, that there is no parallel between the situation of Israel in the Old Testament and modern social questions, and that the Old Testament knows of no superior or inferior races.[9]

Although formally rejecting racism, that synod upheld a "theology of differentiation." It declared that the scattering at Babel was God's method of maintaining human diversity, and Scripture did indeed teach the essential unity of mankind, but this unity was a spiritual unity and need not be reflected in political, social, or ecclesiastical structures.

Hence the ambiguous stand on racially mixed worship. When *verligte* Professor Ben Marais proposed that all church councils open their doors to mixed worship, the move was defeated by a hugh majority. The synod agreed to leave the decision to local church councils, which would act in light of considerations of good order and peace. In practice this has generally meant that occasional "joint services" do occur, but arrangements are difficult.

Blacks are usually not allowed to worship in White churches without prior permission, although Whites are free to worship in Black churches at any time—provided they have a permit to enter a Black area. In White suburbs, where many Blacks live in separate one-room servants' quarters behind their masters' home, the only facilities for public worship may be in garages, because use of White churches by Blacks, even in segregated services, is not acceptable to most White church members. Despite criticisms, a few NGK pastors have insisted on opening their church halls and even their sanctuaries to Blacks. By 1978 the general synod of the NGK had finally come to the conclusion that White churches are free to allow Blacks to attend special services such as weddings and funerals.

Since 1974 the growing rebellion among the "daughter" churches has spurred some NGK leaders to express dissent more openly. A few have engaged in consultation with Black urban leaders, or resigned from the Broederbond, or spoken out against specific legislation such as pass laws. Others have gone so far as to declare the whole structure of apartheid immoral.

Stirrings in the Universities

Many religiously oriented Afrikaner university students seem to be groping for new directions. For example, the Afrikaanse Studentebond (ASB) —founded in 1948 as an organization for Afrikaner students, with a "Christian-national" basis—has become somewhat more progressive. It has talked of reaching out to all Christian brothers and sisters regardless of race,[10] has undertaken studies on controversial topics such as racism and Afrikaner identity, and has even advocated that the Crossroads community not be demolished. The studies have fallen short of recommending power-sharing on an equal basis, however, and sharp differences of opinion emerge at every congress on conclusions reached by them.

In 1977 it was a group of theological students and professors that raised the most explosive Afrikaner challenge to apartheid. It is interesting that this statement, the Koinonia Declaration, emanated not from DRC members, but from some members of the Gereformeerde Kerk (the Doppers), the smallest of the three White Afrikaans churches and also the most theologically conservative. Paradoxically, it is their puritanism that spurs Doppers to stand up for their beliefs, even against the government, when they become convinced that a policy is un-Christian.

The Koinonia Declaration was produced by members of a Calvinist study group called The Loft, located in Germiston (a group that included a few DRC and Presbyterian Calvinists), and a number of students and professors from the Doppers' Potchefstroom University for Christian Higher Education. Other signers included two NGKA pastors and a progressive White DRC theologian, Professor David Bosch. The declaration, a thorough attempt to apply Christian principles to the South African political situation, declared that apartheid could not be justified in terms of Calvinist doctrine, condemned certain aspects of government policy (especially security laws and the Immorality Act) in strong terms, and called for equal political and economic opportunities for all races.

The declaration was warmly received by several English-speaking churches and became an official study document of the United Congregational Church. The response of the Gereformeerde Kerk and the DRC was negative, however. It also sent an electric chill through government circles. Prime Minister Vorster and Minister of Police Jimmy Kruger even went to Potchefstroom and pleaded with the signers: "Why didn't you dialogue with us first? We are brothers!" Eventually most of the professors who had signed the statement resigned or recanted.

Out of this group, however, emerged the nucleus of a new group, the multiracial Reformational Africa Studies Program, which included members not only of the Dutch Reformed family, but of other Reformed denominations as well. A program was set up to study and apply God's word to the judicial, political, economic, social, and ecclesiastical spheres of the South African situation through research and action. Perhaps because it was interracial, some of its younger members were not only working but living together, and it was publishing a provocative magazine, the group was pressured to disband.

Stellenbosch is a three-hundred-year-old town where one can wander down quiet streets, visit homes built in the graceful old Cape Dutch style, and sip wines from local vineyards. It is also the site of the oldest Afrikaner institution of higher learning, Stellenbosch University, the "Harvard and Yale" of the Afrikaners. Six of the country's eight prime ministers were educated here, graduates have been prominent in every field, and professors have served on a variety of government panels and commissions.

By American standards the polite, clean-shaven, neatly dressed men and women students are a sedate lot. Yet in 1980, when Prime Minister Botha reacted stuffily and evasively to students' questions about racial policies, he met hisses and boos—a rare happening in a society inculcating "respect for authority." More recently, Black political leaders such as Ntatho Motlana have been invited to the campus for the first time. A recent study also revealed that while 54 percent of the students polled said they would die to uphold White rule if necessary, 43 percent said they would not.[11]

It is possible that the ferment at the university that played a central role in evolving the ideology of apartheid will lead efforts to move Afrikaners away from it.[12] If so, students and faculty at Stellenbosch's famed theological school will play a leading role. An account of our visit there may furnish some insight into the conflicting ways NGK Whites perceive social change.

We were entertained by a theology student (whom we shall call Hermann) and his wife, and were joined by another theology student. Over a simple lunch in the couple's book-lined apartment, all three expressed their frustration with the conservatism in the church. Together with eighty other Stellenbosch seminarians and a few professors, they had attended the South African Christian Leadership Assembly (SACLA), a "moving experience"; they had been "amazed at the love between the races." Hence it was disheartening for them to witness the opposition to SACLA from many Dutch Reformed circles.

After the Assembly the group created occasions where members of different races could communicate on a purely social level. One of the theology professors, Professor Nico Smith, was called before the Curatorium[13] for suggesting in a sermon that such communication was a necessity for Christian fellowship. Also the church council of the local congregation where he preached took up the matter with him. It eventually seemed that no theological heresy could be proved against him and nothing came of the inquest. He kept his convictions in this regard.

After describing arguments with one of his professors, Hermann suggested that he might be able to introduce us to him. An hour later the professor welcomed us warmly into his spacious, tastefully furnished home.

The persisting point of contention between the younger man and his instructor was the latter's failure to demonstrate to Hermann that there was a genuine difference in point of view between the NGK and the state. After the professor had spent considerable time in explaining pre-Cottesloe NGK history, we also asked him to clarify the difference. "We have a partnership with the government," he conceded. "The government came forth out of the church." Then he added quickly, "Very early we in the DRC talked of positive and constructive segregation. There must be a means of constructing a society in which these people are on their own. But when this was built into a political policy, a Christian sense was not always applied."

When Hermann asked why the government had not been constructive, his professor replied that the government always had to please the voters: "One must remember that the Nationalists got in with a very small majority. The man in the street believed in an apartheid that was not always Christianly motivated."

What did the church do to correct this? "Well, it took time to sort this out. On certain issues a church deputation will go to the authorities concerned and ask for an interview." After admitting that this rarely occurred, the professor pointed to the "distance" between church and state on the "immorality" issue: "We say immorality lies not only in illicit relations between Black and White, but also between Black and Black, and White and White."

When asked for more concrete examples, the professor declared that today the NGK no longer considered a ban on mixed marriages to be good theology.

"We would not go for general sanctification, but we would allow for exceptions—if the parties came from the same culture."

Later he added, "Twenty-five years ago the church would not have hesitated to read its view into Scripture. Today the church is extremely sensitive to biblical interpretations of social issues. Today we are moved to more critical considerations. Take the Day of the Covenant, for example. Lately, it has been studied again and the question has been raised, 'Haven't we perhaps mythologized it too much?'"

The professor was committed to the homelands policy, and was firmly convinced that most urban Blacks wanted to return to their "tribal traditions"—hence to their homelands as well. "One person, one vote" was "completely impractical."

He saw himself as part of a growing "mediating group" between the conservatives and the *verligte*. "But the masses are uneasy," he added. "They are looking to leaders who can lead them in the old ways, conservatives whom they feel they can trust. Many church members feel we are going too fast."

Afterward Hermann sighed. "He really believes that part of the church is moving too fast!"

Dr. David Bosch, professor of missiology at the University of South Africa, sums up five characteristics of the NGK's response to racism and revolution: (1) a conviction of a manifest destiny, (2) a mystical identification with the people of Israel, (3) the idea of a "missionary calling" to other "less privileged" races—a call now being extended to include defending "White Christian civilization," (4) maintaining the purity of the Afrikaner people, and (5) a positivistic attitude to law, a tendency to regard prevailing circumstances as inevitable because they have been willed by God. (For example, a long report by the 1974 General Synod contained a devastating diagnosis of some fruits of racial segregation, such as the homelands policy, but no suggestion whatsoever that the cause of this might be found in the laws themselves.)[14] These factors help explain the internal conflict, and the continuing resistance within the DRC to meaningful change.

On the one hand, there are signs of liberalization (in addition to those already described). Ex-Prime Minister Vorster's brother Koot Vorster, the archconservative whose "awesome visage and stentorian tones made his listeners shiver" (in the words of one DRC member), retired in 1979 from his post as Moderator of the White church, and his successors seem to pursue somewhat less hard a line. A number of DRC leaders have called on the church to return the money received from the Ministry of Information. At the 1978 general synod the DRC declared mixed marriages to be "highly undesirable" rather than "not permissible."

The NGK has become more open to discussion with other churches. For example, it has participated in a meeting with other South African Reformed churches, attended a conference on social justice under the auspices of the

World Alliance of Reformed Churches, met with representatives of the German Reformed Federation, and participated in a consultation with the Swiss Federation of Protestant Churches.

The *DRC Africa News* has begun to include articles on controversial matters such as the churchmen's demonstration over John Thorne's detention, and has even published accounts of SACC meetings.

On the other hand, the ongoing agonized discussions over "reconsidering" the Immorality Act and the Prohibition of Mixed Marriages Act have been interspersed with backtracking on relatively progressive statements. The result has been widespread confusion, and bitterness among the three "daughter" churches. Discussions with other churches seem to have resulted in no real agreement; in virtually every case NGK and NHK delegations have refused to subscribe to majority conclusions. The NGK synod has also rejected proposals by the Federal Council that the latter be changed into a general synod for all four churches. The Whites' rejection seems based on fear of the numerical superiority of "daughter" church members, who in 1978 numbered 1,800,000, as compared with 1,500,000 NGK Whites.

Is the NGK a force for social change? At least one group of studies suggests that the most regular NGK churchgoers are those with the greatest racial prejudice.[15] Perhaps the most accurate conclusion is that the situation is becoming increasingly polarized between *verligte* and *verkrampte*. The "average" White DRC member probably perceives the church as Koot Vorster does—as the "last bastion of the Afrikaner."[16]

II—THE NGKA

For many years Africans of the Nederduitse Gereformeerde Kerk in Afrika (NGKA) were looked upon with suspicion by their fellow Blacks, not only because they seemed to support apartheid, but also because of widespread belief that they were given preferential treatment by government officials. By the mid-1970s that image had changed drastically: the "daughter" churches—especially the NGKA—were asserting that they were no longer tied to the apron strings of their "mother."

The first act of defiance came in 1973, when one hundred Black ministers of the NGKA held a consultation on the theme "A Theology of Development and the Independence of the NGKA." They announced their total rejection of the "un-Christian" policy of apartheid. That declaration shocked the White church and sparked angry rebukes from some of its leaders. The Black ministers, however, stuck to their guns, and a month later issued a second statement insisting that "we should obey God rather than men," but also stressing that "the opposition must avoid all forms of violence or bloodshed."[17]

In the following year, a number of NGKA "rebels" were instrumental in forming the Broederkring, a group of comparatively radical ministers and laypersons from the three "daughter" churches, including a few White ministers (mostly ministers in "daughter" churches). By 1975, when the NGKA held its quadrennial synod at Worcester, the Broederkring and others dissatisfied with the status quo had garnered enough power to convince the synod to pass resolutions attacking detention without trial and demanding unity among the divided members of the NGK family.

The synod also resolved to eliminate tribal divisions in NGKA seminaries and to make English the medium of instruction. NGKA seminaries had been following the NGK policy of using Afrikaans and African tribal languages, and had conformed to the government policy of separating not only Black from White, but Black from Black, with the result that the NGKA's ninety theology students were enrolled in five different schools for five tribal groupings.[18]

Even more significant was the synod's resolution on the status of Whites serving the NGKA. The issue was a thorny one: until then, White clergy and administrators had always remained members of the White NGK, and were ultimately responsible to it rather than to their own congregations' church councils. The White church, not the Black, also exercised authority in cases of discipline over these White missionaries. Henceforth, the synod declared, these men and their families would have to become full members of the churches they served.

In 1975 the NGKA made another bold move: it took full membership in the South African Council of Churches (SACC), a body that to many NGK Whites represented the enemy camp.

It is significant that Ernest Buti, the NGKA moderator who piloted his church into the SACC, was a strong advocate of multiracialism. While praising Black theology for teaching Blacks to see God through their own eyes and in their own circumstances, he denounced the separatism of some Black consciousness leaders as "just as bad as apartheid." Some observers even believe that the period of "withdrawal" from the White church enabled NGKA leaders to confront Whites confidently in a multiracial setting, and that as a result NGKA Blacks are much more in favor of multiracial contacts than are many radical Blacks in the multiracial churches.[19]

Despite these onslaughts, the tie between the NGK and the NGKA remains fairly strong. Among the many bonds is financial dependence: it has been estimated that 70 percent of the budgets of the "daughter" churches comes from the "mother."[20] In addition, over three hundred Whites continue to serve in the NGKA, most of them as parish pastors.

Another sign of White influence is the NGKA's failure to express more than "regrets" over the NGK's rejection of the move for an umbrella synod, although it had been predicted that this would prompt the Black church to sever relations entirely.

Most significant of all was the election in 1979 of a conservative moderator, J. M. Lebone, to succeed Ernest Buti, who had died a few months earlier. The race for the moderatorship was a hot one. Ernest Buti's son Sam, as Scribe of the Church, by custom was lined up for election to the post. But

Buti, leader of the NGKA "progs" and a prominent member of the radical Broederkring, lost by only seven votes.

Viewpoints on the election differed significantly. The *DRC News* cheered the choice, declaring that the new leadership was dedicated to "leading the church on the way to fuller realization of its own potential, but with due circumspection and moderation."

David Bosch, a leading White nonconformist in the NGK and one of the few non-White members of the Broederkring, explained that the choice should be understood partly in terms of an "expediency syndrome" and a "jealousy syndrome." Black ministers were prone to intimidation, he observed, because they had been told "you've been subsidized." Then too, outspoken men like Sam Buti were envied. However, the fact that the Broederkring had come in with a slate and been clobbered was also due to the fact, that in the view of some, it tended to operate as a church within a church, emanating an occasional high-handedness that angered others.

Black and White observers agreed that Dominee Nico Basson, the White actuary of the synod, had been "the power behind the throne." According to Black journalist Goba Ndhlovu, the young progressives were still poorly organized and faced constituencies dominated by older ministers. The conservatives, under Basson, boasted a well-oiled machine, had done their homework, and were financially well-off. Hence they could hold the support of older ministers who were concerned about their own future. This group was also backed by the power of the Black universities, where White NGK professors headed the faculties of theology.

Several issues were hotly debated in a tense atmosphere. Although the 1975 NGKA synod had passed a resolution that a single training college should replace the ethnically divided theological schools, Basson managed to sway the gathering against further action on the resolution.

A resolution calling on members to dissociate themselves from the Broederbond evoked passionate discussion, but in the end was defeated despite Sam Buti's efforts. Instead, a watered-down version was passed, proposing that they should not belong to any secret organization that could be detrimental to the work of God.

The most disputed issue was the status of White clergy in the NGKA. Although the 1978 DRC synod had agreed that henceforth all new White ministers become full members of the NGKA upon their induction, a mutual agreement had not been signed by the two partner churches. When the draft agreement was presented for ratification by the NGKA synod, contention arose over the status of Whites already serving in the NGKA. Sam Buti's group objected to including in the agreement the option of continuing under the new or the old conditions. These Whites, he declared, should also take full membership in the NGKA, or withdraw totally from it. (As it was, Whites who were not full members could still hold executive positions—they could be chairpersons of church councils, districts, and regional or synod meetings.) Buti was defeated; the draft agreement was passed.

However, Buti did retain his old position as NGKA Scribe. He also managed to have the "last laugh" (in the words of one observer) when he staved off a proposal that the NGKA break away from the SACC. Moreover, the "progs" won all seats in the fourteen-member general synod committee that, together with the moderatorship, runs church affairs.

Afterward, a foreign visitor to the synod, Dr. A. G. Hofland, Moderator of the Gereformeerde Kerken van Nederland (GKN), described the synod as a "big disappointment," and noted that the chairperson (Lebone) "certainly was not democratic in his handling of the synod meetings."[21]

Sam Buti

The obvious leader of the progressive forces in the NGKA is Sam Buti. As a guiding force in the Broederkring, he will be expected to take the center stage at the 1983 synod. In 1973 he was recognized as one of the helmsmen of the NGKA's dramatic challenge to the White church. In 1975 he called for a national roundtable conference between Whites and Blacks, emphasizing that the delegates would have to include political prisoners, exiles, and homeland politicians. Buti even urged Blacks to identify fully with "radical" organizations such as the South African Students Organization and the Black People's Convention. In 1977 he became president of the SACC. The position carries little power but considerable prestige, and Buti has used it to make powerful speeches at SACC conferences and other gatherings.

Buti is a controversial figure. Some regard him and many other members of the Broederkring as "power-hungry." On the other hand, some radical Blacks consider him too conservative: nurtured in the tradition of Afrikanerdom, he feels closer to Afrikaners than to English-speaking Whites, is a friend of Minister of Cooperation and Development Piet Koornhof, and seeks Black-White unity. Of himself, Buti says: "I started life as an Uncle Tom, who became a fence sitter, who became an activist."

Buti may go down in South African history as the activist who saved Alexandra township, where he had long been a dominee. When he learned that the government was about to move on its plans to build more huge single-sex hostels for migrant workers there,[22] removing families to other townships, he called a meeting in his own home. When some persons at the gathering expressed fear, Buti reminded them that life was always risky. In the end, the Alexandra Liaison Committee was formed with Buti as chairman. Through patient negotiation (and the threat of unfavorable international publicity such as that gained by Crossroads) the committee managed to persuade the authorities to change their minds, replan the whole town, and even allow residents to build their own houses in the township. Such success is unusual in South Africa—and it was achieved nonviolently.[23]

Despite persistent attempts to meet and talk with Buti, we were unable to reach him. He appeared to leave his home in Alexandra every morning before seven, returning home after ten every night.

Interview with David Bosch

We did, however, obtain an interview with David Bosch, a White NGK minister who belongs to the Broederkring, is a good friend of Sam Buti, and for fifteen years served as a missionary to a NGKA congregation in the Transkei (but has not taken dual membership). Later he was appointed to teach missiology at the University of South Africa (UNISA), in Pretoria, the one quasi-multiracial university in the country (because all courses are taken by correspondence). As editor of *Missionalia*, he has written a number of authoritative papers on the social role of the church, some of which have been presented abroad. To most of his fellow Afrikaners, Bosch is a "radical."

Although SACLA received much of its impetus from Michael Cassidy's Africa Enterprise group[24] and leaders of other groups, it was Bosch, as chairman of the SACLA executive, who organized and set the tone for the mammoth rally. A tall, lean man with a rectangular face and rugged features, he greeted us warmly in his UNISA office. He was obviously delighted to talk about SACLA's success.

"There's a big difference between this gathering and the Congress of Mission and Evangelism organized by Africa Enterprise and the SACC at Durban in 1973. In that year the DRC declined to participate, and only about ten DR Whites, as individuals, appeared. This time there were no official delegations from each church, but DRC members and pastors actually accounted for about 15 percent of the assembly, and were third in numbers there—*despite* the fact that a great many of the DRC authorities warned members not to attend!

"Then too, the presence of 'New Evangelicals' such as the American Ron Sider [author of *Rich Christians in a Hungry World*[25]]added a note of social and political responsibility to the traditionally apolitical approach of the evangelical movement.

"Of course there was a lot of talk at SACLA about the 'crisis' in South Africa. This kind of crisis-language has been making the rounds for years. So people tend not to take notice any more. Then too, till 1974 and the collapse of the Portuguese colonialist regimes, we simply believed in our own survival—as all of us tend to do. Discerning persons, though, see that we are really in the rapids now.

"That made SACLA exciting. A lot of work was done in small groups of ten or twenty. We were divided by computer, so that there was a balance of clergy and laity, men and women, old and young, Black and White. They really got down to the roots of problems.

"The mere fact that SACLA *happened* is a breakthrough. All apartheid legislation was suspended—eating rooms, toilets, everything was integrated. In 1973 the legality obstacles were unbelievable. This time, not more than half an hour was spent on them. Blacks were put up in White homes in Pretoria. We just informed the authorities that they were staying there, and the authorities accepted it, although it was against the law. Another case of government by exemption! For most Whites it was the first time they'd had Blacks in their homes. Also, it was the first time that many of the English-speaking Whites had been guests in Afrikaner homes—and vice versa."

"How do you see the long-range effects of SACLA?"

"Well, the participants resolved that these meetings, on a smaller basis, have got to go on all around the country. And they can, because people start with the shared experience of SACLA.

"I grant that it doesn't change the structures. But a change of attitudes and values has to go along with any change of structures. It's important to realize that all this can't come without preparation.

"On the other hand, there's a temptation to concentrate only on attitudes, as many 'evangelicals' are apt to do. I feel that it's an evangelical heresy to say that if you're born again, all the rest will follow. One Black I know told such a White evangelical, 'All my troubles come from born-again Christians!' It's interesting, though, that while Black and English-speaking White charismatics tend to retreat from social awareness and action, Afrikaner charismatics tend to become *more* socially aware. This is partly because the charismatic movement is inherently ecumenical—so that they move out of their isolation."

When we asked Dr. Bosch to comment on trends in the White NGK, he stressed that one must distinguish between Afrikaans churches and Afrikaans society. "In the 1950s there was an awakening of social awareness in the Afrikaans churches, culminating in Cottesloe. But that was also the high-water mark of the Verwoerd era. The destruction of Cottesloe came from the government, not the church. The DRC got such a fright that for the rest of the decade it couldn't start anything.

"In 1970, however, the Afrikaners split into more parties. Afrikaners were no longer one voice. And for the first time, Afrikaans papers began criticizing the government. In the political field, openness was growing. In the church, however, that wasn't happening to the same degree. Many DRC leaders attacked SACLA—yet all the Afrikaans papers supported it. For the newspapers to be urging churches to become involved represents a real turnabout! In addition to that, the coverage of SACLA was much greater in the Afrikaans papers than in the English press. Religion isn't news for the English papers. The Afrikaner is a religious animal; the English-speaker is not."

Did he see the White DRC as a vanguard for change? Bosch shook his head slowly. "It has that *potential*. But people look at the church as a bulwark. For example, when I was in Namibia I was told, 'First we had integration on the level of sport, and we accepted it. Then the social barriers in hotels, bars, and other places went down. Now we are even prepared to sit down with Blacks at the conference table. But there's one area where we won't allow Blacks—and that's our church!' The church *should* be the vanguard, but it becomes the trench."

"Perhaps you could tell us about yourself. How does it feel to be at odds with your fellow Afrikaners?"

"It's hard to maintain a position of marginality. People don't understand the Afrikaners' solidarity. If you try to remain in your group, you're constantly under painful pressure. You have to become a member of another cultural group, change your church, change your language. Then you can survive—but it is an extremely marginal situation.

"I still get invitations to preach in the White church, but they're few. And I still go to the same White church. At least one of the four ministers groans when he sees my wife and me coming. But we won't leave. We listen intently to the sermon, and then my wife, particularly, will go to the minister's home to pick him up on theological points.

"But the number *is* growing. Right here in UNISA there's a group in the theological faculty.[26] We socialize together, sustain one another. But we also maintain contacts with English-speaking Whites, and with Blacks. It's not a comfortable life. But there are many stimulating, exciting, hilarious moments."

"It sounds like a prophetic community."

He smiled. "Although it may be hubris, I do like to think that."

III—The Sendingkerk

Until recently it has been rare for a Colored to identify with Africans, the group at the bottom of the social "pecking order." True, Coloreds' rights are also restricted: they have been able to vote only for representatives to a largely powerless Colored Persons Representative Council (now abolished), and they are subject to residential zoning, job reservation, and many other forms of discrimination.

Nevertheless, Coloreds' average income, low as it is, is considerably higher than that of Africans, and the government spends more on Coloreds than on Africans for education.[27] It also permits Coloreds to supervise Africans in some work settings, and has designated the Cape as a "Colored Preference Area"—meaning that through secondary job reservation, Coloreds are given preference in obtaining higher skilled jobs when Whites are not available.

Finally, the government has proposed a new constitution that would give the White, Colored, and Indian communities their own parliaments to legislate on matters—such as education and housing—pertaining exclusively to the given group. Matters of mutual concern might be dealt with by a council of cabinets but whether the government actually implements this remains uncertain. It would represent all three racial groups. However, the African majority would be excluded. To most Coloreds, acquiring a little more power and material security is appealing.

On the other hand, relations between Coloreds and Whites have been fraught with ambiguity.[28] Many Afrikaners retain a somewhat paternal affection for Coloreds; some even lament the Coloreds' loss of franchise. For their part, Coloreds have often found it expedient to identify with their "masters" instead of the Black "serfs."

In the "family" of the Dutch Reformed churches, too, the mulatto "daughter" has found it hard to cut the umbilical cord with her White "mother." The bonds are very real. Eighty-nine percent of the Coloreds speak Afrikaans (although only 28 percent belong to the Sendingkerk). In most respects the two ethnic groups share the same culture (although many Afrikaners would deny this). Coloreds have been socialized to look up to Whites.

Most important of all, the White DRC provides the Sendingkerk (like the other two younger churches) with large sums of money for "mission work" and "lends" ministers who are paid through White funds. Indeed, even in 1980 the Sendingkerk still had more White than Colored ministers (112 Whites, 94 Coloreds). Ironically, the White DRC now refers to the daughter churches as "autonomous."

In recent years—particularly since the 1976 "disturbances"—a growing number of Coloreds in the universities have begun to see all non-Whites as Black and to call on Africans, Coloreds, and Indians to take pride in their blackness. A corresponding movement in the Sendingkerk, long considered the most submissive of the younger churches, was slow in coming, however. One reason—in addition to those cited above—is the fact that three-quarters of the Sendingkerk's half-million members are rural people with little formal education and limited access to communication.

By the early 1970s, however, the rise of Black consciousness and corresponding growth of Black theology had begun to touch the Sendingkerk. Many parishioners were coming to church with a highly sensitized political consciousness. Moreover, Coloreds had become tired of being associated with a church that justified racist policies of the government and openly practiced apartheid in its own structures. Perhaps most important, many Colored dominees had come to believe that to acquiesce in a situation of oppression was an act of unfaithfulness to the gospel.

At the Sendingkerk general synod in 1974—a year after one hundred NGKA ministers publicly denounced apartheid—there were rumblings of revolt. The synod rejected government prohibitions on mixed marriages (a particularly sensitive subject to descendants of mixed unions) and also called for an open policy on mixed worship.

At its 1978 general synod, the Sendingkerk went further. It rejected the government's proposal for a three-parliament system, appealed to all ministers serving the Sendingkerk (that is, White DRC ministers) who were members of the Broederbond to resign from that secret organization, and called on the government to repeal the Group Areas Act.[29] Most important of all was a decision to work toward "bottom-up" union of the four Dutch Reformed churches.

The three Black churches had been pushing for such a union for several years. However, some Black churches simply proposed that the Federal Council, a purely advisory body, be replaced by a federal synod with the power to make binding decisions on all four churches. The Broederkring "radicals" retorted that, inasmuch as such a synod would be constituted on the basis of presbyteries, the White NGK—though a minority in terms of membership—would have the power. Moreover, a federal structure still accepted the existence of four racially divided churches; authentic church unity meant involving the whole church at all levels.

The Sendingkerk synod rejected the plan for a federal council in favor of such unity. The decision made the Sendingkerk the first fully open church in the DRC family. It also isolated the White church even further.

Today most Colored ministers believe that they should do their own missionary work among their own people, resent the appellation of "mission," and see the Sendingkerk as a full-fledged church. A perusal of *Die Sendingblad* ("The Mission Journal"), published for the whole Dutch Reformed Church, is revealing. Edited by Whites, it illustrates smiling, well-dressed White ministers and their wives performing various good works. The few Blacks portrayed are usually hymn-singing parishioners or functionaries of new homelands, shown shaking hands with their White benefactors. Although the DRC claims to separate church and politics, the magazine devotes considerable space to stories about the dangers of Marxism, crusades to send Bibles to communists, and DRC attempts to evangelize atheists—for example, Bulgarian sailors on shore leave in Cape Town.

The old mission mentality was dealt a severe blow when the 1978 NGSK synod supported an agreement like that reached by the NGKA: White dominees serving in the Sendingkerk could keep dual membership, but all such ministers called in the future must become full members of the Sendingkerk, forsaking membership in the mother church.

In 1978, too, the Sendingkerk voted to retain observer status in the SACC, but failed to approve full membership. Many delegates cited the SACC's affiliation with the WCC, but a more compelling reason for not assuming full membership may have been that the Sendingkerk remained dominated by the White power structure. At this synod, a White dominee, David Botha, was reelected moderator.

In contrast to most ministers of the White DRC, Botha is *verlig*. In a meeting with us, he expressed his fervent hope and belief that the "daughter" and "mother" churches would eventually come together in one general synod for the whole family. His explanation of the difficulty in implementing that unity, however, did not even include racism, but focused on "culture." The main problem, he said, lay with the concept of what the church is. "In the younger churches we are moving away from the cultural concept, whereas in the White church the cultural concept is still dominant." As for "radical" leaders such as "young Boesak," their ideas needed to be "balanced out" through consultation, and guidance by elders.

He was referring to Allan Boesak, a Colored minister who calls himself Black. He has become president of the Broederkring, and has stirred up a storm with his call for civil disobedience to unjust laws.

Portrait of Allan Boesak

In his third book, *Farewell to Innocence*, Boesak summarizes Black consciousness, Black power, and Black theology:

Black Consciousness may be described as the awareness of black people that their humanity is constituted by their blackness. It means that black people are no longer ashamed that they are black, that they have a black history, and a black culture distinct from the history and culture of white people. It means that blacks are determined to be judged no longer by, and adhere no longer to, white values. It is an attitude, a way of life. Viewed thus, Black Consciousness is an integral part of Black Power. But Black Power is also a clear critique of and a force for fundamental change in systems and patterns in society which oppress or which give rise to oppression of black people. Black Theology is the reflection of black Christians on the situation in which they live and on their struggle for liberation.[30]

Boesak is careful to point out that for him and most other Black theologians the Black experience and Black situation are not realities *within themselves* that have revelational value on a par with Scripture. Rather, "it is the Word of God which illumines the reflection and guides the action."[31] But Black theology is not only "part of" the gospel; it is the content and framework of the gospel of Jesus Christ.[32]

Yet this militant young theologian rejects any idea of a Black Christian nationalism. In fact, he believes that Black theology should include Whites. "Blacks know only too well the terrible estrangement of White people," he says. "They know only too well how sorely Whites need to be liberated—even if Whites themselves don't."[33]

Born in 1946 in Somerset West, Cape Province, Boesak attended the (Colored) University of the Western Cape and the Theological Seminary of the Sendingkerk. After pastoral work in Paarl, he studied at the University of Kampen in Holland and at Union Theological Seminary in New York, obtaining his doctorate from Kampen in 1976. Shortly after the 1976 disturbances erupted in Soweto and the Cape area, he took the politically sensitive position of campus minister at the University of the Western Cape. He has been national chairperson of the Association of Christian Students of Southern Africa, and was a board member of the Christian Institute before it was banned. Perhaps his most outstanding work has been with the Broederkring of the Dutch Reformed churches, a group he headed for several years.

Boesak is rather short, with a well-knit body, light skin, and a modified afro. Perhaps because of his role as chaplain to college students, he tends to dress informally, preferring slacks and turtleneck sweaters to the traditional coat and tie. As he talks, quickly and forcefully, using his hands for emphasis, Boesak conveys enthusiasm for the people, for his work, for the challenge of living in a difficult world.

At our two meetings with him he seemed to welcome the chance to talk of his farewell to his early "innocence"—to ignorance of how the bondage of racism determined his daily existence. "Colored people don't feel completely European or completely African. In my childhood and early youth, I felt I *ought* to belong to the White Afrikaner community, but felt rejected. I had a longing to be White.

"There was also inverted racism in our own community—the lighter ones thought of themselves as better. My own mother looks White, and my father was as dark as any African. Most Coloreds would have tried to neutralize that part—you can imagine the inner conflicts. Fortunately, this kind of tension did not exist within our family. My mother never discriminated among her eight children on account of color. But outsiders, we found, favored the lighter ones in the family.

"My father died when I was six, and my mother had to struggle hard as a seamstress to keep the family together. She taught us what it is to care for each other. There's no jealousy between us—the joy of one has always been the joy of the other.

"As I grew older, I appreciated her more and also realized that though my Black father was only a primary school teacher, he had a great love and understanding of music, art, and poetry. I looked into my family history and learned that the first Boesak—a brown-skinned Khoikhoi—shared with an African the leadership of a slave rebellion. I began to take pride in this, to see myself as a son of the soil. When all things came together, I lost my inferiority feelings. I looked at myself differently. I realized that if I could stop trying to please Whites, I could recreate history, so to speak."

"But your evolution was still not complete?"

"No. In 1973, when I was still struggling with this, the United Presbyterian Church of the U.S.A. sponsored a six-month stay at Union Theological Seminary. In the States I did research on the ethics of Martin Luther King. And I saw that Blacks there could be confident, and have a spontaneous attitude toward Whites. Because they accepted their blackness.

"All this time Black consciousness was growing. Many Coloreds began to realize we're part of a common oppressed community. The whole question of being a Colored, Indian, or African was not just an ethnic, but a political, question. We needed unity in the struggle. We had to make choices.

"I'd always wanted to be a minister—nothing else. As a child, I had a love for God and a sense of calling to the church. And while I was studying in Holland, I began to acquire a taste for theology. Reformed theology is dangerous when it's in the hands of an oppressor. But when it's in the hands of the oppressed, it's remarkably useful. I discovered the excitement of saying things theologically. Toward the end of my doctoral studies, I published in

Holland a book of essays on Black theology and a comparative study of the ethics of Martin Luther King and Malcolm X."

"And you returned to South Africa just before the 'disturbances'?"

"Right. In the Transvaal, it was an African thing. But on the Cape, it was led mostly by Coloreds. The Whites couldn't believe it was 'their' Coloreds who began to riot in the second week of August. Colored high school students living on the Cape Flats climbed into a train to join their brothers and sisters in Cape Town. The police said they would cordon off the streets so the students couldn't come back. But they did come back—Tuesday, Wednesday, Thursday. When the police threatened a trainful of students they simply got off the train and marched into Cape Town via another route. Later theology students summoned the Sendingkerk executive, and as a result, the executive issued a hard-hitting statement stressing that if the government had given these people their rights, this would not have happened."

Since 1976 the Sendingkerk has become more militant, Boesak went on. At the 1978 synod, as one of those leading the fight against an overarching synod for the four NGK churches, he favored unity from the congregational level, and declared it was the duty of the Sendingkerk to invite the White NGK into the family: "Here you stand—come join us." For a "daughter" to take such an initiative was indeed revolutionary.

The Broederkring ["circle of brothers"], too, was growing, he emphasized. The group did not possess a distinct political or economic theory, but saw itself as having a more prophetic witness. Unlike the Broederbond, membership was open. The Broederkring was also open about the fact that most of its financial support came from overseas. At their meetings, members discussed liberation theology as a tool in the struggle. On the practical level, the group helped ministers by arranging study grants and furnishing money for books. Because salaries of Black ministers continued to be subsidized by the whole church, the Broederkring also offered financial support when Black ministers got into trouble for stepping out of line with their White supporters.

Boesak went on, with a sigh, "Frustrations continue. We should have joined the SACC as a full member in 1978, but the Whites tabled the whole move. The White ministers preach and go home to their White areas—even if they *want* to, they can't become really involved with their Black congregations or identify themselves with our struggle. *We* have to face our Black parishioners' questions: 'What are you doing? Where are you moving?' We have a sense of responsibility to the Black community that White 'missionaries' never have. In fact, a large part of the problem is that these Whites have a responsibility to the *White* community.

"Our frustration is aggravated by the lack of real change in the political realm. Take Piet Koornhof, for instance—a charming man, and maybe the most potent secret weapon of the National Party. How can I believe in the man's charming sincerity when he says he wants happy and meaningful lives for all, plus political participation, and at the same time goes around with the Prime Minister trying to get people to accept 'independent' states—the homelands? By the time they get meaningful participation, there will be no Black South Africans left. Everything that Koornhof does is within the framework of a policy we reject."

We knew that at the 1979 national SACC conference Boesak's "non-cooperation speech" had rocked the entire gathering. The church should initiate and support programs of civil disobedience on a massive scale, he had declared, for it no longer sufficed to make statements condemning unjust laws as if nothing had happened. In this endeavor, Whites did have a role. "Those Whites who have clearly committed themselves to the struggle for liberation through their commitment have taken upon themselves the *condition* of blackness in South Africa."

Action was imperative, he had stated. "With tragic inevitability the violence inherent in the system of oppression in South Africa breeds more violence and counterviolence. . . . As peaceful protest is being made increasingly impossible, the belief that violence is the only out is growing. . . . The church must initiate and support meaningful pressure on the system as a nonviolent way of bringing about change. . . . True reconciliation cannot happen without this confrontation. Reconciliation is not feeling good, it is coming to grips with evil. . . . To do all of this in South Africa is to look for trouble. . . . And while we do this we must prepare ourselves for ever greater suffering."

When we asked Boesak how he might implement nonviolent strategy, he looked pensive. "Of course that's the big question. One has to begin with understanding that the system works because we make it work. And because we cooperate. We should begin by looking at areas where we give cooperation. I think of Martin Luther King and his nonbuying campaigns. Here I've been ministering to those involved in the boycott of Fattis & Monis.[34] What we need to do is tell those in charge, 'Look, you guys, you'd better sit down and talk with your workers. Otherwise we'll feel compelled to tell the people from the pulpits not to buy your products.'

"The churches should also exert constructive pressure on the government. Of course it will hit back. That's happening already. Just before we held a meeting with University of Western Cape students on this subject, I had a little friendly visit from the security police. But we simply can't be intimidated by such things. In my own case, I've talked over the dangers with my wife—and she supports me all the way."

He stood up with a smile and briskly began packing papers into his briefcase. Again we were struck by the vigor of his movements, the confidence in his bearing, the togetherness of this man who knew he had a mission to accomplish. "Sorry, but I must run now—another meeting with students." There was one final point: "Some say it's the same old thing, and nonviolence has never worked in South Africa. But in the 1950 campaigns and Sharpeville demonstration, the churches were not really involved. They were content to *react*. Today the church must *initiate* the actions. I'd like to see how the government would respond to two hundred churchmen in their robes, walking down the road to John Vorster Square with ninety-five propositions!"*

*Eight months after our conversation, fifty-three clergy and laity did walk down the road, Bibles in hand, to John Vorster Square, to demonstrate their opposition to the detention of Colored minister John Thorne.

Notes

1. The RCA is a tiny church, with approximately one thousand adherents. Perhaps because it is small, and Indians are not so poor as are Blacks and Coloreds, it is more openly critical of the mother church and the government than are the Sendingkerk and the NGKA. The Rev. Edward Mannikam, chairperson of the synodical committee of the RCA, and the Rev. Shun Govender have been particularly outspoken. The latter wanted to see his church stop accepting support from the NGK, and he advocated a simplified church not dependent on property, a "tent-making ministry." One *verligte* Afrikaner told us that the only church she liked to attend was that of an RCA congregation, for their minister was "relaxed and real."

2. J. H. P. Serfontein, *Brotherhood of Power: An Exposé of the Secret Afrikaner Broederbond* (Johannesburg: Jonathan Ball, 1978; Bloomington: Indiana University Press, 1980), p. 163.

3. Ernie Regehr, *Perceptions of Apartheid* (Scottdale, Pa.: Herald, 1979), pp. 205–207.

4. *DRC Newsletter*, September 1973.

5. *Ecunews*, June 4, 1975.

6. Regehr, *Perceptions of Apartheid*, p. 216.

7. Ibid., p. 220.

8. Ibid., p. 279.

9. Ibid., p. 215.

10. In July 1980, the ASB met with representatives of the Inkatha Youth League. For the first time a Black representative addressed the exclusive Afrikaner organization.

11. *New York Times*, June 10, 1980, p. 3.

12. Ibid.

13. "Curatorium" is a special DRC term for the governing body of a DRC theological seminary, as at the University of Stellenbosch in this instance. When we misspelled the word "curiatorium," a *verlig* Afrikaner commented that our misspelling "reeked of Roman Catholicism!"

14. David Bosch, "Racism and Revolution: Response of the Churches in South Africa," in *Occasional Bulletin of Overseas Ministries*, January 1979, pp. 16–17.

15. Connie Alant, "Die Rol van der Kerk in die moderne Afrikaner Samelewing," in *Identiteit en Verandering*, ed. H. W. van der Merwe (Cape Town: Tafelberg, 1975), pp. 102–113.

16. Heribert Adam and Hermann Giliomee, *Ethnic Power Mobilized: Can South African Change?* (New Haven: Yale University Press, 1979), p. 242.

17. Regehr, *Perceptions of Apartheid*, p. 223.

18. Ibid., p. 226.

19. Ibid., p. 224.

20. *DRC Africa News*, July 1979, p. 1.

21. *Ecunews* 20/79 (June 29, 1979), p. 7.

22. When the distinguished economist Francis Wilson visited such hostels in Alexandra in 1971, he described a switchboard inside the hostel control room: "From this switchboard go wires to all corners of the hostel, where they are connected to steel doors, which are fitted in every corridor in such a way that they can roll down from the ceiling to seal off the corridor from the staircase that leads to the courtyard. Thus at the touch of a button any group of rooms in the

building can be locked off and the men incarcerated. Strikes or riots will, it is believed, be more easily contained by such methods" (Francis Wilson, *Migrant Labour in South Africa* [Johannesburg: SACC and Spro-cas, 1972], p. 43).

23. Christian van der Merwe, "Sam Buti's Hot Seat Is Unique: The Black Afrikaner Who Moved from Uncle Tom to Activist," in *Frontline* (February/March 1980), pp. 28–30.

24. The Africa Enterprise Ministry is an interracial, ecumenical, evangelical group based in Pietermaritzburg. It was founded in 1961 with partial funding from Fuller Seminary in Pasadena, California.

25. Ron Sider, *Rich Christians in a Hungry World* (Downers Grove, Ill.: Inter-Varsity; and New York: Paulist Press, 1977).

26. According to Hennie Serfontein, the Department of Theology of the University of South Africa (UNISA), "which is not controlled by the NG church, as are those of the Universities of Stellenbosch and Pretoria, has become a bastion of those theologians rejected and discarded by the Broederbond [dominated] NGK establishment" (Serfontein, *Brotherhood of Power,* p. 174).

27. In 1977 the comparative figures were as follows. *Income* (annual per capita): Whites, 6,396 rands ($7,355), Coloreds, 2,668 rands ($3,068), Blacks, 1,440 rands ($1,656). *Education* (annual per student): Whites, 654 rands ($752), Coloreds, 157 rands ($180), Blacks, 48 rands ($55) (In Loraine Gordon et al., eds., *A Survey of Race Relations in South Africa, 1978* [Johannesburg: SAIRR, 1979], p. 399).

28. Even more ambiguous are the various subcategories of Coloreds: "Cape Coloreds, Malay, Griqua, Chinese, other Asiatic, other Colored"—a veritable grabbag of ethnic groups encompassed in one so-called racial category. Japanese businessmen who work in South Africa are considered "honorary Whites," but Japanese working-class individuals born in South Africa are generally categorized Colored.

29. Coloreds lived in the District 6 area of Cape Town for over 150 years. Over 30,000 persons were living in the area when it was proclaimed White in 1966. Twenty thousand of them were "resettled" on the bleak wastes of the Cape Flats. Very little development took place in the empty shell that the district became.

30. Allan Aubrey Boesak, *Farewell to Innocence* (Maryknoll, N.Y.: Orbis Books, 1977), p. 1.

31. Ibid., p. 12.

32. Ibid., p. 9.

33. Ibid., p. 16.

34. This factory, located in Bellville, home of the University of the Western Cape, fired ten workers when they went on strike over wages and working conditions. The SACC, Diakonia, and other organizations joined the local forces in a boycott of Fattis & Monis products. In November 1979, after six months of struggle, the Fattis & Monis management gave in and reinstated the workers (*Ecunews* 35/79 [November 16, 1979], p. 9).

CHAPTER SIXTEEN

African Independent Churches

All over South Africa, in the cities and the countryside, you can see them: small bands of solemn worshipers clad in uniforms with religious insignia. Their long, flowing robes may be black or white or pastel, their cloaks may be capes or shawls or blankets, and their headdresses range from baker-type hats to ribboned caps or bright turbans. The bishop usually carries a miter and wears special robes as well as a stole embroidered with a cross and the name of the church. They are members of the Ethiopian, Zionist, or Apostolic "sects"—the African independent churches (those entirely under African control).

In the White sectors of the cities, where most members are lonely domestics living in huts behind the master's residence, they are likely to gather in parks. In the countryside, they usually assemble on a hillside or along a river where they may be baptized or purified. In coastal cities you may see half a dozen figures circle around a half-buried bottle, raising their hands to the skies, then plunge into the cold sea, where the leader pushes their heads into the turbulent waves in a triune immersion that seems to invoke Jehovah, Neptune, and African water spirits.

Traditional African religions have been less concerned with an afterlife than with the explanation and control of space-time events, says Martin West in his authoritative *Bishops and Prophets in a Black City.*[1] A great deal of mission Christianity, however, seemed to Africans more oriented to the next world than to the problems they faced here and now. One reaction has been to form independent churches. The church "prophet," for example, concentrates on this-world activities such as healing the sick, divining causes of misfortune, and predicting future events.

Until recently, leaders and members of the independent churches have shown little interest in political change. One reason is that the great majority are illiterate or have had little formal education. Another reason is poverty; these people rise early for miserable jobs and return home late at night. Politicization is a process that is more likely to occur only when people have free time to think. Finally, the women members—who form the majority—fear involvement in politics.

191

Yet the potential is there. Independent churches have grown so rapidly that they are now thought to number over forty-five hundred, serving some four million Black Christians. Some nine hundred of these churches are in Soweto alone. Indeed, the movement has spread from South Africa to all parts of Black Africa.[2]

Political awareness in the independent churches has been growing, albeit slowly. In the early 1970s Steve Biko and other SASO leaders began to prod the African Independent Church Association (AICA) and the Inter-denominational African Ministers Association (IDAMASA), which includes independent church ministers, to stimulate Black consciousness among their followers.

After the Soweto disturbances, too, demonstrators who were the children of independent church members began to challenge their parents. In 1977 the late Mashwabada Mayatula, an independent church minister and former member of the Christian Institute, became a member of the Soweto Committee of Ten. After the banning of the Christian Institute, which had helped form AICA and finance its theological college, the SACC (by then largely controlled by Blacks) took over the task of developing a greater sense of organization and fostering black consciousness among the independent churches.

The specific task of promoting the education of African independent church ministers fell on the SACC Division of Church Development. Isaac Mokoena, Bishop of St. John's Church near Johannesburg, became the division's director. During an interview with him, Mokoena explained to us that the division sponsored a theological school and correspondence courses. The government, said Mokoena bitterly, saw independent churches as a threat, hence the authorities encouraged secessionism.

"It's so bad that a man who may simply have had a dispute with his minister need only write to Pretoria and say 'I'm establishing a new church'—and the government grants permission *and* allows him to call himself bishop.[3] They establish another file, on a church that may consist of a minister, his wife, children, brother, and a friend or two. This kind of multiplicity tends to weaken the gospel."

Ethiopians, Zionists, and Apostolics

There are basic differences as well as similarities among the Ethiopian, Zionist, and Apostolic churches. The Zionist movement, founded in 1904, has even stronger American connections than the Ethiopian, for its roots lie in the Christian Apostolic Church in Zion emanating from Zion City, Illinois. The Zionists have retained some elements of traditional African paganism, together with a rather Pentecostalist-type Christianity similar to that of "storefront churches" in the United States. Faith healing is of paramount importance, reinforced by dancing, the use of drums, spirit possession during services, speaking in tongues, and testimonies voiced in a half-singing, half-speaking tone.

Both Zionists and Apostolics (a subgroup, fundamentalist like the Zionists, but putting more emphasis on education and theological training) insist more than the Ethiopians on wearing special uniforms, holding communion services at night, and baptizing the faithful in any river available. Some Zionist churches—especially the Nazarites, who virtually deify their deceased founder, Isaiah Shembe, as a prophet—believe in a Black Christ. Some even reverse the color bar in heaven: Whites will be turned away from the gates, for "nobody can rule twice."

The Ethiopian sects are those that broke away from "mission" churches (now incorporated into the traditional churches) or their offshoots; they remain patterned on their parent churches. The Presbyterian Church of Africa, for example, keeps the mission-church constitution, hymnbook, doctrine, and form of service, although it refuses to have anything to do with the parent organization. The Ethiopians also tend to use the color black in their uniforms.

For the Zionists, black, the color of death and disease, is seldom worn. Their uniforms are basically of white, symbolic of cleanliness and purity, together with other symbolic colors such as blue, green, yellow, and red.[4]

The decentralized nature of the independent churches makes them hard to analyze. The rural and urban churches are also somewhat different in structure. For a penetrating analysis of the rural churches, the reader is referred to Bengt Sundkler's *Bantu Prophets in South Africa.*[5] Here we shall confine ourselves to a few generalizations about the Zionist type, because these churches represent a more original African phenomenon.

Prophets, Faith Healers, and Diviners

Most Zionist churches in Soweto have an elaborate leadership system, headed by a bishop, as well as a less formal prophetic presence (prophetic healers and prayer women). Women usually have their own hierarchy and play a very important role, but rarely hold office in the formal hierarchy, or pose a threat to the male structure. Uniforms are usually required.

Congregations tend to be small, partly because most of them meet in private houses or school classrooms. They are also poor. In one church, for example, full members pay the equivalent of five dollars per year, which covers salaries, uniforms, books, candles, communion wine, and wafers, and a fund to help members in emergencies. All officials, even the archbishop, have either full-time or part-time jobs unrelated to the church.

The prophet is of utmost importance, for most members say that the reason they joined is "I was made well there." In addition to the prophet (who has the power to predict, heal, and divine), two other basic types of healer exist in Soweto: the faith healer and the *sangoma,* the diviner. The faithful believe that the power to heal emanates from God, although in some cases it is thought to come from God indirectly, through the shades (specific ancestors who are believed to exert influence on the living). The faith healer is a Christian. A *sangoma,* most often a woman, may be a Christian but usually is not; her healing power is believed to come not from God, but directly from the guiding shades. Some prophets were originally called as diviners, but decided to become Christian prophets by undergoing training with a prophet instead of a diviner.

Significantly, most independent churches, when they discover a diviner in their midst, attempt to convert rather than expel them. Reasoning that if a diviner comes to the church, she or he must believe in God and the Holy Spirit, they suggest that by accepting the power of the Holy Spirit, which can be channeled through the shades, the diviner's power will be greater.

Festival services may last eighteen hours or even longer. West describes one that included the slaughtering of an ox, prayers, hymns, foot washing, communion, gifts of clothing and money to the bishop, and joyous dances calling the Holy Spirit down upon the faithful. After hours of more singing, more drumming, and more elaborate dancing, in which many members became "possessed," the congregation gathered for a feast beginning with meat, rice, potatoes, bread, pumpkin, and several salads, and ending with jello-and-custard, cake, and homemade ginger beer.

This blend of Christian and animistic elements has often been criticized as a bridge back to heathenism. West disagrees. He points out, for example, that while Zionists may appear to have made baptism into a purification rite similar to traditional Zulu ritual, in the churches he studied a clear distinction was always made between purification and baptism. He also refutes the widespread belief that the independent churches have replaced the Trinity by the shades, and quotes an African writer: "The ancestors are not an end, but are there only as witnesses to the strong belief in the continuity of life and human relationships. They are not objects of worship, but of fellowship and mutual relationships."[6] West also cites a Black Methodist minister who continued to honor his shades. According to the minister, if an African slaughters a goat to intercede on his behalf with God, the historical churches condemn it. But was this not like a Roman Catholic's entering a cathedral, lighting a candle, and praying to a saint to intercede for him?

An enlightened anthropologist, West also stresses the many *functions* of independent church rites. Members help each other find jobs or housing, and churches give financial assistance to those in need because of illness or death in the family. Churches often maintain social control by enforcing strictures against smoking, drinking, marital strife, extramarital relations, or quarrels between members. The elaborate hierarchies offer chances for leadership to persons living in circumstances that thwart their human potential. To those whose only certainties are death, taxes, and frustration, the rites of confession, dancing, purification, and spirit possession provide not only links with tradition, but also emotional catharsis. As for the healing that attracts most members to the Zionist churches, a cure seems to be based on the emotional support that comes from a "listening ear"—someone who hears out their troubles, many of which could be called psychosomatic. Finally, says West, the independent church becomes a surrogate family to the alienated urban immigrants, whose ties with former rural kinship groups have been shattered.

This distinguished White anthropologist seems to be expressing a functional point of view. His perceptions are acute, and there appears little doubt that the independent churches perform these functions for powerless Black Africans.

Independents and Whites

But do these churches speak only to the needs of an uneducated, poor, oppressed people? It is interesting that the charismatic movement, which has grown so rapidly in the White historical churches, incorporates somewhat similar emotional elements, particularly in relation to healing and testimonies. Moreover, professionals in some hospitals have shown an interest in discovering the "secret" of diviners' power, and the (White) University of Witwatersrand began a study of their methods, a project halted by the Soweto disturbances. In Natal, we were told, there exists a "hospital" where Blacks and Whites eat and pray together as they are healed by an African *sangoma.*

According to Bishop Mokoena, some members of historical churches have been attending their own services by day and coming furtively to African independent churches by night, for special secret prayers of healing. Even Whites, risking the authorities' displeasure, have attended, and a few have even taken leading parts in the services. Mokoena also related how he himself had prayed four times weekly with a dying White woman, at her home, until she was cured.

It is not only through healing that Blacks have spoken to Whites. An Afrikaner woman told us that she had felt "humbled" when her maid, a member of an independent church, had expressed shock that "madam" did not attend the funeral of a White neighbor. During times of sorrow, the maid always gave food, money, and herself—her presence—to her own kin and neighbors.

A member of the Christian Institute spoke with feeling of the "cleansing of the bitterness built up during the week," of "the deep and resounding joy" he had witnessed at independent church services. "Sometimes I feel a lack in my spiritual life. Their service, with its warmth, complements what we lack in our fellowship. It could enrich *us,* as White Christians.

"Their song, dance, clapping of hands, their openness toward one another, create an atmosphere that makes for mutual support. When the service is over, they sit down in small groups, listen to each other's troubles, and find out what they can do to help one another. Just to leave after a service is unthinkable. Their lack of materialism puts me to shame. They have so little, yet they share it.

"When someone dies, they sit down, talk, pray with the family, and share the sorrow. And in sharing the grief, it is released. We Whites are in a hurry to get a funeral over with. I've heard these Black people say, 'In this long process we work through our sorrow, and find cleansing and victory. You Whites have tensions because you don't work them out. Yes, we see Whites in their homes—they are more lonely than we. We have a greater sense of community.' "

Beyond this, the independent churches have established a "structure" that would be almost unthinkable in the West. It is a religious institution virtually without formal buildings, stock holdings, estates, rectories, or even full-time salaries for its clergy. A church without money. A church so poor that it lies outside the capitalist system, and so decentralized that, although each congregation is organized, there is no umbrella bureaucratic power structure. Yet these possible weaknesses become its strengths. How can a government threaten thousands of half-visible, moneyless, self-sufficient groups of Christians?

Pressures from Blacks for Africanization are growing in the historical churches. In the future, predict some observers, these churches and the African independents will move closer to each other. Black consciousness may provide the link. Black churches have voiced African aspirations through Black theology. Yet it is significant that nineteenth-century independent church leaders were among the first to articulate Black consciousness, and that the Pan Africanist Congress, shortly before it was banned, perceived the possibility of linking the theology of separatism in the independent churches to political goals.[7]

The historical churches have experience with organization and a more developed political consciousness to offer their Black brothers and sisters, whereas the independent church members can stimulate the historical churches to a greater cherishing of the African heritage. Perhaps the two will meet to become a new force with political potential. And perhaps such a force will offer a new vision, for both Blacks and Whites, of the human potential.

Notes

1. Martin West, *Bishops and Prophets in a Black City: African Independent Churches in Soweto* (Johannesburg: Ravan, 1975; New York: International Publications Service, 1976). We have relied extensively on West's analysis for this chapter.

2. According to Lester Van Essen, "Approximately six thousand independent denominations have sprung up in the past twenty-five years [in Africa] which have no relationship to any mission organization" (*Reformed Journal* [October 1977], p. 14).

3. The government has since eliminated this registration process.

4. West, *Bishops and Prophets,* p. 16.

5. Bengt Sundkler, *Bantu Prophets in South Africa,* 2nd ed. (London: Oxford University Press, 1961).

6. West, *Bishops and Prophets,* p. 178.

7. Gail M. Gerhart, *Black Power in South Africa: The Evolution of an Ideology* (Berkeley: University of California Press, 1978), p. 202.

CHAPTER SEVENTEEN

Prophetic Voices

A prophet may be defined as a religious teacher, an advocate of a cause, or someone who predicts the future.

In this chapter we shall be peering into the future through the eyes of several South African secular prophets, chosen somewhat arbitrarily from among the many engaged in the struggle for an end to apartheid and a more just society. Because the initiative for change has shifted increasingly to Blacks, we shall be listening to them. Although they are political leaders, all of them see the role of the church as important.

Even if some of these men are dead by the time the reader sees this page, or even if in some cases their positions have shifted, we believe that the basic issues and the viewpoints they represent will not have changed substantially.

What are the ongoing issues? As Black leaders see them, they are: (1) participation in the homelands policy, (2) liberation movement ties with Moscow or Peking, or the West, (3) inclusion of Whites in these movements, (4) divestment and other sanctions, (5) the politico-economic framework of the future: capitalist, communist, or "African socialist?" and (6) the new political dispensation: federation, consocation, or a unitary system based on "one person, one vote."

Barry Streek observes that although Black rejection of government race policies has been growing, Black political strategies against apartheid remain divided. He classifies Black political groups into four categories: (1) those who join the system, (2) those who use it with qualifications, (3) those who try to survive banning but still have nothing to do with any structure created by the government, and (4) those who have been outlawed and gone underground.[1]

An example of the first category would be the Coloreds' Freedom Party (an outgrowth of the Federal Party).[2] Unlike the anti-apartheid Labor Party of the Coloreds, the Freedom Party agreed to serve on the Colored Persons Council (a totally nominated body that succeeded the partially elected Colored Representative Council).

This first category also includes community councils and some homeland

197

governments such as Venda, Transkei, Ciskei, and Bophuthatswana. Although leaders of these homelands are often dismissed by other Blacks as stooges, some surveys indicate substantial support of their parties, mainly through the conservative tribal structures that the government deliberately reinforces.[3]

In the second category (those saying that they use the system in order to destroy it) belongs the Labor Party. Its efforts to win an executive majority in the Colored Representative Council were so successful that in 1980 the government abolished the council.

Also included in this category would be the Indians' Reform Party and the ruling parties in some homelands such as Qwa Qwa, KaNgwane, and Kwa-Zulu. The controlling party in the last-named, Inkatha, is the most effective of these movements and will be described later.

The second category also includes parallel trade unions (racially segregated unions linked to White unions) and Black sports groups willing to accept a segregated role.

Among "survivalists"—the third category—are the new Black consciousness groups that emerged, phoenixlike, after Black consciousness organizations were banned in October 1977. The new groups include the Azanian People's Organization (AZAPO), the Media Workers' Association of South Africa (MWASA), the Conference of South African Students (COSAS), the Azanian Students Organization (AZASO), and the Port Elizabeth Black Civic Organization (PEBCO). Together with the older Soweto Committee of Ten, the Natal Indian Congress (NIC), and the South African Council of Sport (SACOS), these organizations are the leading exponents of noncollaboration with the system. AZAPO, an umbrella organization of educational and professional groups, seems totally committed to the Black consciousness philosophy, and has been trying to work with trade unions.

Within the noncollaborationist fold, too, might be included the Unity Movement of South Africa, a Trotskyite group originally organized as the Non-European Unity Movement, which advocates that the struggle focus on the factories and looks to an international working-class struggle against capitalism rather than to the "illusory" hope of national liberation. Thus far the Unity Movement has proved to be too intellectual, pessimistic, and lacking in national organization to appeal to many Blacks.

Possibly defying any categorization along the lines of either using or surviving the system are the Federation of South African Trade Unions (FOSATU) and the South African Allied Workers Union,[4] which are involved in building up Black Unions. The former insists on nonracialism, the latter on Black leadership.

The strategy adopted by the exiled groups—the fourth category—is clearly to isolate South Africa on every level, to increase the armed struggle, and eventually to topple the system. To this category belong the ANC and the PAC, both outlawed since 1960. A newer arrival is the Black Consciousness Movement, which formed an exile liberation group in 1979 under the interim leadership of Barney Pityana (a former secretary general of the banned South African Students Organization), then studying theology in London, and Ranwedzi Nengwekhulu, a lecturer at the University of Botswana.

Rank-and-file Blacks are still groping for a stand on these complex questions.

I — SOWETO

One day four young Africans who articulate the frustrations of their people and who must remain anonymous offered to take us on a tour of "the Soweto that the tourists led by government guides never see." For hours we drove up and down unpaved, rutted, dusty streets, looking at desolate fields of rubble, a few dimly-lit shops, and endless rows of uniform four-room "matchboxes" (as the Sowetans call them).

These standardized concrete-block buildings house, on the average, eight to ten persons. (The population of Soweto is officially given as 700,000, but is unofficially estimated at closer to 1,500,000, and its population density is said to be more than twice that of Johannesburg.)

All the houses were roofed with asbestos, a known carcinogen. Less than a fourth of the houses had electricity or indoor toilets. Yet some boasted brick walks, flowers, small trees, or a bit of grass. (We remembered the White Johannesburg couple who had assured us—although they had never been to Soweto—that Africans do not grow grass because "these superstitious people" feared that it would attract snakes.)

We saw homes where enterprising and fortunate leaseholders had installed a toilet in an outhouse, or built a real inside bathroom, or added another bedroom. We also saw a few fairly large homes for comparatively well-to-do Africans, in the section of Soweto that government guides like to show visitors.

Some Black workers paused in their street-cleaning tasks (the streets had no gutters or litter bins) to chat with us in surprisingly friendly fashion. But the prevailing atmosphere was one of alienation: jobless youths tinkering with carcasses of burned-out cars, others squatting around dice or cards, women ferreting tin cans out of junk heaps, and groups of children—unable to afford uniforms or school fees—sitting beside the dusty road or playing beside tall heaps of garbage.

Although Soweto was the third largest Black city in Africa, there were only two small movie theaters, one YMCA recreation center, one fire station, and no parks, we were told. Open spaces are used as unofficial dumping grounds. The one football stadium, our guides said bitterly, was built to co-opt the people—to give them not bread, but circuses.

It was a pity we could not see Soweto by night, they went on. Then the streets were illuminated by huge glaring arc lights, the air became laden with thick acrid smoke from the coal that most Sowetans use for cooking, and the sentries at the six modern sandbagged police stations became even more watchful as they patrolled their fortresses. And in the shebeens—the illegal drinking clubs that form the heart of social and political life in Soweto in the absence of other centers—political discussion reached a high pitch.

In these shebeens there was a certain sense of community. The huge drinking halls, on the other hand, were the scene of personal violence born out of frustration. Whites sneered at the Africans' "innate instinct for drunken violence," but these state-controlled liquor outlets are obliged to turn over eighty percent of their profits to the White government for the purpose of homeland development. After the 1976 "disturbances" the government rebuilt them quickly—to the fury of young African militants.

We made a visit to a "family group" threatened with eviction. In five rooms of a dank former migrant workers' hostel, with no electricity or toilet, forty-five persons were living. In the room we visited, ten persons were huddled, separated by a curtain from the next family. Six adults slept on the four bunks in shifts; the children stretched out on blankets spread on the cold stone floor. The floor was well swept, the room remarkably clean.

A crippled man and his wife told us that they had "no identity." They had no identity cards because, when the river flooded a nearby area, their mud brick home dissolved, and their papers were washed away. With no reference book, they could get no work. With no work, they could pay no rent. Yet government authorities called on them frequently, sometimes at 5 A.M., demanding that they come to pay their "debt."

At the end of the tour, one of our more articulate guides, a young man with an embroidered Muslim cap, asked us to stay in the car and tell them what we thought about what we had seen. When we spoke of the depressing physical conditions, he shook his head. "It's not so much the physical conditions," he began slowly, his voice trembling, as if he had been waiting a long time for this moment. "We're aware that parts of other African countries are even worse. It's the oppression. Even those few of us who go back to fairly comfortable homes are surrounded by ugliness, violence, the knowledge that the police could knock at the door at any time—the endless nightmares of apartheid.

"We've struggled peacefully. Now we feel that the only way is armed struggle. We don't want that. But after three hundred years, we are tired and frustrated. We welcomed you White people when you came to Africa. We even offered you our wives. You didn't care. You just took everything. Even your fine missionaries gave us the Bible—and took our land."

We did not try to answer, nor did he wait for a response. His voice, still trembling, was rising. "May I tell you about those 'Black' shops you saw here in Soweto? Only one-fourth are owned by Africans. Most belong to Whites. The trains are owned by the White government and the buses by White entrepreneurs. No form of African industry is allowed. Almost all homes belong to the government, and even when an African accumulates enough to buy a house, he can only lease the land it stands on. Nothing belongs to us—nothing but our chains.

"We were taking a chance when we took you on this tour, without getting an official pass from the West Rand Administrative Board. You might have been from the security forces. We know they have a worldwide network—you might have been working for them overseas.

"I wish I could hate you White people. I can't. It would be so much easier to hate you. But it's not in me. And we've seen poor Whites, even here—we know they suffer, too. But this—it could go on another three hundred years!"

"No," we responded, "history is on your side. You will find freedom."

"Freedom?" he continued. "Is there any freedom, anywhere? We don't want to copy you. We don't want White culture. We don't want to be plastic Americans, or even plastic Europeans. We don't even want your religion. That's why I've converted to Islam, where all men are equal. We just want to live in peace.

"Freedom? There's no freedom in Africa. It's run by a new form of colonialism. White money rules us. Worst of all are the White Black men, who get a little money, and copy the Whites. We don't want that kind of charade—we don't want capitalism."

"Are you saying that you're turning to Marxism?"

"Perhaps. *They* try to keep us from reading Marx and other socialists. Marxism must be beautiful, because they're trying to keep it from us." He stared out the front windshield; his body was shaking, but his hands clasped the steering wheel tightly. Then he turned and faced us squarely. "Marxism? Perhaps. But don't you understand? We don't want any kind of imperialism, from capitalists or any others. We just want to *breathe*."

We could have asked the young men if they belonged to the African National Congress, the Pan-Africanist Congress, or the Black Consciousness Movement. But such a question would have been pointless, for it is highly dangerous to acknowledge membership in a banned group. Our impression was that they had read little of the underground Marxist literature that does exist (generally at the White university level). What is important is that their rage and their conflicts typify the dilemma of many young Africans today.

II — THE COMMITTEE OF TEN

In 1977 a group of Africans formed the Soweto Local Authority Interim Committee (the "Committee of Ten") to oppose the puppet Urban Bantu Council and plan for a truly representative civic body to run Soweto affairs.

The Committee was headed by Dr. Ntatho Harrison Motlana and composed of leading professionals and church leaders including members of the Christian Institute, National African Federated Chambers of Commerce, and Black People's Convention. Later, a Catholic priest, Lebamang Sebidi, and the late Rev. Mashwabada Mayatula, a leader of the Independent Church Association and former member of the Christian Institute, were among those who replaced members who resigned or were banned. Almost everyone on the Committee has suffered detention.

Although many Nationalist leaders have denounced the Committee as a "Black consciousness organization based on the Marxist revolutionary ideal," most of its members could be described as "moderates." (One White liberal has said that if the government had tried to find a way to solve the racial situation, it could not have dreamed of a better group.) They are by no means in total agreement on all the issues, however.

Today the original Committee of Ten blueprint for an autonomous modern city—almost an urban Bantustan—has been replaced by insistence on the right to political inclusion in the city of Johannesburg.

The Committee has refused to take part in elections for community councils. It has also refused to participate in regional committees to advise the Cabinet Committee on Urban African Affairs on the grounds that it was a maneuver to give apartheid the stamp of respectability and get Blacks to implement separatist government policies. As one member put it, "If Koornhof said that he wanted me to sit on a committee to look at *real* alternatives to apartheid, I'd jump at the chance."

The group has been falsely pictured as eschewing contact with Whites. Committee members speak at White universities, meet White journalists, and participate in think tanks with government officials. In 1978 Broederbond chairman Gerrit Viljoen met Motlana in the first major dialogue between top Afrikanerdom and Blacks totally opposed to apartheid. No policy changes emerged, but most White participants agreed that apartheid's original formula was no longer viable.

Committee members are often perceived as middle-class intellectuals with an outlook that isolates them from the masses. It is by definition a local group, restricted to Soweto. Hence the base of support for the Committee has been somewhat narrow. In an effort to broaden its constituency, the Committee formed the Soweto Civic Association and opened its membership to all greater Soweto residents.

It was the support of a man of the church, Bishop Tutu, that has helped widen the appeal of the Committee to the average Black. It does articulate sentiments that are shared by most Africans. In the words of one observer, "That simply makes it a reliable 'guard dog' to protect the people against 'daylight robbery' by the system."

On our two visits to South Africa, we talked with Committee members Douglas Lolwane, Leonard Mosala, Tom Manthata, and Lebamang Sebidi, as well as chairman Motlana. All are well-educated, articulate men. Over the years Dr. Motlana has remained the group's leader.

It was young Black consciousness militants who put him into his position. The Black Consciousness Movement itself had always been a somewhat "leaderless" movement, with little formal organization. Even before October 19, 1977, when virtually all Black political groups were banned, Motlana seemed to these youths a logical choice: he had been working for Black liberation since his student days as member of the ANC Youth League and activist in the Defiance Campaign, and appeared to be a fearless man who could challenge the authorities.

Dr. Motlana commands a large following in Soweto and some other urban areas. That following includes a great many Zulus who chose him in preference to Zulu Chief Gatsha Buthelezi, for, despite government statements, only a small minority of urban Africans (15 percent, in one study) have strong tribal ties.[5] Unlike Buthelezi, he does not seem preoccupied with a drive for personal power.

When we met Motlana at the coffee bar of the Johannisberger, an "international" hotel where Whites and Blacks who can afford it are permitted to meet, it was obvious from the number of Africans—especially women—who approached our table that we were talking with a well-loved celebrity. He is a handsome man, with a thin wiry body, goatee beard, high cheekbones, and flashing smile. Although his hair is slightly graying, he radiates great youthfulness: he moves with a debonair buoyancy and talks fast, using his eyes and emphasizing his remarks with quick vigorous gestures.

With no hesitancy he responded to our questions about his life and his vision of the future. Denying any bitterness over his detentions and bannings, he described how he had been interviewed by five senior police officers the day after his speech commemorating the Soweto disturbances. "Two of them threatened to kill me as they did Biko. Because I was 'inciting children to violence.' Since then I have been entirely silenced." He laughed. "When I was first arrested, in 1976, eight officers entered my home with submachine guns, and a Zulu translator with a knobkerrie!"[6]

In early 1978, after being released from five months in prison, Motlana had expressed a certain optimism about the possibility of peaceful change. The Afrikaner was an "authoritarian chap," he declared, and would follow the leader; a pragmatic De Gaulle would emerge to lead a reluctant White community into granting full political rights to Blacks. In our meetings, Motlana was less sanguine about basic attitude change, however.

"Afrikaners can't even imagine letting a Black into their suburbs. I was invited to speak at a meeting called by Carel Boshoff, the head of SABRA[7] [the government-oriented South African Bureau of Racial Affairs]. During the meeting he and I chatted and I learned of a house up for sale. I said I'd be interested in buying it. *He* said, 'Impossible! I couldn't live next door to a Black—our cultures are different.'

"I answered, 'Look, I've gone to university for eight years, my children are all at university, I have a car—in fact, more than one—I look at the same TV programs, wear the same kind of suits, eat pretty much the same kind of food, and take a bath every day. What's the difference between you and me? Is it *culture?*'

"The guy couldn't answer. Isn't it true that culture is a euphemism for race? Afrikaners have become mythologized about this thing called color!"

When we asked Motlana how he felt about federation, he shook his head emphatically. "Once I supported it—simply because I could still imagine *regional* division, but not one based on race. But when Whites talk of federation, they mean along racial lines.

"Today some liberals cling to the old idea of a qualified franchise, accepting certain classes of Blacks into the White mainstream the way the Portuguese accepted *assimilados*. Others talk of 'weighted votes.' One guy is seriously proposing a scale of one to twenty-five votes—from one for the illiterate Black to twenty-five for an Oppenheimer! Still others talk about 'gray areas' where people can live in an integrated way if they like. A few chaps talk of consociation, too.

"But *any* change within the framework of separate development is no change at all. Inevitably, there's going to be a single society. And the sooner the Whites realize this, the better. Do they want a few more years of ruling alone, followed by disaster for *all?* The government should level with the people, and tell them that change *will* be painful, but it's the only guarantee of survival. They say we refuse to negotiate. We *will,* when there's something to negotiate. When government leaders are prepared to say, 'We must work together toward majority rule.' "

Did he envision a Marxist or capitalist South Africa under majority rule?

"Most of us think we should have some form of socialism, some state intervention. But I am not a Marxist. Back in my ANC days, we resented communist influence on our organization, an influence that continues to this day. Discussion of the struggle—the African nationalists versus the Communist Party—took place in my consulting rooms. I didn't agree with the breakaway group that became the Pan-Africanist Congress, though I shared their political views. They should have stayed to get rid of the communists and fight from within. My thinking was like Sobukwe's, but I didn't want a new group.

"Today I even fight with my own son. He's at Wits [Witwatersrand]—one of the few Blacks they let into a White university, maybe as a form of blackmail. Since Wits is White, he can study Marxism, and has access to all sorts of banned books.[8]

"I disagree with Marxists on a lot of things. Above all, they don't succeed in convincing me that the typical class struggle fits the South African situation, or any other in Africa. I don't identify with the analysis given by exile movements that see the situation as a class struggle.

"Do you want to know my opinions on Marxism? Six months in detention give you plenty of time to read! One criticism is that Marxism creates another privileged class, one that becomes a permanent clique. I don't see how you can talk of democracy in the Soviet Union, for instance. Another criticism is that Marxists don't recognize that you have to give people certain incentives—so that life will be better for *them,* and better than that of those lazy bastards who sit in the sun.

"Here the problem is that we have crazy extremes of wealth. But at this moment in time I believe more in democratic socialism, like that in Sweden. I believe in private ownership, but some state intervention and services. I don't believe in absentee landowners.

"Blacks have often been farm managers—good ones. I know one who ran five White farms. But now the government is removing Blacks from land they once owned, before they were dispossessed. They must leave their ancestral lands and the graves of their ancestors, which to Africans is like being severed from a vital part of the self. This is just one of the things that must be stopped.

"The state should own land. This is where African tradition is so important. Land should be held in trust for the upcoming generations, by whoever is working it. Private houses and small plots of land—yes, these should be privately owned. And farmers leasing land from the state can make a profit from the effort they put into working it."

"What about commerce and industry?" we asked.

"I think the mines should be nationalized, and maybe some other industries. I don't mean a complete takeover, but a partnership between the state and private entrepreneurs. It works in other countries—and Afrikaner state corporations are an example right here in the RSA."

How did he see these changes coming about?

"Inside, there will be continuous pressures of Blacks against apartheid. Outside, South Africa's friends in the West will become ashamed of such a repressive regime. Their long-term interests lie elsewhere. The United States, for instance, relies increasingly on Nigeria—a leading foe of apartheid—for oil. So the West may be confronted with a choice between support for apartheid and support for the liberation of Blacks.

"If these kinds of pressure—internal and external—fail, the exodus of thousands of young Blacks will result in prolonged urban guerrilla warfare. I hope that won't happen. I'm a man of peace, and I don't want to see the country destroyed. But when Andy Young appeared on the scene, I began to have more hope about America. She *could* support the winning side."

What about the role of Whites in a majority government?

"That's a question that scares Whites. They shouldn't feel that way. It's true that *some* young Blacks look for Black rule. Personally, I don't want to throw Whites into the sea, or create an Afrikaner homeland. I'd welcome them into the government, and could see some as cabinet ministers. But they won't have special protection, either.

"A White South African is a South African—no less, but no more. And I must point out that if the Whites resist *real* change—change that is inevitable—the more bitter will be the conflict, and the more likely that an extreme Marxist regime will take over."

And the role of the church in change?

"I was born a Lutheran, and I'm sorry to say that the White Lutherans who ran the school I attended did not really believe in Black education, but instead supplied Black children to farms as labor. Because my marks were good, my uncle took me away to an urban high school run by the Methodists.

And later I read about the role of the missionaries in the policy of conquest.

"Only recently have I come to read about what Christianity really means, and to realize that Jesus was the real revolutionary of the first century. From reading the *Institutes,* I've also come to understand that Calvin did not discriminate against color.

"Unfortunately, many young Africans haven't had the chance to read, so they reject Christianity and its morals, which they equate with the regime. And while you can see a little change in many churches, the NGK is where church people are *resisting* change most. How many cabinet ministers have been *church* ministers?"

As he stood up to get another cup of coffee at the cafeteria serving bar, we became aware once again of the erect way he carried his thin, taut body; it was the bearing of a man who has no time to waste on fears for the future.

He sat down again, pondered for a moment, and clicked his tongue. "The church. Who knows where it will take us? Tutu and the SACC have redeemed it. If the government persecutes an institution, Blacks will perk up and say, 'There must be something there!' The SACC has become a new force in liberation."

Since our visit, Dr. Motlana began writing a column for a new multiracial magazine, *Frontline,* a column in which he elaborates on the outlines of a new society. He emphasizes that for most Blacks "gradualism" is a bad word. Some even criticize him for talking with Whites, and perceive improvement of the ghettoes as dividing Blacks into haves and have-nots, thus defusing Black anger.

Yet, says Motlana:

The older and more conservative people such as myself feel that any progress is progress, even if it is very limited. And we feel that we should not refuse to upgrade our environment or cooperate in its upgrading just because it is not answering the principal problems. . . . I do not believe that the older generation's acceptance of marginal improvements means that they will be satisfied with these marginal improvements and nothing more. They also want real power and the real substance of citizenship in their own land. . . . The abolition of race distinctions is a part of the process of liberation—only a part, and in many respects a very small part—but it is still important. In South Africa's circumstances liberation is not going to come overnight, and all parts will mount up to contribute to it.[9]

Did this mean that Blacks would reject any form of timetable for liberation? Dr. Motlana confessed that he does not know. He felt that no timetable to partial liberation would be acceptable. The change to majority rule in Zimbabwe stimulated Black South Africans to insist that there is no justification for further "pussyfooting," he pointed out. He himself would welcome the government's laying down a clear timetable, provided that it occurs in a reasonable amount of time, and the end is total liberation.

However, Motlana asserted, there is no need for group reassurances, like those obtained for Whites in Zimbabwe. Individual rights will be protected; group rights are morally wrong. The absence of Black revenge under the Mugabe regime should convince Whites that it is rubbish to believe that when Blacks get power they will suppress Whites. Mugabe's ten years in jail did not poison him against his jailers.

Ntatho Motlana represents a convergence of the ANC and BCM lines. Indeed, in his own words, the latter is "a distillation of African nationalism, in a continuous line. Our sons have gotten more sophisticated, but it's basically the same kind of thinking."

III — GATSHA BUTHELEZI AND INKATHA

The most bitter rival of the BCM leaders is Chief Gatsha Buthelezi, chief minister of KwaZulu and president of Inkatha. Inkatha, with 250,000 paid-up members, is the second largest political party in South Africa's history—second only to the National Party.

Although the Chief explains his assumption of KwaZulu leadership as the result of "pressures of my people," it occurred largely at the urging of ANC leaders who felt that inasmuch as homeland status was inevitable, KwaZulu should be headed by a man with an independent spirit and an ANC background. Yet today many ANC and BCM leaders denounce Buthelezi as a "traitor" who "collaborates" with the homeland system and uses his position for his own ends. Buthelezi hotly denies the charge, pointing out that unlike most other homeland leaders he has not accepted independence.

Whereas Buthelezi and other Inkatha leaders think that the homelands policy is unjust but should be used as a means to ultimate liberation, BCM opposes the policy entirely: it is not interested in "desegregation," but in the "national question"—that is, land. Inkatha (and to some extent ANC) would say that the land belongs to the people of South Africa. BCM insists that it belongs to the indigenous peoples of the country—namely, to those peoples of any color who identify themselves as "African," and that until that fact is recognized there is no way that an understanding between Blacks and Whites can come about.

Buthelezi makes numerous speeches to White businessmen and university students and he has met with Progressive-Federal Party leaders, signers of the Koinonia Declaration, Broederbond leaders, and government officials. Urban Black leaders, in particular, complain not only that Buthelezi cooperates with separate development, but that he is cultivating tribalism and Zulu nationalism. In 1976, they point out, he directed Zulus living in KwaZulu townships near Durban not to participate in actions such as those of the Soweto and Cape Town students. In 1980 he threatened to close schools in Durban's Black townships (over which KwaZulu has control) if students continued boycotting classes.

Critics also accuse Buthelezi of prolonging apartheid by encouraging multinationals to invest in KwaZulu, and entrenching Inkatha hegemony so firmly that no civil servant who is not a member of the party can expect to be promoted. Although the Chief claims that Inkatha has stopped KwaZulu from accepting independence, opponents recall that he once supported federation, that the stated aims of the movement do not include specific rejection of autonomy, and that in 1977 KwaZulu accepted the second and last stage of preindependence self-government.

Many Blacks also believe that Buthelezi was behind the gangs engaged in assaults on Inkatha opponents, such as the tarring and feathering of a man mistaken for Dr. Motlana. In any case, there is no doubt that he launched a campaign to discredit the SACC, claiming that there was deep dissatisfaction on the part of overseas donor agencies with the administration of funds given to the SACC.[10]

Equally important, though less openly expressed, are fears about the Chief's personality. Most persons who have met him describe him as an egotist and a man extremely sensitive to criticism. His speeches are replete with denunciations of Black consciousness leaders, liberals, and the SACC. About half of one Soweto speech—which lasted six hours—was devoted to certifying good relations with the ANC and attacking Dr. Motlana, whom he described as a "political delinquent" and a "babe in the woods" who "has not even begun to understand that in politics you cannot get away with aiming attacks on prominent people." In the light of his own attacks on prominent figures, the charge was somewhat ironic.

At our meeting with the Chief in his office at Ulundi, the KwaZulu capital, Buthelezi presented himself as a reasonable, patient, farseeing man, ever ready to negotiate and committed to nonviolence. He is a powerfully built man, with a trim figure, ready smile, neat beard, and quick emotional gestures. Within a few minutes he had plied us with dozens of speeches, articles, public letters, and other Buthelezi documents. He pointed proudly to photographs of himself with President Carter, Kenyan Prime Minister Jomo Kenyatta, Nigerian Brigadier Murtala Mohammed, and other notables.

A major portion of our talk was devoted to defending himself and criticizing others as a way of defining his own position. For example, he emphasized the distinctions that must be drawn between himself and homeland leaders who accepted independence and added that his stand had encouraged other homeland leaders to reject independence. He also denounced Motlana and other Black consciousness leaders: "In effect they want *Black* majority rule, whereas I accept a Black-White future."

As for Desmond Tutu, his defense of the militant youths who tried to attack Buthelezi at the funeral of PAC leader Robert Sobukwe still rankled: "Tutu tried to get in touch with me for a one-to-one talk afterward, but there's no use in discussion, for it's an ideological problem. I have no hard feelings against him. He is a pathetic figure." (At other points during our talk, Buthelezi declared that, unlike many other Black leaders, he was willing to talk with anyone.) The "so-called Christians at the SACC" disgusted him.

Buthelezi emphasized that he had assumed leadership of KwaZulu because he saw the homelands as a power base from which to begin an assault on apartheid. Yes, many detractors accused him of working within the system—but he could point out that *all* Blacks work within the system. (Those "detractors," we remembered, insisted that there is a great difference between submitting to law under compulsion and voluntarily accepting its platforms.)

With considerable vehemence, Buthelezi denied the charge of tribalism.[11] "The Zulus have a colorful history. They are a warrior people. So some say I am trying to dominate with a Zulu imperium, because they fear our past reputation. But we are not a tribe. The Zulus were the mightiest *nation* here in the nineteenth century. And I am the great-grandson of King Cetshwayo, who defeated the British at Isandhlwana, and the grandson of King Dinuzulu on my mother's side. My mother was Princess Constance Magogo Zulu. ANC was founded in 1912 by a Zulu, Pixley Seme, who was married to my mother's sister, Princess Harriet. We Zulus have the best case for wanting independence. But we do not see a Zulu destiny. We see a common destiny, not only for all Blacks, but for Blacks and Whites in one nation."

Inkatha's participation in the South African Black Alliance (SABA), of which Buthelezi is chairman—making his third "hat"—should prove his lack of interest in Zulu hegemony, he added, for SABA also includes the Coloreds' Labor Party, the Indians' Reform Party, and the parties of two homelands, Qwa Qwa and KaNgwane.

Buthelezi made much of the fact that unlike his rivals he has a strong visible constituency. "No leader whose support comes from his *constituency* can support disinvestment. Only political cowards do that. My people must survive. *I* favor constructive engagement of foreign enterprise, which offers work opportunities. It should be based on the Sullivan Code [drawn up by the Black director of General Motors, the Rev. Leon Sullivan, for U.S. multinational corporations in South Africa] or even better, the European Economic Community Code. I am not necessarily against *selective* disinvestment. It should be tied to concrete things. I do believe that corporations can help a people move toward economic justice, by demanding enforcement of codes of conduct and engaging in other nonviolent pressures."

Smiling broadly, the Chief expounded on nonviolence, a customary emphasis in his talks with foreign journalists. Throughout history, the *people* had never chosen violence unless there was no other choice, he asserted. Moreover, surveys of South African Blacks had shown that the majority want peaceful change. Furthermore, the state was too powerful for armed struggle alone to succeed. Finally, as a committed Christian he could not espouse violence. Instead he believed in nonviolent pressures such as getting foreign investors to adhere to codes of conduct, monitoring employment practices, and pressing Whites to sit down at the negotiating table. If these did not work, Blacks should use consumer boycotts, or even widespread strikes. But if they too did not succeed, then one could hardly expect Blacks not to use violence.

Buthelezi's vision of the future appeared somewhat vague. It included equal opportunity, majority rule, and redistribution of wealth. When we asked whether he favored a socialist or capitalist model, he replied that he was committed to curbing unbridled capitalism. At the same time, he believed in free enterprise—modified to a certain degree by African communalism.

And "one person, one vote"? Again he seemed to hedge a little: "We must all sit around the table at a constitutional conference and look at the models of how to get to majority rule. You can't just impose it on a group. Just to say 'one man, one vote' is too simplistic. We must have checks and balances, compromises, to advance to 'one man, one vote' in a unitary system. We must use consensus. I am thinking, of course, of a Black-White future."

In all this the church had a role, as a conciliator between man and man and between mankind and God, declared Buthelezi. Although he himself was a lay deacon in the Anglican Church and assisted his priest in communion, he felt that the churches as a whole had not faced up to their responsibility. Only individuals such as Beyers Naudé and Archbishop Hurley had done so.

Gatsha Buthelezi seems to fall within the liberal tradition of making improvements in the existing economic structure. However, some observers maintain that Blacks have benefited very little from multinational projects in KwaZulu. For example, a German plant turned out to be highly labor-intensive, employing mostly skilled German expatriates and only a few Zulus.

Moreover, although Buthelezi talks about boycotts, strikes, and the monitoring of employment practices, there has been virtually no action.

Buthelezi is showing his muscle in other directions. Unlike Motlana and others who refused to join regional committees set up by the Ministry of Cooperation and Development, Buthelezi agreed to join one for Natal, commenting that "Inkatha members would serve on the committees to prevent sellouts from misleading the people." Because his only real rivals refuse participation on principle, Inkatha dominance in the Natal region is virtually assured, and could give the committees more credibility. Buthelezi has also hinted that Inkatha would take part in community councils.

Although ANC leaders tend to be suspicious of Buthelezi, they met him in London, England, in late 1979, perhaps in the belief that it is better to keep the powerful Zulu chief on their side than to force him into the hands of the enemy. Whether an alliance could develop between Buthelezi and the ANC (which is committed to socialism and to any expedient means—including armed struggle—to liberation) is highly problematic. Some ANC leaders suspect that the government's seizure of their guerillas near the border of Swaziland and KwaZulu may have been instigated by the man most likely to see himself as a rival to ANC's Nelson Mandela—namely, Gatsha Buthelezi.

Since Robert Mugabe decisively defeated Bishop Muzorewa, the "Whites' choice" for the leadership of Zimbabwe, some observers have concluded that leaders who work inside White-created structures are rejected by most Blacks, and that Buthelezi's star is setting. The chief himself appears to be ever more on the defensive. Yet Inkatha retains formidable assets: numbers, organization, experience.

According to *Frontline,* Buthelezi and Inkatha should be telling South Africans far more specifically what they stand for:

> The rhetoric of liberation is not enough. South Africa is coming to the crunch and everybody knows it. The needs have moved on: now we need close examination of change and where change ends up. . . . Anything Inkatha could possibly come up with would either scare Whites or enrage its Black opponents, and more probably do both. But Whites as much as anyone else need a clear idea of what fundamental change might come to. White suspicion that liberation is mere camouflage for an underlying intention to turn the tables creates unnecessary resistance. And as Buthelezi knows, those who blithely dismiss the Whites as irrelevant obstructionists with no role in the future are living in a fool's paradise.
>
> To spell out the specifics would cause White upset. But Inkatha's life expectancy is high enough to sustain a fair amount of upset. . . .
>
> And South African society overall would be better for the existence of a concrete, practical, alternative proposition which it can get its teeth into and chew over.[12]

Yet another big question is: could Buthelezi work with other leaders? Could he accept anything but the top-dog position?

IV — BLACK MOVEMENTS IN EXILE

How do the exile movements differ from Streek's categories of the "survivalists" and from those who "use the system in order to destroy it"?

Since 1961, when ANC leaders became convinced that armed struggle would be more effective than nonviolence, the influence of the South African Communist Party (SACP) with the ANC seems to have grown (largely as a result of difficulty in obtaining financial support except from the Soviet bloc).[13] Hence Whites are not excluded, and some of them—such as SACP members Joe Slovo, a former Johannesburg lawyer, and his ex-wife Ruth First—have attained positions of power in overseas offices of the banned organization.

ANC leaders also tend to see the South African conflict as a class struggle and the present situation as a special kind of colonialism. Hence national liberation should be the goal of the first stage, to be followed by a socialist revolution. All "progressive forces," even the emerging Black bourgeoisie, should be seen as allies in the struggle during the first stage.

However, ANC militants harbor suspicions of Inkatha, fearing that it might offer to take part in an internal settlement as an alternative to the liberation movement. Unlike the Black Consciousness Movement (BCM), with its emphasis on mass uprisings at the right moment, the ANC favors tight underground organization and outside training to prepare for guerrilla war.

Observers agree that the PAC has a far weaker following than the ANC, especially since the death in 1978 of PAC charismatic leader Mangaliso Robert Sobukwe. (The PAC, it should be recalled, was less than two years old when it was banned, in 1960.) After frustrated attempts to get financial backing in the West, the PAC obtained substantial help from China. Hence Moscow-Peking rivalry shapes the competition between these two movements. The PAC looks to the revolutionary potential of the peasant sector and the Bantustan contradictions within the system.[14]

Until 1979, the Black Consciousness Movement was more a movement affiliating various Black groups than a political organization as such. The BCM approach is still characterized by greater spontaneity and a looser power structure than the tightly organized ANC and PAC. The BCM philosophy has been that this less bureaucratic approach allows greater freedom from detection.

Refusing to see itself as a party, the BCM has drawn adherents from the proscribed ANC and PAC, and even the Unity Movement. The BCM has always sought the inclusion of Coloreds and Indians, whom it defines as "Black" because of the discrimination they have experienced.

Theoretically, one could grade the perspectives of the four leading movements on a descending scale. ANC leaders, many of whom were educated under the British Empire, have welcomed the support of Whites, including communists, and they have an international outlook. The breakaway PAC narrowed its purview down to Africa, yet retained a transnational approach. Young Black Consciousness adherents, products of Bantu education, have less knowledge of the world beyond South Africa, and focus on conscientizing the Blacks within its borders. Inkatha is primarily concerned with Zulu aims. However, such a formulation is an oversimplification, for each one of these groups has shown subtle changes over the years.

The ANC now has more Blacks in its London, England, office than it did a few years ago, and insists that its members give their allegiance first to itself, and only secondarily to the SACP. The PAC has admitted not only Coloreds and Indians, but Whites such as Patrick Duncan (whose father was Governor-General of South Africa). In the early 1970s White activist Basil Moore played an important part in the Black Consciousness Movement as editor of *Black Theology in South Africa*.[15] And today BCM includes Indians and a few White exiles.

It is true that the primary emphasis of both PAC and BCM has been on independence from Whites. Yet in his first speech as head of PAC in 1959, Sobukwe declared that anyone who "owes his basic loyalty to Africa, and who is prepared to accept the democratic rule of an African majority, would be regarded as African." Then he added, "We guarantee no minority rights, because we think in terms of individuals, not groups."

In the same vein, BCM's Steve Biko declared, "The [White] liberal is no enemy, he's a friend—but for the moment he holds us back, offering a formula too gentle, too inadequate for our struggle. . . . While we want to work to establish a country in which all men are free and welcome citizens—White as well as Black—we have to concentrate on what means most to Blacks. So at this stage we are preoccupied with Black sensitivities, not White sensitivities."[16]

Although Chief Buthelezi is fond of saying that his movement, unlike the others, is nonviolent, such a categorization is also an oversimplification. We recall a conversation in Lesotho with Phyllis Naidoo, a banned ANC Indian leader who had fled there by swimming the icy river between the two countries. Although she had recently been wounded by a bomb placed in a package sent from Europe, but routed of necessity through South Africa, Mrs. Naidoo welcomed us into her rondavel for two long talks.

"We decided for armed struggle in 1961 only after agonized discussions, asking ourselves whether we had exhausted every alternative," she stressed. "And today, the struggle is many-pronged—it does *not* depend on armed conflict alone. We are working in other ways inside South Africa." Although it would have been dangerous to elaborate on this, she pointed out that the ANC had been active in the 1973 Durban strikes, and spoke with respect of nonviolent actions such as recent consumer boycotts, as well as the work of the SACC.

Although Mrs. Naidoo had scant praise for Chief Buthelezi, she felt that there were no irreconcilable differences between the ANC and the BCM, pointing out that almost all SASO students who escaped to Lesotho joined the ANC forces.

It is interesting, too, that many Black consciousness advocates have supported the campaign to free Nelson Mandela, the ANC leader imprisoned on Robben Island since 1964. The campaign originated with Percy Qoboza, the dynamic editor of South Africa's only Black daily newspaper, the *Post* (liquidated by the government in 1981). Qoboza is also known as the "faceless godfather" of the Committee of Ten, for although he is not a member himself, the meeting that spawned it took place in his office in 1977.

Qoboza, a plump, nattily dressed, genial man whose career includes early studies for the Catholic priesthood and a year at Harvard University on a Nieman fellowship, speaks pessimistically about the future: "The lines are being dangerously drawn. The White political structure has been thrown into a state of utter confusion. Their confidence in separate development has been shattered, and there's a growing realization among them that it cannot work. But they don't know what the alternative is. And the greatest danger is their refusal to think of alternatives."

Despite this gloomy outlook and the fact that he has been imprisoned, Qoboza has not lost hope; he continues to make efforts to dialogue with Whites. On the other side, Qoboza tries to take the role of mediator between quarreling Black political groups. "My counsel to the Ten," he says, "is not to look down on Buthelezi, but to extend the hand of fellowship. He's basically a good man, and has talent. I don't think there are monumental differences between us."

From the foregoing it might be concluded that the bitter rivalry that has hamstrung "survivalist" and exile liberation groups (to the delight of the government) is more a question of personalities than strategies. The groups seem able to agree to disagree on liberation movement ties with foreign powers, the inclusion of Whites, and the politico-economic framework of the future. They do agree on the value of economic sanctions (although it is treason to support them in South Africa). They also share a rejection of homelands policy and of any form of federalism.

The Issue of Federalism

To understand their attitude toward federalist proposals, it will be helpful to look at one that is actually far more "enlightened" than the consociational[17] plans advocated by the government. Its proponents, Heribert Adam and Hermann Giliomee, question the conventional opinion that the antagonists will inevitably collide with a force that will destroy the country in the process.

Conceding that the dominant group—the Afrikaners—does not by itself have the power to determine policy, they nonetheless focus on that group in the belief that currents within it, rather than actions of the Blacks, are more likely to influence South Africa's future in the short run. Adam and Giliomee examine the underlying cleavages within Afrikanerdom and the growing tendency of the younger bureaucrats and entrepreneurs to be concerned with pragmatic problems of survival. They point out that foreign threats such as sanctions impress the need for solidarity on elites in divided societies only when the threats are directed against society as a whole. In the case of South Africa, foreign threats are correctly seen as a danger by the ruling minority, but as a benefit by the majority.

Outside interference, then, exacerbates latent cleavages in the ruling oligarchy, and the cleavages lend themselves to various possibilities of splits. Pressures from the West, particularly if they include carrots as well as sticks, could cause the past ethnic mobilization of Afrikanerdom to fade into pragmatic survival calculations.

Adam and Giliomee declare that the present plans for consociation do not include the preconditions for success, because under those plans group membership would be imposed, segmental leadership would be restricted, and power and resources would be distributed unequally. They believe that a *negotiated* federalism may be the most feasible constitutional formula to reduce conflict and alleviate anxieties among minorities.

Widely decentralized autonomous decision-making in a federal state would be paralleled by a proportional exchange of revenue at the central level. Although the federal units would have a high degree of ethnic homogeneity, they would have to avoid any reference to race or ethnicity as the rationale for constituency. Moreover, there would be no restrictions on mobility; influx control would be abolished.

Adam and Giliomee conclude that "together with affirmative action [a concept on which they do not elaborate] in an expanding economy there is no reason why all of South Africa's people could not benefit from such a gradual change of policy."[18]

The trouble with such a plan is that it is indeed a picture of South Africa's future in the short run. Black leaders among both the survivalists and the exiles dismiss with contempt even this more enlightened version of federalism. It might have worked a few years ago, they concede, but the Whites let opportunity after opportunity for such a compromise slip by.

Increasingly, Blacks see all blueprints for a federalist solution that would preserve "ethnic unity" as a rationale to preserve White hegemony. Even the Adam-Giliomee proposal for a just and proportional exchange of revenue at the central level they regard with skepticism, because it seems to them unlikely that the exchange would be implemented radically enough to correct the enormous inequalities between racial groups.

In the end *verkrampte* and *verligte* seem to agree on what one Afrikaner called "the inner nonnegotiable core": rejection of "one person, one vote" in a unitary state. On the other side, surveys show that Blacks are increasingly convinced that attainment of "one person, one vote" is *their* "inner nonnegotiable core."

Is there no way out of this impasse? ANC and PAC leaders speak in uncompromising terms, but many "survivalists" inside the country would probably agree with Dr. Motlana that majority rule could be implemented gradually—provided that Blacks were given a timetable.

Interviews with Bennie Khoapa

One vision of the future that falls short of a holocaust "too ghastly to contemplate" comes not from a White liberal but a Black who has been immersed in the struggle for freedom for many years. He is Bennie Khoapa, who founded both the short-lived *Black Review* and Black Community Programs (BCP), in which he was Steve Biko's boss. After five years of banning, he fled to exile in the United States. Today he is an important figure in the overseas activities of the Black Consciousness Movement, and makes frequent trips to the African continent for consultations with leaders working inside the republic.

Born in the Transkei near the Lesotho border, Khoapa did social work in the 1960s. Realizing that SASO needed to reach beyond its student constituency, Biko persuaded Khoapa in 1971 to become nonstudent advisor to the group. A year later Khoapa was also organizing the BCP.

In our talks with him, Khoapa made it clear that he speaks only for himself and should not be considered a spokesman for the BCM.

One of his principal goals is to unify the strife-torn liberation groups because, like many other Blacks, he sees dissension as a cardinal African weakness. He also sees the splits that occurred at the ratification of the Freedom Charter as a source of current divisiveness. It will be recalled that the

Charter was passed in 1955 at the Congress of the People, which brought together the ANC, the South African Indian Congress, the South African Colored People's Organization, the multiracial South African Congress of Trade Unions, and the (White) South African Congress of Democrats, a leftist organization that had emerged after the banning of the Communist Party and had pledged to work for equal rights for non-Europeans.

At the meeting it became clear that the Congress of Democrats was trying to take over the ANC. As a result, others (mostly from the ANC Youth League) seceded from the ANC in 1959 and formed the breakaway Pan-Africanist Congress. It was not so much the inclusion of the Whites as the possibility of control by forces outside Africa to which these dissidents objected. Nelson Mandela shared Sobukwe's fears of international domination by the Communist Party, but decided to stay with the ANC and fight from within.

At the Congress of the People, the ANC—which previously had operated by passing down issues to grass roots groups for discussion—railroaded the Freedom Charter through with very little debate. A key sentence read: "All national *groups* [italics added] shall have equal rights." A group was defined along tribal/ethnic lines. Thus the Charter, says Khoapa, would perpetuate categorizing people according to ethnicity, instead of recognizing—as the PAC did—that all South Africans can be "Africans," regardless of color. Khoapa believes that Buthelezi is seeking not "majority rule" but majority Zulu rule, and that the Chief might base his claim to supremacy on the implication in the Charter that, if a leader can claim the largest group, he will have more clout at the center. The Charter, he says, should be redebated.

Aside from personality differences, there is no good reason why the ANC, PAC, and BCM should be divided, Khoapa believes. In the first place, he says, the PAC and BCM are not really anti-White, as is so often believed. Secondly, the ANC leadership now is visibly Black. It insists, however, that the ANC be a national organization where any person, regardless of color, is welcome.

To Khoapa, federalism or any other plan based on ethnic power is "racist." "People everywhere have begun to realize that the world is a community. Even a superpower like the United States can't run the show. We do belong to one human family. But we must begin in our own backyards, and then link up with others."

Khoapa foresees a new kind of leadership emerging in African countries, and he is attempting to work out a relevant leadership theory. Some elements of the Black Consciousness Movement would be taken as models:

"Black consciousness defies the bureaucratic ethos that characterizes the ANC. During the 1976 disturbances it was the inabiity of the police force to identify the leaders that led to its failure to stem the tide. The police are always out after 'leaders.' But even Biko was never named 'the leader' by us—the media did that. All of us should be potential leaders. We need great people, not just office-seekers. A real leader is both a leader and a follower.

"The basic need is for supportive structures. People at the grassroots have to be involved in decision-making. And we must see this as a continual, open-ended process. The experts on high say confidently that they can solve problems. But like the great Brazilian educator Paulo Freire, I believe that problems can't be solved, but only managed.

"In Africa that would also mean submitting problems to the group. The African is a social being. For example, in traditional communities and even many urban areas, we don't make an appointment with a neighbor or a friend—we just drop by. Whites, with their individualism and sense of privacy, don't understand that. Nor do Marxists understand that we are a religious people. Individualism and Marxist secularism are essentially Eurocentric. We need ideas relevant to Africa."

Although he would like to see a form of African socialism emerge out of the struggle, Khoapa predicts that instead there will be a so-called compromise solution. After prolonged guerilla warfare, the White South Africans will wish to negotiate. The many non-African capitalist interests involved in the situation will also not wish to see precious resources destroyed through escalating warfare. Although a military solution would be the best as far as Blacks are concerned, says Khoapa, such a solution will not be "allowed".

"Whites feel that unless White rights can be guaranteed they can't trust Blacks. It will take a long time to convince South African Whites that Blacks can be democratic. So the government will approach the world community to act as referee—to find a solution that will pass some internationally accepted criteria of 'fairness.' It will be somewhat like the conference the British called to effect a settlement in Zimbabwe.

"Discussion will include a broad spectrum of actors and experts, including academics like Adam and Giliomee, and representatives of the Organization for African Unity, which actually has a Western perspective. Out of this will come a unitary state, the dismantling of apartheid, and probably acceptance of a Western-type government. The world community will require that the position of Whites be protected as was the case in Zimbabwe.

"The process leading to that 'solution' will include the seduction of some Blacks and some Black political organizations by dangling before their noses the ethos of money and power. The ANC in its present form runs the risk of falling victim to such a courtship. Although the criteria of fairness will be better than those prevailing, they will certainly not coincide with what the majority in South Africa consider acceptable.

"This scenario outwardly appears good. But any arrangement that emphasizes the special protection of 'special' people is in fact a sellout. That a White majority should either be 'trusted' with government of the majority (provided that they treat the majority with fairness) or be given 'special assurances' is indication of the arrogance of Western thinking when dealing with African peoples.

"If education becomes free for Blacks, and the right to mobility is guaranteed, and programs are set up to help compensate for inequities, Blacks, over the years, may begin to catch up. The chief problem is that this 'solution' leaves the *basic* economic structure untouched—still in the hands of Western capitalism. True liberation means getting rid of neo-colonialism; it means developing African socialism. Then we could contribute to world civilization from our own perspective."

Notes

1. Barry Streek, "Black Strategies against Apartheid," in *Africa Report,* July-August 1980, pp. 35–39.

2. In October 1968 the Broederbond sent out a special circular urging Broeders to assist with the registration of Colored voters. . . . The Christian de Wet Fund—the secret 1,000,000 rand fund of the Broederbond—contributed 50,000 rand to finance the election of the Federal Party" (Ivor Wilkins and Hans Strydom, *The Super-Afrikaners* [Johannesburg: Jonathan Ball, 1978], p. 163).

3. Cf. Newell M. Stultz, *Transkei's Half-Loaf: Race Separatism in South Africa* (New Haven: Yale University Press, 1979).

4. Joseph Lelyveld, "South Africa's Black Unions Gaining Political Role," in *New York Times,* December 21, 1980.

5. According to the *Survey of Race Relations* for 1979, Inkatha had 250,000 card-carrying members, of whom little more than a thousand lived in Soweto (*Survey of Race Relations, 1979* [Johannesburg: SAIRR, 1980], p. 40). One Black observer has pointed out that the fact that Inkatha is the only black political organization the government allowed to endure for a long time makes its membership of a quarter million (out of five million Zulus) seem not so significant as was commonly assumed. More recently, the Johannesburg *Star* reported on a poll it had taken in Soweto: "An overwhelming majority of Soweto residents would support Dr. Nthato Motlana and his Committee of Ten if they stood in Soweto council elections, a *Star* poll has found. . . . The Committee of Ten also emerged in a three-way contest including Chief Gatsha Buthelezi's Inkatha Movement and Mr. David Thebahali, current council chairman. Asked which group they would back in Soweto council elections, 69 percent of the random sample said the Committee of Ten; 9 percent said Inkatha; 5 percent said Mr. Thebahali's men" (*Star* [weekly air mail edition], November 15, 1980.

6. A short club with a knobbed end, used by tribal groups, especially Zulus, as a weapon.

7. Professor Boshoff succeeded Gerrit Viljoen in 1980 as the head of the Broederbond. Thus it would appear that there has been a shift from *verlig* to *verkramp* leadership in this powerful Afrikaner secret society. Boshoff is an advocate of an "Afrikanerstan." The White homeland would be situated in the Orange Free State. No Blacks would be allowed to work there. In this manner, Whites would be truly self-sufficient, and no longer dependent on Black labor.

8. Professors at white universities have been permitted to import radical books that are forbidden for general consumption. This elitist exception is apparently based on the idea that the South African intellectuals need to know the literature of the enemy.

9. Ntatho Motlana, "Separate Dilemmas and White Rights," *Frontline,* May 1980, pp. 22–23.

10. *Ecunews* 4/79 (February 25, 1979), p. 1.

11. Subsequent to our interview, Inkatha's constitution—which assured Zulu priority, while recognizing other "African brothers"—was revised, and "Zulu" and "African" were changed to read "Black." There is no racial restriction on membership at any level, but well over 80 percent of Inkatha members are Zulus, and there is no question that they dominate the organization.

12. *Frontline,* December 1979, p. 26.

13. The extent of the SACP's influence within the organization is largely unknown.

14. Gail M. Gerhart, *Black Power in South Africa* (Berkeley: University of California, 1978), p. 195.

15. Basil Moore, ed., *The Challenge of Black Theology in South Africa* (Atlanta: John Knox, 1974).

16. Donald Woods, *Biko* (London: Paddington, 1978), p. 55.

17. Newell Stultz defines consociationalism "as a political union of segmented groups such that none loses its identity or substantial control over its own affairs, and within which interelite cooperation occurs with the deliberate aim of counteracting 'the centrifugal forces at the level of the masses' " (Stultz, *Transkei's Half-Loaf,* p. 147).

18. Heribert Adam and Hermann Giliomee, *Ethnic Power Mobilized* (New Haven: Yale University Press, 1979), p. 300.

Part Three
The Future

CHAPTER EIGHTEEN

What Does the Future Hold?

Most revolutions occur unexpectedly. The revolution in South Africa is an exception. For decades distinguished writers such as Alan Paton, politicians such as Alex Boraine and Helen Suzman, magazines such as the forthright *South African Outlook*, and even mass circulation newspapers such as the *Rand Daily Mail* have warned of a holocaust unless the government instituted fundamental change. No South African can say, as "good Germans" did after the Nazi atrocities, "I did not know."

The truth is that the revolution has already begun. There is the guerrilla warfare spreading at the borders and in the cities. And there is the piecemeal relaxation of petty apartheid, the crumbling of job reservation, the discussion of self-governing rights for Indians and Coloreds, and the somewhat equivocal collective bargaining rights obtained by Black unions. True, most of these are labeled "cosmetic changes" by Blacks who will settle for no less than complete power-sharing, a decent standard of living, the elimination of the homeland policy and of influx controls. The gap in perception has the quality of Greek tragedy: changes that seem so monumental to one side seem merely palliative to the other.

Nevertheless, one should not minimize the psychological impact of these palliative measures. For Blacks they are a tangible sign of progress that can occur when they unite. For Whites they represent a realization that power *can* be shared, that their cherished vision of the world can be altered, and that social change is not necessarily disastrous.

Changes in attitude should be measured not only in reference to the point where one has arrived, but also in reference to the point from which one has started. It was only a few years ago that it was common for Whites to refer to Africans as "Kaffirs." In 1980 when a minister declared that Blacks should not be included in the proposed constitutional talks, because "their thought processes are still slower than ours," the overwhelming reaction forced him to apologize and withdraw his remarks.

Even Prime Minister Botha is on record as saying that he would not object in principle to interracial marriages. Considering the difference in the starting points of Americans and South Africans (and the fact that Blacks constitute 11 percent of the population in the USA and 83 percent in the RSA), perhaps the most comparable situation would be one in which a White American is asked to approve the marriage of his daughter to a Black.

More fundamental is the revolution in the way Blacks look at themselves. Today young urban Africans, particularly, display a pride, a conviction that the future is theirs, even a certain disregard for death, that separates them from their parents. As they view the liberated countries of Africa and other young nations around the world, they know that they are moving with history. And they sense that they are a part of a wider world revolution.

It is almost as difficult for White Americans as for White South Africans to accept this reality. White Americans live in a society in which only a minority of their fellow citizens are Black. Moreover, Black Americans are incomparably better educated and better integrated into the economy than their counterparts in the RSA. Yet after twenty-five years of integration efforts, American Blacks suffer from unemployment rates twice as high as those for Whites, and are "ghettoized" in decaying urban areas. Discrimination in all aspects of life persists, and even the Ku Klux Klan rides again. Other minorities live only marginally better. Americans have not come to terms with the Third World in their own midst.

Equally hard for Americans is to adjust to the rise of a new spirit among Black, Brown, and Yellow peoples in the rest of the world. Most Americans condemn the deployment of Cubans in Angola, ignoring the fact that South African forces are also fighting in that country. Such a double standard is partly rooted in racism. During the Vietnam War, American servicemen were taught to regard the Vietnamese—who later outfoxed them—as "gooks." It is not hard to imagine that today the U.S. military educates its worldwide Rapid Deployment Force with a more wide-ranging set of pejorative terms bolstering American contempt for those who have the misfortune not to be born White.

On several counts South Africa is not a problem unto itself, but a problem that belongs to the whole world. In the first place, the RSA is obviously dependent upon industrial countries for investment capital and export markets. Secondly, the West is even more dependent on South Africa than the latter is on the West, in certain respects. According to the government-sponsored *South African Digest*,[1] the republic produces 81 percent of the West's chrome (an anti-corrosive additive), 73 percent of its gold (used in electronics and other industrial fields), 86 percent of its platinum (used in oil refining and catalytic converters), 48 percent of its manganese (a basic raw material in steel), and somewhat smaller percentages of other vital mine als.[2] It is also the greatest source of gem diamonds.

Thirdly, in the words of Father Gerard de Fleuriot, "South Africa is the best place on the globe for capitalism, because it contains a Third World within a First World. It has the sophistication of a European economy—an articulate infrastructure, with a sophisticated banking and monetary system, a stable administration, good communications and harbors—combined with a Third World pool of abundant cheap labor. In addition it has almost all the minerals . . . the world [wants], except oil."

The RSA is currently reducing its dependence on oil by producing "SASOL,"[3] liquified gas produced from coal, of which the country has an abundant supply.

Obstacles Resistive to Change

With such ideal conditions for capitalism, it is not surprising that the rate of return on investment has often been higher than 20 percent. However, the present revolutionary situation seems to be deterring some U.S. multinationals from further investment. In fact, in 1979 there was a net divestiture of $164 million. According to Robert Manning, "the combination of anti-apartheid critics, constraints imposed by the apartheid government, continuing strikes and guerrilla attacks, and political uncertainty has begun to make these companies wary of future commitments."[4]

As long as apartheid exists, capitalism will seek cheap labor that is supplied from a migrant labor system codified by pass laws and by influx control that dumps redundant workers into bleak resettlement camps in the homelands.[5] Although most American government and business leaders probably disapprove of apartheid, they rationalize that the country has vital raw materials—from chrome for reinforcing steel to uranium for nuclear bombs—that American consumers cannot dispense with.

South Africa also reflects a problem seemingly inherent in the human condition. Perhaps the urge to experience superiority by underlining one's membership in a "superior" group—an urge often expressed through racism—is a common human need. In any case, it is a worldwide phenomenon.

The land of apartheid is also a microcosm of the global struggle between the "haves" and the "have-nots." It is a reflection of the human unwillingness to relinquish power. True, sharing of power is not tantamount to yielding it entirely. To a *volk* that has always perceived the world in ethnic terms, however, to share power with a numerically stronger group is to lose it forever.

Perhaps, too, the Afrikaners' desperate clutch on their dominant status differs only in degree from White Americans' reluctance to admit minority persons into their unions and school boards, or from a government policy that deliberately fosters unemployment to balance middle-class woes, a policy that primarily victimizes Blacks and other minorities.

Even more basic is fear of change—that all-pervasive amorphous anxiety that grips us all when we face the unknown. In truth, no one can accurately predict what changes will be wrought in the "South African way of life" after the shift to majority rule. Whites like to believe that they will maintain the same high standard of living. Even liberals who advocate bringing the Blacks' standard of living "up" talk rarely, if ever, of scaling their own lifestyles "down." A surprisingly high number of Blacks, too, imagine that simply because the country is so rich in natural resources, virtually all of their people will live at the level now enjoyed by Whites.

Change will hurt, however, for it means transforming both structures and attitudes. Which takes precedence? Like their counterparts in the United States, South African liberals such as Archbishop Hurley have tended to focus on attitudes, in the belief that if attitudes change, structural changes would follow. In recent years more liberals in both countries have come to believe that economic, political, and legal structures are primary.

A simple example: in the early days of desegregation most Whites in a certain New Jersey community could not entertain the thought of using an outdoor swimming pool that a new law had opened to all races. On the first hot day, only Blacks appeared for a swim. On the second hot day, a few Whites dabbled their toes in the cool water. On the third day a few took the plunge. Two weeks later, Blacks and Whites were paddling around the pool as if tension had never existed. It is true, of course, that attitudes have not always followed the lead of new laws, but in many cases that is because the laws have not been implemented firmly or wisely.

All of this should not be taken to denigrate the value of efforts to change attitudes, for obviously they are important in dealing with a problem as fraught with emotional undertones as is racism. Rather, it suggests that racial attitudes are more likely to be changed indirectly, as the result of pressures or the realization that other interests—survival, comfort, status, and the like— are more important. It also suggests why the political liberalism of both Blacks and Whites—a tradition based largely on Christian moral suasion— has not been very effective in the past.

Today, even within the churches, the younger liberals (or progressives, a term that many would prefer) are more sophisticated about political and economic issues, more aware that the struggle must be many-pronged. Realizing that grassroots democracy is poorly developed in South Africa and that most Whites tend to follow the leader, they are also more concerned with reaching opinion-makers—politicians, newspaper editors, business leaders, university professors, dominees of the NGK hierarchy. Some of these liberal/ progressives have been active in think tanks dealing with South Africa's future.

Although the transition to majority rule will be psychologically painful for Whites, that attitudes *can* change gracefully is suggested by the lives of several persons portrayed in this book. Perhaps the most notable example is Beyers Naudé, the NGK dominee who abandoned his post as Moderator of the Southern Transvaal Regional Synod to head the multiracial Christian Institute. In late 1979 he took another "impossible" leap, renouncing his membership in the White NGK in order to join the Black NGKA. He thus retained the same confession of faith, while moving into another milieu. Perhaps this is symbolic of the leap that Whites will need to make as the nation moves toward majority rule.

Naudé has long been considered a "prophet" by those who have followed him over the years. With his rugged build, square jaw, intense blue eyes, and deep resonant voice, he indeed has the bearing of a prophet. In any gathering his presence is felt immediately: one senses that this is a man who has reflected, and suffered, and dared to look into the future—and yet retains a quiet centeredness.

Despite his banning, Naudé has managed to retain a remarkable awareness of what is going on in the country and the world, as well as a tough-minded ability to appraise events. Although extremely pessimistic about the course the government is taking, he is optimistic about developments in the NGKA. For years he was troubled by the isolation of the NGK from its so-called daughter churches and from the SACC. But the NGKA, as a member of the SACC, could become an even more important element in the ecumenical fellowship of churches, he realized . It could also take the lead in establishing organic unity of the three "daughters." Then they could challenge the White NGK as to whether it wished to join the majority and become a multiracial institution—or stay out. By insisting that Blacks and Whites worship together, the NGKA would be taking a stand in direct opposition to that of the White church, and the very act of worshiping together would become a challenge to separate development. Thus the NGKA could play a more meaningful role.

Together with CI activist Roelf Meyer, Meyer's wife, and a few other NGK members, Naudé crossed what might be called "another Blood River." To Whites the step represents one of the most crucial challenges of all.

The Role of White Liberals

If the initiative is passing to the Blacks, is it true that White liberals, inside and outside the churches, are "irrelevant"?

The term "liberal" itself is vague, often used pejoratively in South Africa to describe Whites who pass resolutions and then go home to cocktails in their suburbs. It is true that many members of the "liberal" Progressive-Federal Party (PFP) stop short of "one person, one vote."[6]

It is also true that almost every liberal organization in South Africa—from the PFP and the Urban Foundation to small welfare groups and scholarship funds—seems to be heavily subsidized by Harry Oppenheimer,[7] the billionaire head of the vast South African-based multinational Anglo-American Corporation. Oppenheimer is moving to eliminate job reservation (apparently in the belief that it is both immoral and uneconomical). Yet he has done virtually nothing to eliminate single-sex hostels in the mining industry.

Still, it should be remembered that many White liberals have taken courageous stands, and some have been banned and imprisoned. We believe that they are still relevant.

The real task of White liberals, say Black leaders, is to prepare Whites in their own communities for political change. Already some Whites in the National Union of South African Students (NUSAS) are attempting that task, albeit with little success. The Black Sash, led by dedicated women such as Jean Sinclair, her daughter Sheena Duncan, and Joyce Harris, continues to join multiracial protest demonstrations, work with Blacks threatened with deportation to homelands, and warn the White community of the need for fundamental change.

For example, in February 1980, Sheena Duncan described the reaction of Blacks to the new laws (following the Riekert Report) making it virtually impossible for "illegals" to work in "White" areas:

> We are now watching the fuse to the powder keg burn shorter every day. . . . Never in the sixteen years since this office was opened have we experienced such anger expressed by Blacks or such a sense of impending catastrophe. Never have we felt more urgently the need to communicate to White South Africans the realities of what is happening.[8]

Under the vigorous leadership of director John Rees, the South African Institute of Race Relations is rapidly changing from a largely White liberal organization to an aggressive multiracial but Black-dominated institution. It should be noted that over the years, not only English-speaking Whites, but many Afrikaner liberals have been active in the SAIRR—notably journalist/ historian René de Villiers, economist Sheila van der Horst, and Christian Institute member Fred van Wyk. Although few Blacks played a leading role in the past, the Rev. E. E. Mahabane and D. D. Tengo Jabavu were elected to the executive.

Today the Institute's wide-ranging activities include research (such as its invaluable annual survey of race relations), preparing young Blacks for university entrance exams through the use of volunteer tutors, publishing the lively, informative monthly *Race Relations News*, and even supporting the call to free ANC leader Nelson Mandela (in an issue that was temporarily banned).

Visitors (and some insiders) often wonder why these organizations and progressive newspapers have not been banned. One reason may be that they perform a useful function for the government by pointing to potential friction points in the system before they become explosive.[9]

Although the contributions of Jewish leaders such as Progressive Party spokesperson Helen Suzman, writer Nadine Gordimer, and *Rand Daily Mail* editor Benjamin Pogrund have been important,[10] the majority of White liberals have been committed Christians.

Will South Africa be better off under Black rule—or is it possible that one tyranny will be exchanged for another?

That question has been posed by many Whites, *verkrampte* and *verligte* alike. It is a pertinent question for both Blacks and Whites, because it is basically a question of the human condition. In this struggle there are no "good guys" and "bad guys."

Still, to pose the question as one for all South Africans to grapple with is one thing; to use it (by invoking the image of Idi Amin) in order to forestall majority rule is another. Blacks have as much right to make mistakes, and to learn from them, as do Whites.

Obviously, Blacks who are well educated and have a democratic orientation will be less likely to engage in destructive power struggles or corruption. The onus, then, is on the White power structure in South Africa. Liberals in the West, and their governments, can also play a part, by making it possible for more South African Blacks to study in their countries. Here the churches can play a particularly significant role.

Notes

1. Extract from a report published by the Subcommittee on Mines and Mining of the United States Congress, reproduced in a special newsletter enclosure in *South African Digest,* September 5, 1980.

2. American and Russian geologists dispute these figures. In any case, it is clear that South Africa is a giant in the worldwide mineral production industry.

3. The term "sasol" is an acronym for the South African Coal, Oil, and Gas Company, Ltd., a state-owned company formed to oversee South Africa's oil-from-coal program. The two plants bombed by the ANC are called SASOL I and SASOL II. American firms known to be supplying equipment or expertise to SASOL plants include Fluor, Babcock & Wilcox, Raytheon, Chicago Bridge, Honeywell, and Goodyear. According to the American Committee on Africa, Fluor committed itself to the Sullivan Code, but in 1979 Black Welders at the SASOL plants were being paid $2.20 per hour, while workers from other race groups were paid $4.00 per hour ("Fluor: Building Energy Self-Sufficiency in South Africa" [a pamphlet of the Africa Fund, associated with the American Committee on Africa], August 1979).

4. Robert Manning, "South Africa Tries to Regain Confidence in Foreign Firms," *Christian Science Monitor,* December 18, 1980, p. 11.

5. In July 1980, when over 10,000 Black municipal workers went on strike, the Johannesburg city council broke the strike by deporting 1,200 workers to their homelands. More than 50 percent of all Black workers in the RSA are migrant workers.

6. In 1977, even famed author Alan Paton declared, in direct reversal of the policy his Liberal Party (since dissolved) had always espoused: "Universal suffrage and a unitary state imposed from without is not—for me—compatible with the liberal ideal" (*Reality,* September 1977, pp. 6–7).

7. Henry Oppenheimer is recorded in Jewish birth records, but has since converted to Christianity, and is a member of the Church of the Province of South Africa (CPSA).

8. "Resettlement and Influx: The Fuse Burns Shorter," in *Black Sash,* February 1980, p. 5.

9. Heribert Adam and Hermann Giliomee, *Ethnic Power Mobilized* (New Haven: Yale University Press, 1979), p. 282.

10. One hundred twenty thousand South Africans identified themselves as Jewish in 1970. According to Allie Dubb, there were few South African Jews until the gold rush in the 1880s brought in a heavy influx from Western Europe and Great Britain. This was soon followed by an inflow from Eastern Europe. In 1937 immigration was severely restricted, and by 1970 Jews constituted only 3.1 percent of the White population. More than half of those questioned in a survey of Johannesburg Jews in the late 1960s felt that discrimination could eventually be transferred to them, and nearly half expressed doubts that they would remain in the republic. Antisemitic cartoons appear in some Afrikaner newspapers, indicating a residue of prejudice from the early gold-rush days when the cartoon character "Hoggenheimer" was portrayed as plotting with English-speaking colonialists. Although some Jews have been involved in the banned South African Communist Party, labor unions, the PRP, and NUSAS, the great majority are silent and conservative (Allie A. Dubb, *Jewish South Africans* [Grahamstown: Rhodes University Institute of Social and Economic Research, 1977], pp. 24–55).

CHAPTER NINETEEN

Violence, Nonviolence, and the Churches

The church mirrors society. In the words of David Bosch, "The key to the understanding of history as God's revelation lies in the eyes of the beholder." God can be seen as One who "nationalizes" all humanity, or as the Great Revolutionary. The church can be a pillar of the status quo *or* a force for social change.[1]

All over the world today groups in the Catholic and Protestant churches have become vital elements in the swing to the right, and the fear-ridden resistance to change. Thus in some churches there have emerged a rigid insistence on top-down authority, a growing concern for conformity, and an obsession with "order."

On the other hand, the churches have also spawned the growth of what Brazilian Archbishop Helder Camara calls "Abrahamic minorities." In some Third World countries, particularly in Latin America, these minorities have had a powerful impact on the majority. In South Africa, these prophetic groups have pushed their establishments to stand up for measures leading to the gradual dismantling of apartheid. Although oppression continues, it is chilling to think of what might have happened without the prophetic witness of the multiracial churches.

Abrahamic minorities in South Africa have encouraged the emergence of Black leadership, notably in the SACC. Among other things, this has demonstrated to society at large that Blacks can exercise such roles responsibly and that Blacks and Whites can work together harmoniously. In a ghettoized society, the church remains the one important institution where Blacks and Whites can meet on an equal footing—if they make an effort to do so. Thus its very existence has served to keep hope alive.

Even the multiracial churches that challenge the status quo retain many weaknesses. All of them have a middle-class orientation. For example, they fail to recognize the basic reality that church membership is largely made up of workers. Pastoral activity is geared toward building community in residential areas, without reference to industry, even if factories are located within parish boundaries. Priests and ministers have little or no relationship with the

Black working class, particularly men, and are ignorant of developments in the Black trade union movement.

This covert class orientation of the churches is also evident in the fact that in all of them—to varying degrees—the power structure lies with the Whites. Another is the dependence of the structure on money. Still another is the fact that only rarely do rank-and-file members carry the banners of eloquent resolutions into the field of action.

Yet it is precisely because of this prophetic leadership that Christianity retains some credibility among the angry youth in the townships. Even many of those who have lost faith in the institution itself frequently consult with their minister or priest. One could say, then, that the church has exercised a "moderating" influence. Such a phrase is loaded, however. It is more accurate to see the church as a link between generations, in a time when "sons know not their fathers, and fathers know not their sons." For young people maimed by the narrowness of "Bantu education," the multiracial "European" churches also serve as a link with the rest of the world.

Finally, the church is one place where nonviolence is discussed and where some nonviolent action originates.

The Future of Nonviolence

It is often said that nonviolence is dead in South Africa. Nothing could be further from the truth.

Why does this myth persist? The news media usually prefer to feature the "excitement" of bloody riots. Few journalists recognize nonviolent action—as such—when it occurs. With the exception of Chief Buthelezi, Black political leaders do not use the term, for they tend to identify it with passivism, or at least pacifism, and to blame the failures of the early ANC on its adherence to pious Gandhian principles. They cannot afford to be regarded as Uncle Toms who plead with the oppressor. Yet these leaders call for "noncooperation" or "resistance" through specific actions such as boycotts and strikes. By whatever name, nonviolence is alive in South Africa.

In 1980 alone, examples were legion: the months-long boycott of schools by thousands of Colored children; the boycott of classes by African and Indian university and high-school students who sympathized with the Coloreds; the multiracial march led by Bishop Tutu to protest the arrest of Colored Congregational minister John Thorne after he had publicly supported the protesting students and teachers; the consumer meat boycott to support striking workers demanding the right to choose their own nonracial grievance committees; bus boycotts protesting hikes in fares; a work stay-away in Cape Town commemorating the 1976 uprising, a stay-away that became 90 percent effective; auto industry strikes in the Port Elizabeth area; dockworker refusals to load cargo in Cape Town; persisting noncooperation with the military draft; ongoing support from the churches for the SACC's 1974 conscientious objection resolution; continuing endorsement of the 1979 resolution calling for noncooperation with the state "in all those areas in the ordering of our society where the law violates the justice of God"; the refusal of the Anglican priest David Russell to comply with his banning orders, resulting in a court conviction.

Most of these actions were built with multiracial cooperation and all have been infused with a new militant spirit.

If nonviolent struggle in South Africa has not been so effective as it might be, it is partly because training in the principles of nonviolent action is rare, and has been confined chiefly to Whites. Moreover, communication between action groups is weak, largely because the government plants informers in circles suspected of subversion—or bans such groups entirely.

Another factor is that of limited understanding of the dynamics of non-violent action among White Christian liberals, many of whom identify it with an emphasis on conciliation and conversion of the "enemy", rather than on confrontation. Some even regard confrontation in any form as "violence." The few small groups in South Africa that show interest in nonviolence tend to gather for Bible study meetings, where they spend more time on seeking justification for action in some scriptural passage than on planning the action itself. (It should be noted that Bible study groups are ubiquitous in this unusual country.)

Blacks rarely attend such meetings today. They are wary of the government's suspicion of multiracial gatherings, and they are impatient. After centuries of oppression, must they wait for the conversion of White hearts and minds?

Yet without using the word "nonviolence," Blacks seem to be turning to a more pragmatic approach to nonviolent action. Although few have heard of James Farmer, of the Congress of Racial Equality (CORE), they would recognize the import of his words:

> We must show that nonviolence is something more than turning the other cheek, that it can be aggressive within the limits a civilized order will permit. Where we cannot influence the heart of the evil-doer, we can force an end to the evil practice.[2]

A leading exponent of the pragmatic approach is American political scientist Gene Sharp, who catalogues no less than 198 different methods of non-violent action that men and women have already used successfully in struggles for national liberation, civil rights, better living conditions, disarmament, and fundamental changes in an oppressive regime.[3] Emphasizing that nonviolent action is *action* that is nonviolent, he asserts that advocates of nonviolent action do not seek to abolish power; they recognize the necessity of wielding it in order to control the power of threatening political groups.[4]

Refuting the idea that power depends on a ruler's ability to impose his will on his subjects through forceful sanctions, he maintains that a government or a system is dependent on the people's goodwill and support. Political power is always dependent on replenishment of its sources by the cooperation of institutions and individuals—cooperation that may or may not continue.[5]

In one chapter of *Social Power and Political Freedom*, Sharp addresses the question of South Africa.[6] Considering the Nationalist government's repression of nonviolent protest and the weak international response to Black pleas for economic boycotts and for ostracism of the government, the feeling that one must fight back is eminently understandable, he says. However, recognition of the difficulties of nonviolent struggle and of the inadequacy of the movement in the past is not in itself an argument in favor of violence. Defeats and stalemates also occur when violent means are used.

A cardinal point is that although military superiority does not guarantee victory—especially in guerilla warfare—the government does possess a vast preponderance of armed power. Indeed, it is an advantage to the government for Blacks to resort to violence, for that provides an excuse for extremely harsh repression. It was precisely because the killings at Sharpeville were perceived as committed against peaceful unarmed demonstrators that such vigorous protests were roused around the world. If the government could have shown that those shot were terrorists, the effect would have been radically different.

It is naive, says Sharp, to think that if opponents of a regime struggle nonviolently, the oppressive regime will quietly acquiesce. Nor is it true that nonviolence avoids suffering, or that the movement has been defeated if the opponent retaliates with brutal repression. On the contrary, suffering and death must be expected. Active nonviolence requires more inner strength and self-discipline than does armed struggle.

It is the willingness to persist that produces what Sharp calls political jiu-jitsu: the government's supposed greater power is rendered ineffective and turned to its own disadvantage, because the repression of nonviolent people tends to alienate sympathy for the government (provided that this is known to a wider public).

One must also ask whether a technique of struggle is likely to replace one dominating minority with another, he stresses. True freedom requires the diffusion of power. Concentration of power, even in the hands of the most benevolent ruler, makes it easier for a usurping despot to impose absolute tyranny. In contrast, nonviolent struggle tends to diffuse power through the population as a whole, for the struggle itself depends on voluntary widespread popular participation. At the end of the struggle, military power is not concentrated in the hands of the commanders, and the population is trained in effective ways of struggle by which it can maintain its freedom against new usurpers.

While Sharp is not optimistic that the struggle in South Africa will be basically nonviolent, he makes specific proposals concerning dissemination of knowledge on the use of nonviolent methods, organizing for group action, promoting awareness of what others have done in difficult situations, and ways in which international groups can support liberation in the RSA.

Although Black Consciousness Movement leaders have not taken a firm position on the option of violence or nonviolence, they have expressed the hope that revolution would be as peaceful as possible, and have spoken of crippling the economy as one way of promoting liberation.

It is interesting to note other parallels between Sharp's ideas and those of the BCM. Both Sharp and the BCM base their thinking on the principle of conscientization: helping an oppressed people to think critically, recognize themselves as dignified human beings, and develop an *active* awareness that can turn them into subjects who can transform their oppressive situation. Both call for enhancing Black pride, strengthening Black institutions, and building the will to resist. Both are concerned with diffusing power among the populace—or, as Bennie Khoapa would put it, making every activist a potential leader. Sharp and BCM activists see the capacity to act in solidarity as both a means and an end.

Finally, Sharp's basic thesis—that a regime is dependent upon the willingness of its subjects to continue to cooperate with it or submit to it—is echoed by Barney Pityana's declaration that the Black man is an accomplice "in the crime of allowing himself to be misused and therefore letting evil reign supreme in the land of his birth."[7]

All these common factors refer only to the conscientization, education, and organization steps of a campaign. Sharp seems to go further by exploring the execution of strategy. Since Black Consciouness theory is still evolving and it is difficult to know what is happening underground, it is impossible to tell whether a similarity of tactics will emerge.

ANC leaders, too, concede that even after building alliances with other nationalist groups, they could not amass enough armed power to fight the enormous military machine in the RSA. Victory will come not only from acts of sabotage (which thus far have been largely confined to objects rather than persons), but from pressures of world opinion, international isolation of South Africa, and relentless strikes, they believe.[8]

Although all of these tactics fall under the rubric of "nonviolence" it is hardly likely that the ANC, BCM, or PAC would adopt a term that has fallen into such disrepute.

Nonviolence as Ingredient of Success

Is nonviolent struggle unrealistic? Consider the demonstrations by the Coloreds in the Cape in 1980. As long as they remained nonviolent—that is, during the school boycott—even the Afrikaner press pointed to the legitimacy of Coloreds' grievances, and the Prime Minister himself vowed to satisfy them. When rioting broke out, many Whites were seized with fear. Minister of Police Louis LeGrange denounced "skollies" (an Afrikaans pejorative for Colored hooligans), implicitly labeling the whole group of demonstrators, and the authorities were provided with a rationale for repression.

The likelihood that some of the rioting was instigated by *agents provocateurs* only serves to underline how well an oppressor recognizes that violence can alienate the populace. Militants trained in nonviolence refuse to be provoked.

If the participants in the many boycotts, strikes, stay-aways, and demonstrations that occurred in 1980 had been schooled in nonviolent discipline, none of the actions would have degenerated into counterproductive riots. If the actions had been coordinated on a nationwide scale, the country might have been brought to a standstill.

To be really successful, nonviolent action in South Africa should be coordinated with action in countries that help sustain apartheid. For many years church-based groups such as the American Friends Service Committee and the Interfaith Center for Corporate Responsibility, together with the American Committee on Africa and the International Defense and Aid Fund, have appealed to Americans to engage in divestment and other pressures.

On the other side, the Sullivan Code (sponsored by American Zionist Baptist minister Leon Sullivan), as well as the EEC Code and the Urban Foundation Code, call on multinational corporations to agree to measures such as nonsegregation of work facilities and equal pay for equal work. Basically, these codes operate "within the system."

Critics say that such codes are a public relations success that helps to secure the multinationals' presence in a basically unchanged system (one that depends on migrant or "commuter" labor, deprivation of political rights, and division of the country into homelands and White areas).[9] These critics maintain that divestment represents the quickest and least violent path to eradication of apartheid.

For discussions of the pros and cons of these approaches, the reader is referred elsewhere.[10] It is important to note, however, that studies show that multinational firms have not adhered to the codes closely, and some have engaged in lively code-dodging. All the codes, too, ignore the crucial problem of migrant labor. Like the government in its policy of building up a Black middle class as a buffer against revolution, the implementation of the codes seems to result in giving advantages to skilled labor and passing over the poorest workers.

Even more important is the fact that these companies are not concerned with their involvement in the political system, but only with how they treat their employees. A crucial question is, what impact does the enterprise have on society? For example, does it sell oil to the military (as the Gulf Oil Company does)?

Significantly, increasing numbers of Blacks are following religious leaders such as Bishop Tutu by defying sedition laws and advocating divestment. In lieu of total divestment, some favor partial divestment, or spotlighting companies where conditions are particularly bad.

Another proposal is "phased withdrawal." Pressure would be exerted upon multinational firms to adhere to the Sullivan, EEC, or Urban Foundation codes. If the firms do not comply at once, pressure groups could set deadlines for each of the conditions to be met. All of this would be accompanied by well-organized publicity about life under apartheid, working conditions in that particular enterprise, and the purpose of this nonviolent action. If the firm fails to respond, the ultimate weapon—pressure for total divestment—would be applied. Designing a strategy based on a timetable (perhaps three or four years) would have the advantage of providing the company with time for adequate planning and maximizing the value of the accompanying educational campaign.[11]

Multinational corporations operating within the capitalist system will not carry out any new code of practice unless the cost of cooperating with apartheid outweighs the cost of change. A new balance of power is emerging, however. In the past few years Third World nations—including oil-rich Nigeria, an articulate foe of apartheid—have emerged as important trading partners for the West. If these nations join together, and the threat of Soviet involvement grows, the traditional silent alliance between White South Africa and the West may crack.

As John Marcum points out, "If it [the United States] does not join in international sanctions to induce peaceful change, the political, military, and economic realignment of a very large part of the African continent will take place despite and against the United States."[12] Moral questions, then, do play a role in *Realpolitik*. By the same token, nonviolent action becomes relevant on pragmatic grounds.

Nonviolence is not a panacea. It cannot achieve revolutionary goals without revolutionary conditions. That revolutionary conditions are multiplying, however, is suggested by a look at the basic contradictions in the system. For example, despite the policy of "separate development," Whites have become even more dependent on Black labor, and the *Star* reveals that "after almost three decades of official separate development, Blacks are outnumbering Whites more than ever in the country's so-called White areas."

Because the government needs administrators and small businessmen in the homelands, it has set up universities there. Yet these schools have spawned Black consciousness leaders, and have been the scene of continuing revolt. Apartheid becomes more confusing, costly, and inefficient. Half-empty buses have often passed by persons waiting for "their" color. The pass system has cost the equivalent of $150 million a year.[13] To promote the notion that Blacks are happy in South Africa, the government has allowed some to travel abroad—where they absorb new ideas and develop new relationships.

"Job reservation," which guarantees protection from competition with Blacks, has brought headaches to entrepreneurs, as industrial expansion has created shortages of White labor. With increasing industrialization, White entrepreneurs have become more dependent on Black consumers—on a market that cannot develop unless Blacks receive higher wages. And as the cost of fuel to transport its products has increased and threats of sanctions have multiplied, South Africa has become even more dependent on its internal market. As "White" Africa has shrunk, the RSA has also become more dependent on selling its goods to Black African countries that condemn apartheid.

Herding Blacks into separate townships and homelands is designed to protect Whites, yet that very ploy has precluded infiltrating Black groups with White agents. Although Black informers have been used, as liberation draws nearer and Black solidarity grows, it has become increasingly more difficult to recruit any who will not eventually turn against their White patrons.

Capitalism needs alert workers—but apartheid generates fear among Whites, a climate that breeds alcoholism, neuroses and coronary disorders (White Johannesburg has the highest heart-attack rate in the world), and a nightly retreat behind the barricades of one's home.

Moreover, the system is ultimately based on control by armed force—an approach that contains its own contradictions. The more that any nation or group arms itself, the more it becomes a threat, and thus a target for an armed opponent. The more money an embattled minority spends on weapons, the less it spends on the impoverished majority—thus escalating the need for greater "defense." The more a group uses arms, the more it becomes psychologically dependent on them, thus insulating itself from empathy with the oppressed, and from understanding the causes of their hostility.

The more a minority government depends on might to defend itself, the more it needs to incorporate members of the oppressed majority into the armed forces. In South Africa, the government is trying to build up indigenous battalions among the very groups to which it denies full citizenship.

The Future

Three scenarios of the future can be conjectured.

In the first, urban and rural guerrilla warfare mounts steadily, and in reaction the *verkrampte* hard-liners press for harsher retaliation. *Verligte* Whites, caught between the heightened militancy on both sides, are pushed into *laagers* with their *verkrampte* colleagues. Conflict escalates, martial law is declared, fighting Black youths are machine-gunned from the turrets surrounding Black townships, and helicopters mini-bomb suspected resistance areas. The bombing escalates. In the process, however, it destroys a large segment of the labor force upon which the economy depends, and alienates world opinion as well.

The outcome of guerrilla warfare is, of course, difficult to predict. Conventional weapons and methods were not too effective against Vietnamese guerrillas. David Halberstam observes that perhaps the Black armored cars of this war will be garbage trucks driven by Black men through the streets of the rich.[14]

Moreover, although Afrikaners are commonly depicted as "tough," today South African White youths live in the city, train for careers in business and government, and are accustomed to being waited on hand and foot by servants. A few years ago defense force recruits were taught how to survive in conditions comparable to those of the "terrs" ["terrorists"]. The lessons included making a fire without visible smoke, killing snakes, and eating them. Six months later the rate of breakdown had increased 40 percent. Psychological casualties among White South Africans fighting at the Namibia/Angola border have also been heavy.

In the second scenario, the defense force feels pushed to do the "unthinkable": it drops a nuclear bomb. A mushroom cloud descends on the populace indiscriminately, with little sensitivity to the superior qualities of the White race.

The third scenario projects the possibilities of nonviolent action under ideal conditions. Africans, Asians, and Coloreds organize their constituencies, and then demand a timetable for the gradual dismantling of apartheid. They warn the authorities that if their demands are not met, they will proclaim a general strike. When the ultimatum is refused, the militants call the strike—and the entire country comes to a standstill.

Zimbabwe, Tanzania, Zambia, Nigeria, and other African countries close their borders to South African goods. A well coordinated boycott of South African goods is touched off around the world. Workers refuse to load or unload South African Airlines freight and passengers. Dockworkers refuse to handle South African cargo. Postal workers disrupt the mail and telecommunications between South Africa and their countries. American and European consumer groups join the boycott of South African products.

Students demonstrate before the United Nations, South African embassies, and major RSA consulates. Conscienticized groups converge on shareholder meetings of multinationals involved in South Africa. The companies agree to withdraw. Citizens with "Apartheid No!" banners march upon Washington, where they demand stricter application of the United States embargoes against selling arms and nuclear technology to South Africa.

An international brigade of civilian volunteers is airlifted into South Africa. It has three functions: to bring information and support from the rest of the world, to bear witness to events, and, if necessary, to forge a "living chain" around demonstrators. As prominent persons whose deaths could shock the world join the brigade, tension mounts.

Confronted by an opposition so well organized and coordinated, the government agrees to the demands.

Although such an ideal scenario is hardly likely to occur, it is significant that there are precedents for every ingredient of the action. For example, in 1974 the United Mineworkers Union (USA) brought suit in federal court to stop the importation of South African coal on the basis of a tariff law barring goods produced under conditions of forced labor. South Africa quickly repealed the law.

In 1977 the International Confederation of Free Trade Unions, which represents fifty million workers in the noncommunist world, threatened (but never carried out) an international boycott. At the same time, British postal union leaders promoted a refusal to handle South African mail (but they were suppressed by British authorities). General strikes, shareholder actions, refusals to unload cargo, embargoes, "living chains," and even small international brigades have all taken place around the world in response to injustice. The problem is that they have rarely been coordinated, and have seldom occurred on an international level.

What would happen if this unlikely scenario were played out? Lives would surely be lost. Thousands of people would suffer. But millions of lives could be saved.

It is probably not a fitting role for clergy to lead strikes and boycotts. But as church leaders such as Bishop Tutu and Allan Boesak would point out, it is surely their role to conscienticize parishioners and to support such action when the goal is social justice.

Over the years the South African churches have been somewhat equivocal in their attitude to nonviolence. For example, most of them have upheld the doctrine of the "just war." Moreover, the SACC's so-called conscientious objection resolution supports the right of selective objection—with which no thoroughgoing pacifist would agree. Today, however, the churches seem to be moving toward support of both pragmatic and "principled" nonviolence. It is also significant that SACC resolutions support both "conscientious affirmation" and the need for confrontation.

It is not necessary to have a deep religious faith to engage in nonviolent action. Yet there can be no question that over the years Christian moral conviction has given many South African clergy and laypersons the courage and staying power to follow this difficult path. It is a power based on respect for the adversary and on recognition of "there is that of God in every person."

Notes

1. David J. Bosch, "Racism and Revolution: Response of the Churches in South Africa," in *Occasional Bulletin of Missionary Research,* January 1979, p. 20.

2. James Farmer, *Freedom—When?* (New York: Random House, 1965), p. 101.

3. Gene Sharp, *The Politics of Nonviolent Action* (Boston: Porter Sargent, 1973); see especially Part 2, "The Methods of Nonviolent Action."

4. Ibid., p. 64.

5. Ibid., p. 8.

6. Gene Sharp, *Social Power and Political Freedom* (Boston: Porter Sargent, 1980); see Chap. 7: "What Is Required to Uproot Repression? Strategic Problems of the South African Resistance," pp. 161–180.

7. Gregory Jaynes, "Blacks in Exile Carry on War against South Africa," *New York Times,* June 20, 1980.

8. Heribert Adam and Hermann Giliomee, *Ethnic Power Mobilized* (New Haven: Yale University Press, 1979), p. 301.

9. Workers "commute" daily from nearby homelands such as KwaZulu to Durban, or Ciskei to Port Elizabeth, or Bophuthatswana to Pretoria. Migrants predominate in Johannesburg and

Cape Town, where they live in single-sex hostels on nine-, twelve-, or eighteen-month contracts. No homelands are near these two cities.

10. Probably the most objective analysis was done by M. G. Whisson, M. C. Roux, and C. W. Manona, "The Sullivan Principles at Ford." All three teach at Rhodes University in the Eastern Cape, near the Ford plant. The study was commissioned by the South African Institute of Race Relations, and published in early 1980.

11. When the Rev. Leon Sullivan, author of the "Sullivan" principles, gave the prestigious annual Hoernlé lecture at the University of the Witwatersrand in September 1980, he said that U. S. companies were moving at a "possum pace" in South Africa. Sullivan added, "I will be returning to America and turning screws more and more. I will be pushing all the companies harder and harder to implement the policies faster and faster, because the needs of Black people in South Africa are beyond description" (*Race Relations News,* September 1980, p. 2.)

12. John Marcum, "African Frontline States Forcing the Pace," *Nation* 225 (November 12, 1977): 492–495.

13. "Pass Law Costs SA $112,8-m a Year," in *Star* (weekend, airmail ed.), January 15, 1977, p. 2.

14. David Halberstam, "The Fire to Come in South Africa," *Atlantic* 245 (May 1980): 95.

CHAPTER TWENTY

The Future of the Churches

The real revolution of our time is the rise of Third World peoples determined to take control of their own lives. They are growing in numbers, in expectations, in power. For a time their aspirations can be frustrated through manipulations of the media, the labor market, the money market, and the unequal international exchange of goods.

But in the final analysis, Sharp reminds us, any government or system is dependent on the people's support. The revolt of the Iranian people after a century of oppression by foreign governments and their surrogates is only one example of the principle that it is the ruler's subjects who hold the ultimate power.

Whether western Christians like it or not, the Christian church is part of the revolution. Moreover, the structure of the church itself will be affected by changes in the relationships between peoples. And South African Christendom will surely be a microcosm of the changes to come.

In the future, we believe, Blacks will continue to come into more positions of leadership in all the multiracial churches. Many Whites in church hierarchies feel that Blacks are not "ready" for so much responsibility. Yet it is significant that in Mozambique and Angola Black clergy took over when the colonialists lost power, and seem to be working effectively.[1]

It seems inevitable that Christians and Marxists will engage in more frequent dialogue. The two ideologies share many goals, and as Lebamang Sebidi has observed, Marxism's anti-religious stance is almost incidental to its overall critique of Western society.

By the same token, the churches will probably come to recognize the implications of social class for pastoral action and focus more on the values and needs of workers.

The brittle bureaucratic structures of the historical churches will almost surely be shaken by new forms of worship emerging from the independent churches. Already the idea of a "tent-making ministry"—one no longer dependent on church buildings, church property, or even a regular salary for clergy—is beginning to gather support in the Indians' Reformed Church in Africa (RCA), and in other denominations. Moreover, if the Christian

241

church is to survive at all, it will need to recognize that many Africans express their reverence for God through drumming and dancing and making joyful noises unto the Lord.

Despite the Vatican's ambivalent attitude toward basic communities, they will probably grow among both Catholics and Protestants. Such communities respond to a profound need of human beings for participation in decisions that affect their lives in the spiritual, social, and political realms.

What will happen if church and state collide over the question of seeking government permits affecting the life and work of the church? After the decision by the Anglican Cape Provincial Synod that the church could not subject itself to a system of racial discrimination that required such permission, Archbishop Bill Burnett warned that the synod's decision could cause the disintegration of the present structural life of the church:

> It is my longing that we should not be so concerned to save the institutional church that we in fact do violence to what obedience requires in our lives. . . . So I just thought to share with you what to me is the greatest burden of my office—keeping the institutional church—which in a sense (although one does believe in the incarnation of Christ) I don't believe in, in which I have no investment in the real sense. In the Body of Christ, yes, but is this the same as the institutional church that I know?[2]

If Catholic and Protestant churches go further than refusing to apply for permits—if they continue to support the principle of civil disobedience and the right to selective conscientious objection, for example—they may face such persecution that the institutional church could well disintegrate. Yet to many Christians the church will not be true to its prophetic role if it is not prepared for that possibility.

In any event, the church will continue to need prophetic groups such as the Christian Institute and the South African Council of Churches, for there will always be a need for criticism of itself and of the society that Christians create. After the advent of a new regime, too, the church will be called to criticize the almost inevitable abuses of power among new rulers.

Both today and tomorrow that prophetic role includes not only criticism of the violence that human beings perpetrate on each other, but also the violence they wreak on Nature. In rich South Africa, where Whites have displayed an almost callous disregard for husbanding the earth, a new awareness of the relationship between human beings and Nature has been growing among a perceptive minority in the churches.

What kind of future will the churches face if an extreme leftist government should take over some day? It is worth noting that "Marxist" Zimbabwe is headed by a pious Catholic, and that the purge of Christianity by "atheistic communists" as predicted by rightists has not taken place. Beyers Naudé foresees that if extreme leftists take power, the church as *institution* may be badly crippled—but the church as *faith* may well come out stronger. Its witness may be more meaningful.

Archbishop Hurley agrees. "In Mozambique, the church in terms of buildings, schools, hospitals, and holdings is not what it was. But a good deal has been going on in basic communities, at the grassroots level. Perhaps that's the healthiest kind of Christianity. In South Africa, too, the church as people will survive."

The horizontal role of the church will always be more than that of carrying a prophetic vision of justice. It will also include taking the initiative to achieve reconciliation—reconciliation based on *caritas* and on concern for one's opponent. This is particularly true in South Africa, where those engaged in maintaining oppression have destroyed their own freedom and become captives of the system themselves. They, too, need liberation.

South Africa is a world problem. To the extent that Americans support its exploitive system through their own appetite for a high standard of living, they are part of the problem. To the extent that Americans take steps to rid their own society of racism and exploitation, they help South Africans see that it can be done.

South Africa also mirrors the human reluctance to share the "good things in life." Bishop Tutu might have been addressing the rest of the world when he told a group of White students at the University of Witwatersrand:

> We are committed to Black liberation because we are committed to White liberation. You will never be free until we are free. . . . So join the liberation struggle. . . . Uproot all evil and oppression and injustice of which Blacks are victims and you Whites beneficiaries, so that you won't reap the whirlwind. Join the winning side. . . . Oppression, injustice, exploitation, all these have lost, for God is on "our side"—on the side of justice, of peace, of reconciliation, of laughter and joy, of sharing and compassion, of goodness and righteousness.[3]

Notes

1. A somewhat analogous parallel is the implication in South African government propaganda that if Blacks had the vote, the country would be taken over by inept leaders or a foreign (read communist) power, and the West's mineral supply would be cut off. Yet the West has maintained a brisk trade with Marxist Angola and with other newly freed African nations.

2. "What the Archbishop Actually Said," in *Seek* (January/February 1980), p. 1.

3. *Ecunews* 13/80 (June 8, 1980), p. 11.

Epilogue

Many South African White voters went to the polls in the April 1981 general election with a sense of foreboding: this might well be the last under White minority rule. Bishop Tutu put it more bluntly: "Within five or ten years, South Africa will have a Black prime minister."[1]

The Nationalists' victory (capturing 131 seats in the nation's 165-member Parliament) was eminently predictable. Almost as predictable was the bolting of White voters from Nationalist ranks. The extent of that flight exceeded the expectations of many observers, however. The Progressive Federal Party gained nine seats, bringing its total to twenty-six. More worrisome to Prime Minister P. W. Botha was the showing of the far-right Herstigte Nasionale Party. While neither the HNP nor Connie Mulder's splinter Conservative Party won any Parliamentary seats, between them they managed to attract over 200,000 voters, more than five times as many as in the 1977 elections.[2] Whites opting toward the far right were clutching desperately at symbols of the old order. Under the circumstances, would Botha feel hamstrung—unable to push through even moderate reforms for fear of splitting the party?

Perhaps. He could interpret the elections as a mandate, however, since a closer look at the HNP and Conservative Party reveals that their growth emanates from the large number of extreme rightist refugees from Mozambique and Rhodesia.

The suppressed anxiety among the Whites was mitigated by the sense of power that comes from riding the wave of an exuberant economy. Gold continued to sell at high prices. Coal exports increased sixfold since the mid-1970s.[3] Even trade with Black African countries reached an all-time high. Although most of them were avowed foes of apartheid, they were more dependent than ever on goods that the continent's most industrialized nation could offer—a reality over which RSA continued to gloat.

Nevertheless, in early 1981 the country was plagued by 16 percent inflation—reflecting the low productivity of an apartheid economy. Many economists were stressing the need for a free market economy that would permit Blacks to compete with Whites, who have enjoyed protected status. (Even though formal job reservation for vacancies or reclassified positions no longer exists, the rule that no White can be replaced by a Black still protects the present work force.[4]) Moreover, direct investment by American companies continued to remain at a near-standstill. It was clear that guerrilla attacks, pressure from anti-apartheid groups, and the ambiguity of Botha's policies made American corporations hesitant to invest further.

Anxiety among Whites was also stoked by ongoing unrest in RSA. During the first half of 1981, African workers continued to strike at a number of plants, Black students called for work-stayaways in urban areas, and authorities stepped up their crackdown on such activists. Over five thousand people gathered at the Regina Mundi Catholic Cathedral to commemorate the 1976–77 Soweto uprisings with impassioned speeches, most of them supporting Mandela—whereupon police fired tear gas into the Cathedral. Thousands of Colored pupils continued their boycott of schools, and Colored leaders and academics with reputations as moderates continued to be detained—confirming the recent dramatic rise in militancy among people whom the Nationalists had been hoping to bait by means of relative privileges.

On the international level, anxiety among many South African Whites was heightened as they looked over the border into Zimbabwe. Under Marxist leader Robert Mugabe the nation was doing surprisingly well—perhaps too well for Whites accustomed to viewing Africans as inferior. Despite tribal rifts and economic problems, Zimbabwe was producing enough corn to export half its crop, and was doing so with an incentive-based non-Marxist approach. South Africans could take all this as a sign that it is possible for Whites to live and work with security in a Black-dominated society—or they could take it as an omen of the dread day when Black power would take over in their own land.

Some changes in South Africa did go forward in 1981. For example, plans were launched for an all-race sports complex situated between White Johannesburg and Black Soweto. After years of united Black and White demonstrations, twenty thousand Crossroads residents were finally promised a permanent status. The Security Police arrested several alleged members of the Wit Kommando, South Africa's own Ku Klux Klan. As student protests continued, authorities began responding to their grievances: schooling was not free, books were not provided free as they were to Whites, protest leaders were imprisoned, and Bantu education was designed to train Africans for inferior status. The government expanded teacher-training, and even began free compulsory education on an experimental basis in some two hundred African schools. Increasing numbers of Africans, however, declared that they did not want "separate but equal" Bantu education, but parallel curricula at the very least. The SACC went further, calling for a unitary, non-racial educational system. The authorities also talked of opening more universities to Blacks. Yet even at the liberal English-speaking University of Witwatersrand, where 10 percent of the enrollees were non-White, less than a quarter of that quota were African, the largest population group.

To Africans, all these reforms were the same kind of change that had been grudgingly offered during the last decade. The Nationalists were still not talking about reforms of "influx control," or of the Internal Security Act, or of the Group Areas Act, or of the Prohibition of Political Interference Act barring multiracial political parties.

More significant, perhaps, were certain attitudinal changes among sectors of the White intelligentsia. Students at the University of Witwatersrand shouted down Minister of Co-operation and Development Piet Koornhof. The editor of an Afrikaans newspaper warned readers that one day the Nats would almost certainly have to negotiate with the banned African National Congress, while another Afrikaans editor declared that it was useless for Whites to believe that they could maintain their privileged position by force. Even General H. van den Bergh, former head of the Bureau of State Security (BOSS), asserted that while Marxists may exploit the country's internal political and social circumstances, the real threat lay in the very real grievances experienced by Blacks. The systematic removal of discriminatory measures, he added, would inevitably lead to removal of political discrimination—in other words, to Black majority rule.[5]

On the level of action, however, almost every progressive move has been fraught with contradictions. As Joseph Lelyveld observes in a perceptive article, the government eases up on censorship of Black authors, but bans Black newspapers; it authorizes Black unions, then harasses their leadership; it admits that the homelands policy has failed to produce economically viable states, yet thrusts more of these "tribal groupings" into meaningless independence; it promises a new deal for urban Africans, then proposes legislation denying them access to courts to defend the rights they already have.[6]

It also curbs random police checks of "passbooks," yet pushes the Riekert Commission proposal that the right to stay in cities be conditional on having government-approved housing and employment. As Sheena Duncan of the Black Sash points out, this means that government control over Black people moves from the streets to their homes and places of employment. Actually, only about 10 percent of the total African population now qualify for urban residence rights under these conditions. (It was this 10 percent that Riekert hoped to elevate into a middle class too fearful of losing privileges to rebel against the system.) Moreover, the earlier government policy of providing no further family accommodations for Blacks in urban areas has produced a great shortage in housing. As for other Black workers, the Riekert Commission's recommendation that government effect a more systematic control over the flow of non-urban workers to the towns had already resulted in police arrests of thousands of unregistered African workers, many of them from impoverished rural areas, despite protests of employers desperate for labor. The contract workers who do manage to get temporary residence rights will be increasingly tightly controlled and will remain segregated in squalid single-sex hostels.

Although the privileged urban Blacks have enjoyed little tangible benefit from the new policy, the government's hope of deflecting political unrest may be satisfied in another way. Some urban Blacks feel that the large force of casual contract workers from rural areas has a depressing effect on wages, gets used as scab labor, and makes the organization of stay-aways more difficult—thus leading to a possible breakdown in solidarity between urban families and those confined to rural areas.[7]

In other words, the "contradictions" may not be so contradictory, after all. More sophisticated control of the work force is central to neo-apartheid.

Another device for control is to hang the threat of expulsion to the homelands over the heads of African workers. When Black municipal workers went on strike in Johannesburg, over one thousand of them were deported to their homelands.[8] Still another device is to tie recognition of Black unions to stringent conditions, such as bureaucratic delaying procedures in the collective bargaining procedure. Hence the most effective Black unions have refused to register.[9]

Behind all this lies the central issue, the homelands policy, which clearly is based on Whites' fear of being overwhelmed by the "Black danger" and robbed of their high standard of living. Hence amid all the talk of "reforms" persisting through 1981, the government continued its policy of forced removals of Africans to areas where, in the words of Bishop Tutu, "they are dumped like bundles of rubbish." (Tutu, who has made forced removals a rallying point, pleads that every White person should visit one resettlement camp.) In the Ciskei, for example, unemployment has reached 45 percent. The Cillié Commission found "that there was a high level of infant mortality and a widespread incidence of malnutrition in the Ciskei. In the 6–23 months age group, rates were as high as 27 percent for kwashiorkor. The residents of the Thornhill, Sada-Ntabathema relocation camps, although comprising 7 to 8 percent of the Ciskei's population, had no doctor."[10]

Is this perhaps tantamount to writing off entire populations as expendable? Is it genocide?

That people squeezed into such misery may nevertheless rise up one day out of sheer desperation remains a distinct possibility. Nor does the strategy of co-opting 10 percent of the Africans remain more than a gamble, since the privileges offered may only whet their appetite for complete political equality. The government has not yet come up with a workable plan for political incorporation of the excluded majority. As Heribert Adam observes, "Increased economic integration continues to contrast with enforced political segregation, which runs counter to the policy of co-optation in the interest of preserving free enterprise."[11]

The Alternatives

What options is Botha considering in the search for an exodus out of this impasse? At this point one can only speculate. Although the National Party is sharply divided over the need for change, several "think tanks" have been set up in RSA to discuss models that could be drawn from as the basis for an eventual plan. Publicly, Botha is talking of moving ahead to some form of loose confederation, an economic association joining the African homelands and the provinces. The latter would include not only Whites, but Coloreds and Asians, who would now enjoy a direct vote in national affairs. The exact form of such a confederation is the subject of considerable debate.

A far more radical design is that envisaged by Progressive Federal Party leader Frederick van Zyl Slabbert in a 170-page treatise analyzing constitutional alternatives. It envisions a nonracial constitution and universal suffrage with a federal government and proportional representation in voting—a system that gives minority parties representation in a legislature in proportion to their popular vote, thus offering safeguards against the dangers that Whites perceive in a winner-take-all form of majority rule.* Perhaps more important, these proposals would not be imposed, but supporters would seek approval for them at a national convention of all important political groups, including the leading African nationalist movements.[12]

At present very few Whites even among the "reformers" would agree to such a scheme, since it foresees not a confederation of ethnic "nations," but a unitary state and eventual majority rule. Moreover, it emanates from the leader of a minority White party, one associated with English-speaking "liberals" (although, significantly, van Zyl Slabbert happens to be a "born again" Afrikaner).

A third option, less radical than the van Zyl Slabbert plan but world-shaking to Afrikaners, is one that seems to be bruited about in top government circles, according to Gary Thatcher of the *Christian Science Monitor*. It would involve (1) the transformation of the Republic into a strong confederation (with Botha—or conceivably even a Black—as president) consisting of a White-ruled state and the homelands, (2) expansion and consolidation of the homelands, (3) changing Soweto into a kind of "city-state," with considerable autonomy from surrounding "White" areas, (4) giving all South Africans, Black and White, a sort of dual citizenship, whereby an African, for example, could obtain a South African passport, but be eligible to vote only in his or her "tribal" national state, (5) abolition of most racial discrimination, (6) basing the confederation on a shared economy, with regional "growth points" and minimal barriers to commerce between each subdivision.[13]

Since such a plan has not yet been publicized, one can only conjecture about its details. However, one observer, exiled Black Consciousness Movement leader Bennie Khoapa, finds it basically similar to an option that he once predicted that the Nats would consider. He believes that the blueprint would involve (1) speeding up the process of granting "independence" to the homelands and buying off homelands leaders attracted to power and privilege; (2) dividing the four White provinces into smaller units, so that their size would approximate that of the homelands; (3) perhaps setting up part of the Orange Free State as a kind of "Afrikanerstan" for purist Afrikaners willing to live without Black labor (the Free State happens to contain much of South Africa's mineral wealth)[14]; (4) modifying influx control so that it emanates not from the central government, but from industry and the migrant worker's

---

*The latter form prevails in the United States, since at the local level the winning contestant represents all the electorate from his or her district.

"national state" (a pattern already established with workers from Mozambique, Lesotho, and other southern African countries); (5) shifting control of African dissidents to the "national states" (a process already begun—for example, the Ciskei bars union activity, the Transkei has been operating full-fledged machinery of Pretoria-style bannings and detentions, and the Ciskei has launched a computerized system that keeps track of each worker's employment history, including any record of "trouble-making"[15]; (6) giving the central government authority over matters pertaining to industry, foreign affairs, defense, transport, and mining; (7) decentralizing functions such as social services and education to the "national state" level; (8) setting up a system allowing Black chiefs to get together after "consulting" their people (rather than making decisions through direct vote).

To manipulate such a plan, the present government would crack down even harder on both the left and the extreme right. This might demonstrate to anxious Whites that they were still protected against radicals. The HNP and the Conservative Party would be too small to resist Nationalist leaders, and the latter would presumably be able to convince the bulk of White voters, those in the center, that they *must* change, since now the African majority and world opinion stood behind the plan.

On the surface, the plan appears to be a solution with liberty and justice for all. Since Africans would be able to vote for president of the federation, the president would probably be Black. The new power stucture might even find a Black foreign minister and Black ambassador to the United Nations who would be acceptable to all the dominant interests. The African territories, which have changed names over the years from tribal reserves, to bantustans, to homelands, would finally be baptized as "national states," thus removing the international stigma. Black leadership would appear to be in control. "Minority rights" would be protected.

But just what would protection of minority rights really mean? asks Khoapa. If every African is forced to relate to some homeland, and if the federation is based on existing homelands and provinces, the economically rich areas are still left in the hands of the Whites. The fact that the White-run provinces might be divided into states no larger than the average homeland (in an effort to demonstrate to the world that Whites held no more territory than Blacks) would not alter this fundamental discrepancy. One comparatively small White (or at least non-African) group, then, would wield at least as much political power as a much larger African population group. More important, the Whites would retain economic power. Already there are signs that many White politicians and entrepreneurs could go along with so-called Black rule, as long as the existing economic order is left intact. In other parts of Africa Black nationalist governments are in fact dominated by the world capitalist system.

Control of Africans would still persist, but it would be carried out by a variety of more sophisticated economic devices. Moreover, leaving social services and education of Africans (for which the government now spends a fraction of what it spends for White services) to the impoverished "national states" would mean depriving average Africans of their principal means of catching up with Whites some day. In other words, this "contingency plan" would protect the economic status of Whites and do little, if anything, to reconstruct the economic order. Indeed, the Whites might become richer still, for funds could pour in from abroad in response to the arguments that stability now prevailed and that foreign capital was needed to advance Blacks.

Could such a vision become reality? It is noteworthy that all these possible positions are "White positions." Khoapa says that a great deal of arrogance persists on the part of many Whites—including members of all parties in South Africa, many Western government officials, heads of multinationals, and even some academics in the West. Such arrogance suggests that Whites hold the key to the future of South Africa and that therefore they have a responsibility to produce a "plan." The fact is that no acceptable plan can be formulated unless a Black position is also solicited, he declares. In reality, the Black position is a very simple one—just recognize the worth of everybody in the country regardless of race, color, religion, age, and sex, then live together in one country, developing its resources intelligently for future generations. There is nothing complicated about that, he asserts, except to racist minds that equate sharing with Blacks with "loss."

A basic difference between these "White positions" and PFP policy is that the latter calls for a national convention to renegotiate the constitution from scratch. In essence, the PFP is saying, "Let's try to find out together what kind of future we all want."

It is true that *verligte* leaders are talking in terms that would have been unimaginable ten years ago. The report of the Rockefeller Foundation-sponsored Study Commission on Policy Towards South Africa—an exhaustive report published in 1981 after two and one-half years of investigation—found that while most South African Whites resist fundamental change, a real ferment exists. The authors suggest that in the future the real clash might be between *verligtes* and those who advocate what the Commission calls "genuine reform"—i.e., an order in which Afrikaner power is not entrenched, but "legitimate interests" are protected. While only a handful of members of the National Party parliamentary caucus advocated such far-reaching change *publicly,* their ranks include Afrikaner intellectuals, and the significance of the "genuine reformers" is greater than their numbers would suggest.[16]

In any case, despite losses to the left and right Botha probably has a clear enough mandate from the all-White electorate to gain its support for such a program if he so wills. Afrikaners traditionally tend to follow a strong leader.

Yet resistance would be strong. Why, then, would Botha go ahead? Khoapa believes that any such move would be primarily a move to placate international opinion. In this scene, the United States is a principal actor. Clearly, the advent of the Reagan administration has encouraged Pretoria to believe that it could count on Washington for support in resisting what the Nationalists like to call "the Communist threat." President Reagan delighted them when he asserted that the United States could not "abandon" a country that "strategically is important to the free world." After Black African countries reacted angrily to the statement, Reagan backtracked by calling apartheid "repugnant." Nevertheless, various Administration statements suggesting that the U.S. could work toward a more open alliance with South Africa— one with military dimensions—providing that RSA institute more change in its racial policies, leaves little doubt that Washington foresees an *entente cordiale.*

Reagan's Assistant Secretary of African Affairs, Chester Crocker, believes that "American interests and principles cut across the shifting ideological and color lines of southern Africa," and that most African governments use Marxist verbiage, while pursuing ideologically eclectic policies. More preoccupied by "Soviet threats" to the Third World than Carter Administration Africanists, he does favor a preventive apprach—i.e., not only military assistance, but economic investment and support to many countries in southern Africa, in order to discourage radicalization and forestall Soviet combat pressure in the region.[17]

Crocker sees the question of Namibia as inextricably intertwined with that of Angola. He seems to favor the Angolan anti-Soviet guerrilla group UNITA, or at least to oppose allowing UNITA to be weakened to the point where any reconciliation between the group and the MPLA-led government would be merely the reconciliation of victors and vanquished. The ultimate goal should be to eliminate communist combat presence in Namibia and Angola. (He does not appear to be concerned about the very active presence in Angola of South African search-and-destroy battalions sent in to support UNITA.) Crocker and his colleagues have been pressuring South Africa to return to the Namibian conference table, asserting that the United States will "disengage" from negotiations on independence for the territory if South Africa continues to delay on an internationally acceptable settlement. What seems to be emerging is a new formula somewhat similar to the plan for Zimbabwe: a solution with "guarantees" for a White minority, i.e., a multiracial rather than a nonracial system.

Thus the new Washington/Pretoria scheme would provide that instead of holding elections for a constituent assembly, as envisaged by the original United Nations plan, a constitution and a rule of law would be negotiated first (obviously from the existing base of power), followed by elections for the government. True, the process would be almost certain to end—eventually—with a situation unpleasant to Pretoria: the installation of a government dominated by the South West People's Organization (SWAPO), the Marxist-oriented insurgent movement that commands an overwhelming popular following in Namibia and with which South Africa has been fighting a guerrilla war in Namibia and parts of southern Angola for many years. Nevertheless, establishing a rule of law and constitution guaranteeing the Whites political rights would entrench their economic "rights" and put them into an even better position to co-opt Blacks.

There are obvious similarities between this vision for Namibia and the "contingency plan" conjectured for South Africa. If Washington and Pretoria push through this Namibian blueprint, which is modeled on the Zimbabwean settlement, then the new agreement could in turn become the prototype for South Africa itself.

Pretoria seems anxious to secure international approval. Under the "contingency plan" its losses could be more than offset by gains: military security, increased economic investment in an atmosphere of "stability," even the moral/psychological satisfaction derived from acceptance in the international community.

If Reagan's administration is subtly pressuring South Africa to put its house in order because someone reminded him that some people find apartheid "repugnant," then the Administration is itself responding to pressure. Indeed, France and Sweden have threatened to step up sanctions against South Africa. Anti-apartheid organizations have intensified efforts to discourage individual athletes and national teams from competing in sports events in RSA. Several states in the U.S. have passed legislation prohibiting funds from being invested in institutions giving loans to that country. In February 1981 Harvard University sold approximately 51 million dollars in Citicorp issues because Citibank, the corporation's banking subsidiary, participated in a direct loan to the South African government. Support for divestment has continued to grow on other university campuses. Even the Study Commission on U.S. Policy on South Africa recommended that the UN-sponsored arms embargo of South Africa (to which the U.S. subscribed in 1977) be widened to subsidiaries of American corporations in countries that do not observe it, that large American companies in South Africa make no further investment there, that other potential investors stay out, and that barring export of U.S. technology be explored as a means of inducing social/political change.[18]

American church groups and religious leaders continue to be an important element of this pressure for change. The Philadelphia Yearly Meeting of Friends (Quakers), for example, has recommended divestment of securities in companies involved in RSA that refuse to conform to certain criteria such as the Sullivan principles, while the Rev. Sullivan himself has sharply attacked corporations in South Africa for not fulfilling their commitment to his code and has threatened to back selective divestment if necessary.

If a deal between the Nationalists and the West should emerge, churches and other groups opposed to apartheid may be called on to sharpen their analysis. They may need to perceive and explain how the policing apparatus can be taken over by White employers and Black national states, how old mechanisms of repression can be transmuted into new ones, and how such designs fit into the world capitalist system.

The Role of the South African Churches

Within RSA, church groups and individual leaders likewise continued to support or even instigate pressures. In 1981 the Southern African Catholic

Bishops Conference resolved that the church back sports boycotts and also boycott the Republic Day festival. The SACC, treading warily on treasonable ground, called on all concerned with foreign investments and trade agreements with South Africa to base their economic decisions on commitment to the goal of establishing full human rights among all inhabitants of a united country.

Further proof that sanctions can be a real weapon and that South Africa is genuinely worried about them is the government's second revocation of Bishop Tutu's passport, this time in March 1981 after an overseas visit in which he told audiences that foreign investors must know they were buttressing "one of the most vicious systems since Nazism." Bearing messages of international Christian support from Archbishop Robert Runcie of Canterbury and Pope John Paul II, whom he had met on the trip, and resigned to the fact that the government's actions would prevent him from going to Greece to receive the annual Onassis Peace Prize, the Bishop remained cheerfully defiant: "There is nothing you can do which will stop us from becoming free!"

Other signs of creative ferment have continued within the churches. For example, the Methodists chose Rev. Stanley Mogoba, a former Robben Island inmate with radical views, to the most important position in the denomination, that of secretary. The Catholics made the daring move of appointing Rev. Smangaliso Mkhatshwa, a banned priest known to be articulate and aggressive, to succeed Father Dominic Scholten, O.P., as secretary of the SACBC—even while Mkhatshwa continued to be banned. The Congregationalists announced that they would marry any two persons, even mixed couples. And Dr. Frans O'Brien Geldenhuys, who had resigned as chief executive of the White NGK, attacked his church for not using the scriptures to explain to its members why it is essential to make fundamental changes in the existing order.

It is a fascinating phenomenon that the void created by the banning or detention of most Black political leaders should be filled by a man of the church, that Bishop Tutu should emerge—in the words of one conservative editor—as "the most articulate and the most visible spokesman of extra-Parliamentary dissent in South Africa today."

The upstart little cleric could be eliminated in a variety of familiar old ways. He has no secular power. He even favors nonviolence. Yet it is unlikely that the government will dare to ban this "politically pesky priest," if for no other reason than that such a move might enhance his chances of receiving the 1981 Nobel Peace Prize (for which he was nominated by the American Friends Service Committee and Quaker Peace and Service, London).[19] His position vis-à-vis the state, then, represents the paradox of power. In the long run, power based on forceful sanctions alone becomes a helpless giant.

Today the White "First World" within South Africa continues to build a laager, isolating itself against the "Third World" in its midst—just as a militarized United States isolates itself from the Third World in the global community.

Recently, Peter Storey, a White Methodist minister who became Tutu's right-hand man when he was elected the new president of SACC, pointed out that White South Africans are more heavily armed than any other civilian population in the world. And yet, he went on, "Every day that people are arrested for a pass offense, detained without trial, turned out of their homes, resettled against their will, separated from wife or husband, denied access to work, or informed they are no longer citizens of the land of their birth, catastrophe is one day closer." Ironically, "there comes a point when protecting your privilege is such a full-time task that there is no time to enjoy it."[20]

He might have added that the cost of "defense" involves not only a loss of time, but a loss of finite resources. (For example, meeting the defense budget has been made possible only by stepping up the extraction and export of South Africa's minerals.) It involves the loss of consumer goods and services, as funds are shifted to the military (the cost of which has quadrupled in the last decade). It takes White manpower from civilian jobs, leaving them unfilled or open to Blacks. It means loss of human lives. Finally, pursuing a military approach to human conflict only asks for a military solution—rendering the defenders more vulnerable to attack. There comes a point, then, where armed defense is no longer defense, where it becomes transmuted into weakness.

The growing number of leaks hinting at a "contingency plan" suggests that some of South Africa's more far-sighted leaders recognize the paradox of power. On the other hand, a "nonviolent" transition to a new order is not necessarily synonymous with justice. One must also ask whether structural violence will be perpetrated. A new dispensation that only modernizes the rules of racial discrimination does violence to human beings.

What should the role of the church be if such a new dispensation does come to pass? Quite simply, to continue the same prophetic role: to seek that justice prevail. This is not tantamount to assuming a political stance in the sense of supporting or leading a party. Such direct involvement could be tantalizing to church leaders dedicated to the struggle against oppression. Bishop Tutu, for example, might be pushed by supporters and the inevitable gratifications of political leadership into political activities in much the same way that Bishop Muzorewa was thrust into a similar role in Rhodesia/Zimbabwe. Such a development might even be congenial to the interests of Nationalist leaders, who could then proclaim to the rest of the world that in the "new democratic South Africa," a radical Black cleric was allowed a role within the framework that they had created.

In other words, the horizontal role of the church should be—as Wolfram Kistner of the SACC suggests—to continually re-examine itself and the society that it reflects. In the case of South Africa that means working to eliminate injustice, whether perpetrated by White or Black, and it means attempting to make men and women in the rest of the world aware of their part in the process.

As tensions heighten, as oppression becomes more subtle and sophisticated—to all appearances, more color-blind—such a watchdog role will
become even more difficult and challenging. It will require the wisdom of
serpents, the patience of doves.

The role of the prophet will always be difficult.

Notes

1. Johannesburg *Star* (weekly airmail edition), March 28, 1981.

2. Dr. A. S. Herbst, "Election 1981: In Facts and Figures," *Position Paper* of Southern African Forum, Vol. 4, No. 12, pp. 1-4.

3. Joseph Lelyveld, "Exports Spur South African Mine Growth," *New York Times,* February 26, 1981.

4. Heribert Adam, "Minority Monopoly in Transition: Recent Policy Shifts of the South African State" *Journal of Modern African Studies,* Vol. 18, No. 4, p. 619.

5. Johannesburg *Star* (weekly airmail edition), March 7, 1981.

6. Joseph Lelyveld, "Anxiety Over Apartheid," *New York Times Sunday Magazine,* April 26, 1981, p. 18.

7. "The New Apartheid," *Africa News,* June 1, 1981, pp. 3-6.

8. Steven Friedman and Denis Beckett, "Dumping the Dustmen: The Johannesburg Strike," *Frontline,* Vol. 1, No. 5, September 1980, pp. 9-11. The Johannesburg strike began when six hundred workers at Soweto's Orlando power plant walked out. After they were fired, eight hundred Electricity Board employees quit in protest. Within a few days, up to ten thousand city workers were out, as garbage piled up around the city. Francois Oberholzer, the city's overlord, "crushed the strike . . . by the simple expedient of lining up every worker and asking him if he wanted to work or not. Those who demurred . . . were escorted to a homeland bus."

9. Examples of these unregistered African unions are the South African Allied Workers Union (SAAWU) centered in East London, the Motor Assembly and Components Workers Union (MACWUSA) in the Port Elizabeth area, and the Western Province General Workers Union (WPGWU) in the Cape region. Over sixty members of SAAWU were detained by the Ciskei authorities, since Mdantsane, the African township of East London, is located in the Ciskei. These broad-based general workers unions upset the government, which is attempting to have legislation "requiring unions to restrict their activities to one industry or trade, thus out-lawing" unions such as SAAWU and WPGWU. "Police Move on Black Leaders," *Africa News,* July 6, 1981, pp. 3-5.

10. Loraine Gordon (ed.), *Survey of Race Relations in South Africa,* (Johannesburg:SAAIR, 1980), p. 404.

11. Adam, "Minority Monopoly in Transition," p. 625.

12. Joseph Lelyveld, "Botha Opponent Has It All—Except a Chance to Win," *New York Times,* April 26, 1981.

13. Gary Thatcher, "South Africa's White Rulers Plan New Confederation," *Christian Science Monitor,* February 25, 1981.

14. A few years ago a group of Afrikaners did propose establishing a "pure Whitestan" around the area of the Orange River Project on the Southwest of the Orange Free State, where all "dedicated Afrikaners" would start an Israel-like "nation," creating a city and a way of life completely in tune with their extremist views. The plan was discussed but does not seem to have received much practical support. There is no way that the Free State as it exists could operate in this way; its economy is completely dependent on Black labor.

15. "The New Apartheid," *Africa News,* June 1, 1981, p. 11.

16. Juan de Onis, "Private Report Recommends U.S. Expand Embargo on South Africa," *New York Times,* May 22, 1981.

17. Chester A. Crocker with Mario Greznes and Robert Henderson, "A U.S. Policy for the 80s," *Africa Report,* January–February 1981, pp. 7–14.

18. de Onis, "Private Report Recommends U.S. Expand Embargo."

19. The documentation used by AFSC in presenting the case for Tutu to the Nobel Committee was an article by Marjorie Hope and James Young, "South Africa's Doughty Black Bishop," *Christian Century,* December 31, 1980, pp. 1290–1294.

20. Johannesburg *Star* (airmail weekly edition), May 9, 1981.

Index